Silent Tears

Silent Tears

Silent Tears

A Journey of Hope
in a Chinese Orphanage

Kay Bratt

MARINER BOOKS
HOUGHTON MIFFLIN HARCOURT
BOSTON   NEW YORK

First Mariner Books edition 2011
Text copyright © 2008, 2010 by Kay Bratt
Author photo by Kay Bratt, 2005

www.hmhco.com

First published, in a slightly different form, by Booksurge in 2009
Published in 2010 by AmazonEncore

Library of Congress Cataloging-in-Publication Data
Bratt, Kay.
Silent tears: a journey of hope in a Chinese orphanage / Kay Bratt.—
1st Mariner books ed.
p. cm.
Originally published: Las Vegas, NV: AmazonEncore:
Produced by Melcher Media, © 2010.
ISBN 978-0-547-74496-4
1. Bratt, Kay—Diaries. 2. Orphans—Abuse of—China. 3. Orphans—China.
4. Orphanages—China. I. Title.
HV1317.B73 2011
362.73'2—dc23
[B]
2011029334

Printed in the United States of America
DOH 10 9 8 7 6 5
4500610021

DEDICATED TO CHINA'S ORPHANS.
YOU ARE NOT FORGOTTEN.

Introduction

A two-year-old child dangling precariously from a third-story window . . . a little boy tied to a chair for hours . . . abandoned children begging for a crust of bread . . . most of us will live our entire lives without witnessing such blatant cases of emotional or physical child neglect and abuse. Instead, we live in relative comfort, far removed from such horrors and perhaps feeling we are doing our part to help suffering children by sending an annual tax-deductible check to some charitable organization. While this is certainly a worthy undertaking, there is much more that needs to be brought to the world's attention and addressed.

I used to be one of those people, sympathizing at a distance with the plight of less-fortunate humans the world over while tending to my own personal dramas in my middle-class neighborhood in Greyhill, South Carolina.

I was perfectly content for my family to continue its slow crawl toward the American dream—or so I thought. I am not an overly adventurous woman. My idea of a daring journey is lying on the beach with a thick novel while protecting my children from the dangers of sunburn.

However, fate had other plans for me. Late in 2002, I learned I would not be lingering in my safe and easy life much longer. When my husband Ben's company offered him a management position starting up a manufacturing facility in a third world country, we were both excited and terrified. Our families thought we had lost our minds when we accepted and began planning our move to China, a land that then seemed mysterious and wonderful to us. I always believed God had a plan for us, and I quickly realized that this could be my chance to do something memorable with my life. Immediately I set three goals: to learn to speak Mandarin, to volunteer in an orphanage, and to chronicle my time overseas by keeping a journal.

Our lives changed dramatically in 2003, when, after months of anticipation and preparation, we relocated to Shengxi.[1] We embarked on this journey fully realizing it was going to be an unforgettable experience; we just never bargained for the adventure to be so fraught with frustration and turmoil. Once we arrived, the culture shock and isolation we faced were overwhelming. After several weeks, we believed we had made a terrible mistake by leaving our simple, untroubled lives in America. It was a far more difficult transition than any of us had anticipated.

The often nerve-racking, trying times and sometimes extraordinary adventures left us emotionally drained. Even after a few months, my family was not adjusting in the way I had imagined. My young daughter, Amanda, constantly begged to return to the States, and Ben was struggling with the many cultural differences of managing a Chinese business.

Our commitment of eighteen months began to feel like a prison sentence, and my family looked to me to make it all better. At the five-month mark, I knew we needed to pull ourselves out of our mostly self-imposed misery before it turned us against our

---

1 All Chinese city names in the book have been changed. I chose not to reveal the real name of the orphanage or the city to ensure future volunteer efforts would not be compromised.

circumstances and one another. We had resisted enrolling Amanda in school, but once we did, we realized it was the best decision for all of us. Among peers, she began to blossom and return to her extroverted self. A few months later, a little girl moved in to the house next to ours, and she and Amanda instantly became best friends. Knowing Amanda was adjusting helped Ben and me to begin to relax and come to grips with our new circumstances.

With the help of an expatriate friend who had contacts with city officials, I was eventually accepted as a volunteer by the local orphanage. Thrilled and a little frightened, I started out as a hesitant observer, but after experiencing the shock and horror of finding a tiny baby dead from neglect in her crib, I had to decide whether I was going to fight this outrage and try to make a difference or turn a blind eye to protect my delicate position as a foreigner. I left the orphanage that day profoundly discouraged at the utter disregard for human life, yet filled with an exhilarating sense of purpose I had never known before.

At this crossroads in my life, I saw clearly the challenge placed before me. I was driven to try to change the lives of these children whose parents had cast them aside like the day's garbage. I wanted to transform the often vacant, detached expressions on their innocent faces to ones of animation, of joy, of life. My new goal became demonstrating to each child how it felt to be loved and nurtured. I put behind me the memories of my comfortable life in America and threw myself wholeheartedly into my work at the orphanage and my task of making Shengxi a real home for our family.

Using email correspondence and an expatriate website, I began to raise community awareness of these helpless children's miserable existence. Gradually, I began building the volunteer group, one person at a time. Friends and family forwarded my weekly email updates to more and more people, and the trickle of donations that began to arrive helped us to implement many changes at the orphanage. On occasional visits to the States, I spoke at churches and further broadened our support group. Time passed imperceptibly quickly, and I was soon busy coordinating the volunteer schedule, surgeries, and incoming donations.

Silent Tears: A Journey of Hope in a Chinese Orphanage is a collection of my journal entries during my family's time in China. My memoir shows the vast range of emotions I faced during our four-year assignment in China. Countless times, I wanted to quit everything and jump on a plane back to the U.S. Some of the cases of abuse and neglect were so severe they caused me to spiral downward into depression. However, because of the bonds I had formed with so many of the children, I simply could not bring myself to walk away. After a time, I became an expert at hiding the anguish I felt after each death—each entirely preventable death—of one of our babies. I learned through practice to summon an inner strength and stoicism that enabled me to push on.

Some of the children we nurtured went on to become part of "forever families" and to live normal, happy lives. Not all were so lucky. The faces of many children destined to remain in the orphanage—many of whom I deeply loved—return at random to haunt my days and occasionally my dreams. Often, particularly at the beginning of my mission, I would come across a child or baby in distress, tears flowing down his or her cheeks, but unable to utter a sound. I would never fail to be astonished that a child so young could cry so silently, without movement or expression, while so clearly craving human touch. It was as though they had given up on the hope of receiving even a moment of comfort or attention to alleviate the misery of their prisonlike existence. Those memories will linger forever in the corners of my heart. I titled this memoir *Silent Tears* as a tribute to the Shengxi orphanage children, now and in the future.

Silent Tears is based on my recollection of events from March 2003 until the summer of 2007. Some names have been altered, and when dialogue is used, it is based on my recall of specific conversations.

Child of Regret and Sorrow

BEIJING, CHINA, 2006

Her dainty hands were numb from too many hours sitting outside under the bridge. The temperature had not risen with the noontime sun as it usually did. Today's begging had so far brought her only enough money to feed the child and not herself. What little effort it took to teach the child to stay put in her lap and look hungry! But most of the pedestrians were not swayed by the toddler's beseeching eyes, and only a few elderly women gave generously to the cup.

It had been a day with too much time for her to contemplate her circumstances and arrival at such a low place in her life. Several times since this morning, she had daydreamed about how comfortable and happy she used to be. She remembered her small apartment and the satisfaction of shopping and cooking for her new husband. But this line of thought was dangerous; it always led to the painful memories of the birth of her daughter and the drama that had ensued.

Mei Li had been a bright and pretty girl of nineteen when she met her husband. He was studying at the university and she worked as a server in a Western restaurant. One night he came in with a group of his foreign friends. When she accidentally spilled soup in his lap, he was compassionate and took pity on her embarrassment. He did not make a scene and kept the accident quiet. She had been relieved, for such a mishap could have cost her the job. Jobs for the uneducated were not easy to come by and her parents desperately needed the additional income this position brought in. She was thankful that her becoming face was at least beneficial in securing her a job in a sheltered place, keeping her from the degrading work in the questionable trades offered to most young women of her background.

That evening, as the kind young man left the restaurant, she longingly wondered if she would ever again meet such a handsome and considerate man. When Le Ming arrived at her station again the following evening, she was overcome with shyness. After his meal, he asked her to meet him at a local park and she agreed, knowing that if her parents were to discover the tryst, she would be reprimanded for such overt conduct.

They began a whirlwind courtship. When their schedules would allow, they spent many hours together flying kites, walking near the lake, or just sitting and talking of their dreams. She knew she loved him deeply, and when he proposed marriage, she immediately said yes. Within a year, he had saved enough money to rent them a small but cozy apartment. They were married and she began her new life as a wife to an aspiring executive. She kept her job because he had one more year at the university before he would begin working full-time. The part-time work he did as a sales clerk in the telephone store did not make enough to meet all of their financial burdens. This did not trouble her, though, for she knew they would soon be living a much better lifestyle.

When Mei Li discovered she was pregnant, she and her husband were alarmed. It was too soon in their marriage and they were not prepared. The young couple talked to Le Ming's parents and were relieved that they would stand behind them and support them through the first year. His parents were excited to be expecting a grandson who would carry on the family name.

At first, this further worried Mei Li because she knew that there was a chance she would not have a boy. When she tried to talk this over with her husband, he assured her that he knew of a doctor who would perform an illegal ultrasound when it was time, and confirm for them what his heart already knew: that they would indeed have the coveted son. She convinced herself to put the worry out of her mind and concentrate on the future and the joy it would bring.

In order to save for upcoming expenses, she began to cut her diet drastically. She would cook meat, rice, and vegetables for her husband but would eat only rice herself. She was a healthy young woman, so what harm could that do? The extra pennies she saved would buy their son the many things he would need that first year.

When they were unable to bribe a doctor to do the ultrasound, she should have known that bad luck was upon them. After much contemplation, they decided male births were dominant in her husband's family and thus it would be safe to continue with the pregnancy.

The night of the birth, the grandparents took great care in performing every step according to custom, in order not to upset the ancestors. Le Ming was their only son and his child would probably be their only grandchild; they wanted to make sure that nothing went awry.

The birth did not go well. Mei Li labored for close to twenty hours before the doctor finally anesthetized her and performed a cesarean section. As the gas took effect, she watched her husband's eyes and thought of how happy they would soon be.

When she awoke, however, it was to a silent and empty hospital room. She had expected that her baby would be lying next to her, awaiting his first meal from his mother. A look around the room proved her child was nowhere in sight. With increasing alarm, she called out for someone to come. Eventually a nurse entered and, with a frown upon her face, approached the new mother to check her pulse.

"Where is my son?" Mei Li demanded.

The nurse briskly walked to the window, raised the blind, and looked out over the city. The defeated stance of her body indicated she had given this speech many times.

"You did not give birth to a son. You had an unlucky little girl."

As reality set in, Mei Li became very agitated. "This is not true! Where is my husband and where are his parents?"

The nurse sat on the bed and looked at the young mother. "They have all gone home. Your husband says you must have done something to cause this tragedy. Your girl child is not normal— she was born with a deformity."

The room became so quiet that Mei Li could hear her heart pumping blood. She was shocked to learn that the child was a girl, but to hear she was crippled was almost too much to absorb.

"What do you mean? How is she deformed?"

The nurse looked away once again and said, "Her leg is twisted and unnatural. She will be an outcast. I'm sorry to say, but your family does not want her."

"I don't care if they want her or not. She is my child!"

The nurse just shook her head unsympathetically and walked out of the room.

When the time came for Mei Li to leave the hospital with her child, she did so with a heavy heart. She had not had a single visit from her husband nor anyone else in his family.

She had no money to take the bus, so, with the baby cradled in her arms, she began the long walk home. A slow but steady rain fell and she feared for the health of her daughter. As she picked up the pace, her mind whirled with the anticipation of what her husband would say to her.

Drenched with rain, she reached her building and stopped outside to gather her courage. Looking up at the tall building, she tried to pick out their window. Was he there? Would he be happy to see her, and would he put her mind at ease? Would he help her care for the baby so she could rest her aching feet?

Climbing the many stairs, she frequently paused to ease the pain from her stitches. With each floor she reached, her anxiety increased as she prepared what she would say to her beloved husband. She was sad for letting him down; she knew his heart had been set on having a son. If he would only listen, she knew she could convince him everything would be all right.

She wanted to remind him that these days in China, many baby girls grew up to be successful women who went on to help support their parents. Things were changing and they did not have to live according to the old beliefs and customs that valued a boy so much more than a girl. With the love they had for each other, it was only natural that they would work through this and make the best of their situation. They would save their money to find a doctor who could help with their daughter's disability. She hoped he would listen and not be swayed by his parents' abject disapproval.

When Mei Li arrived at the door, she stopped to make sure the baby's leg was covered. She wanted Le Ming to see the beauty of his daughter's face first and not the deformity that might cause a lifetime of worry. She turned the knob, took a deep breath, and walked into her home. Her initial feeling was that everything would somehow work out, for she was back in her comfortable, familiar little apartment. She looked around and saw her husband sitting at the kitchen table with his head in his hands. Her mother-in-law sat beside him with red-rimmed eyes. It was obvious they had been grieving. Mei Li could scarcely believe all this was because they did not have a healthy baby boy! This was not China of twenty years ago—what were they thinking?

Her mother-in-law looked up and with a glare of disgust

ordered her out of the apartment. Mei Li felt a shiver of foreboding as the atmosphere became heavy with hatred.

"Le Ming, please don't let your mother talk to me this way. Please, look at how beautiful your baby girl is. She has your eyes."

Her husband looked at her with eyes full of sorrow. "Mei Li, you must go. You and your baby have caused my family very bad luck. My father died of a heart attack the night she was born. You must leave this house and never come back."

Mei Li backed away in disbelief. She knew well the ancient belief that the death of a family member on the same day as the birth of a baby meant the life of that child was the cause of the death. The deformed leg only added to their certainty that her child was indeed unlucky.

As she turned to leave, the love of her life faltered with his decision and gave her an ultimatum. She could see the pain in his eyes as he delivered what he knew would be an unheeded request. There was no question of his love for his young wife, but it could not be stronger than his loyalty to his mother.

"If you get rid of the baby, you can return and we will try to work this out. Do not bring her back into my house again."

Mei Li cradled her small and innocent daughter close to her body. She pleaded with Le Ming, but he denied her the comfort of rest, food, and dry clothing. She was to leave immediately and to take nothing from her husband's house. With a last withering look, she shut the door on her previously perfect life and turned to begin her new destiny.

"I will name her Yintong," she said. The name meant regret and sorrow, so fitting for this child's life and all the ripples of dark feelings she had caused.

Since that life-changing day, Mei Li and her daughter had spent many months sleeping in doorways, at train stations, and under bridges. Autumn had set in and the temperatures sometimes plummeted to freezing. Their only source of milk, food, and clothing was from begging for small change or digging through putrid garbage. Many times there was nothing to eat for more than a day, and both of them had become weak and sickly.

Mei Li would never have thought that her life would come to this. When she used to lay her head on her clean, warm bed in her cozy home, she never imagined one day—so soon!—she would find herself living in the filth and grime of the streets, washing in the canals and scrounging from meal to meal. Though she was still young, the new burden she carried made her feel exhausted and old.

The first day after her husband had forced her departure, she had gone back to her childhood home to seek refuge. Her parents had reluctantly agreed to give her shelter, but they, too, wanted nothing to do with the handicapped child. They would take her in only if she would give her baby away. But Mei Li was not prepared to do this and decided that, for Yin Yin, a life on the streets was better than a life in the local orphanage. She had heard the stories of abuse and neglect, and wanted to protect her daughter from that kind of future.

However, after the reality of living this destitute life had set in, she couldn't help but wonder if the stories about the local orphanages were embellished. Someone wouldn't hurt a small and defenseless child, would they? Perhaps not having a family was a small price to pay for a warm bed and a hot meal every day. In an orphanage, Yin Yin could grow up around other children and she would have a roof over her head each night. Perhaps Le Ming had been right and the child was born with bad luck. Mei Li only knew that to see her daughter continually cold and hungry was a torture no mother should have to endure.

That night, as Mei Li cradled Yin Yin's head in her lap and stroked her daughter's downy hair, her thoughts were in turmoil. She tried to quiet her stomach's rumblings as they huddled in the doorway of a produce store in a derelict neighborhood. It was not comfortable but it was at least dry. Being much too cold to sleep, Mei Li concentrated on transferring her body heat to the little one nestled in her arms. So many thoughts rattled around in her mind that there was no chance for her to close her eyes and relax.

How could she possibly be thinking of abandoning her own child? How could her husband, a man recognized for his compassion, treat them so unfairly? Must he believe in the ancient superstitions that his mother pressed on him? Why had her own family turned her away? What had she done in her previous life to be punished so severely in this one?

As day finally broke across the sky, Mei Li had made up her mind. With her child wrapped and tied across her back, she began to make the long trek across the city. She would leave Yin Yin in the park close to the orphanage. If she hurried, there would be many hours of daylight for her child to be found. She would not leave her in the dark to cry in fear.

As she made her way through the busy streets, Mei Li wept silent tears of bitterness, remorse, and shame. In the hordes of people who passed her by, no one noticed her distress. She succumbed to a torrent of tears and sobbed for the loss of her innocence and her marriage, and for the tragedy her life had become.

She continued crying over the betrayal of her parents and the impending goodbye to her precious child. Between bouts of tears, she wrestled with her conscience to find forgiveness for what she was about to do. Yin Yin could have a good life, she argued. She would no longer have to beg or go to sleep with an empty belly. She would not have to feel the bite of the cold wind through her worn clothing. Mei Li tried to convince herself that she was giving her child a gift, a second chance at life. She picked up her pace and, her baby bouncing against her back, hurried toward her destination.

At the park, Mei Li was grateful to find someone's picnic leftovers poking out of the refuge bin. She found a tree and settled down for a much-needed meal. As she ate, Mei Li watched every move her daughter made, trying to memorize every feature of her little face. When Yin Yin had finally eaten her fill and emptied her bladder, Mei Li laid her down in a pile of leaves for a nap.

Thankfully, they had the park to themselves. As Yin Yin drifted off to sleep, her mother whispered one last fairy tale about a little lost girl who had found her way to a safe place and lived happily for the rest of her days.

Mei Li took off her coat and used it to cover her child. She gently pressed her lips to Yin Yin's brow while her tears fell over the tiny nose. She traced her daughter's profile and murmured a soft goodbye. As she disappeared through the stand of trees, a grief so profound struck her that her heart felt shattered.

As Mei Li silently crept away, she knew that a dozen lifetimes could pass, but she would never recover from this tragedy. Nevertheless, tonight her daughter would have food, warmth, and shelter. It would be Mei Li's only solace for years to come.

She chose to take the long way home so that she might better prepare what she would say to her husband. She wanted him to know how much anguish this decision had caused her and she hoped he would feel regret for his part in it. However, every word that came to mind was useless to describe the emptiness in her arms where her child had lain, and she could not banish the picture of the tiny, dearly loved face. Had Yin Yin been found yet? Would she be safe? Was she crying for her mother at this moment? These questions and others—forever to remain unanswered— were agony to Mei Li.

As the apartment building came into view, her heart began to pound wildly. What would she do if he would not take her back? Perhaps he no longer loved her. There was only one way to clear away the fears that threatened to choke her. She climbed the many stairs and softly knocked. At the sound of Le Ming's footsteps, Mei Li lost her nerve and turned to run. Before she could get to the stairwell, the door swung open and there he stood. His familiar face arrested Mei Li in her tracks.

Le Ming looked startled at the sight of his young wife with her ragged clothes and tear-stained cheeks. Hesitating only briefly, he held his arms open wide as a gesture of both apology and forgiveness. Mei Li ran into his arms and they clung to each other tightly. She cried, heaving with great sobs of sorrow, while Le Ming's tears were those of relief that she had finally come home. They both knew they would never discuss the child; the abandoned daughter would be an unspoken secret between them to the end of their days.

1

Two more months and we will be on a plane to China with one-way tickets in our hands. It does not yet feel real. My husband, Ben, my daughter, Amanda, and I are excited but also frightened of the unknown. Ben's company, which is sending us there, has one manufacturing facility and is planning another, where Ben will supervise the installation process.

It is an enormous change for a man who has spent his entire life living and working in one small town, but Ben has worked hard for this promotion. He started on the lines eighteen years ago here in Greyhill, South Carolina, and has made regular advancements. This promotion to work in China was the ultimate compliment, even if at first he was rather overwhelmed with the idea.

Ben was extremely surprised that I was open to such an adventure. I am usually the one who likes to stay close to home. However, when approached about this possible move, I immediately felt it was the Lord's way of pushing me to fulfill a dream of helping children. I just never thought He would send me to China to do it!

Before we accepted the offer, I searched the Internet to see if there was an orphanage listed in Shengxi, the city we were considering. Indeed there was, and the moment the new manufacturing facility's site was confirmed, the wheels starting turning inside my brain about the possibilities for charity work there.

It has not been an easy decision; it has been fraught with a complex array of emotions. We have second-guessed every move we've made so far. We have sold our house and vehicles and put most of our belongings in storage. We have had cultural training and language classes, which, alas, for the most part, we have not been able to absorb or retain. Most of our family and friends are skeptics, convinced we will not go through with it. They should know us better—that kind of attitude has only deepened our resolve. Are we doing the right thing? We do not know, but we will find out soon enough. Let the adventure begin.

* * *

MARCH 7, 2003

We have been in China for almost a week. I have gone from exhaustion to exhilaration and back to total exhaustion. The flight over was torturous—we left our southern hometown in the wee hours of the morning knowing we wouldn't arrive in Beijing until twenty-two hours later. On the plane, Amanda finally fell asleep and slept for eight hours. But for a seven-year-old child, that much travel was a nightmare. I only slept for small periods at a time. I cried so much at the airport that my eyes were in no shape to watch the in-flight movies; in any case, I could hardly concentrate. My thoughts tumbled incessantly between my secure past and uncertain future.

* * *

The night before we left, I visited my eldest daughter, Heather, to say goodbye. Leading up to this day, she had been excited about living with her real father—my ex-husband—for the first time.

Moving into his house was a thrilling time for them both. He and I had divorced when Heather was three, and though they had maintained a strong relationship, her time with him had been limited to weekends and holidays. When we made the decision to move to China, it was her wish to have a chance to live with him full-time. No amount of arguing or begging on my part would change her rebellious thirteen-year-old mind. Ignoring my many fears, I conceded to her wishes, with the agreement that after one year she would come to China. She would spend a year with us there, after which we would all return to the U.S. and she would again live with Ben, Amanda, and me.

When I arrived, she was in her newly decorated bedroom, crying and refusing to come out. Until that night, she'd clung to her confidence and proclaimed her independence, but on this last night of goodbyes, the reality of it all had set in. Finally, I joined her and she hugged me furiously, wailing, "Mama, I don't want you to leave." She had regressed from a cocky thirteen-year-old to a clinging child in a matter of minutes.

We both cried and held on to each other, my heart aching so much that I felt physically ill. At that point, it was far too late to change our plans, but it was difficult to walk out that door and leave her. As I passed through their house, her father and stepmother did not try to engage me in conversation; they knew I would not be able to communicate coherently. Heather had given me a letter to read on the plane, and I gave her a scrapbook I had created with a sentimental letter hidden in the back. As I backed out of her father's driveway, I heaved huge sobs of anguish. When I returned home to Ben, he looked at my face and said nothing, just held me in his arms. He knew that no words would alleviate my pain.

Leaving the rest of the family was equally emotional. My sister, Lisa, cried too. I had known this separation would be very difficult for us. As twins, we have shared a bond never threatened by distance. Both of my sisters, my brother, and I are very close; being without them is going to be yet another hurdle I will have to overcome. Last night was heavy with tears; my mother hugged me tightly and retreated to her room to grieve that one of her children was moving away when for so many years we have all lived so close.

The previous day we had said goodbye to Ben's family, but somehow it was different; they were more excited than sad for us. But as Ben hugged his mother one more time, her smile turned to tears and she was at a loss for words.

The next morning, after all the suitcases were loaded, Dad hung his head and cried. I had never witnessed such emotion in him and it tore at my heart. My stepmother watched from the porch and I could see her chest heaving with sobs. Once we were able to extract ourselves from Dad's embrace, Amanda and I wept all the way to the airport. I worry about him and Mom so much; they are not yet old, but the years are creeping up fast. The farewells were more heart-wrenching than I ever imagined they would be, and I felt drained before the voyage had even started. Ben tried to break the tension by teasing that he was beginning to feel as if he were kidnapping us.

The flights felt endless. After the first twelve hours in the air, I began to feel numb. After the twenty-hour mark, with only sporadic sleep and with the lingering memories of leaving my family, I was beyond any fatigue I have ever known. I didn't care what faced us on the ground as long as I could get out of that plane and into a bed.

Once we'd arrived and disembarked, we found ourselves amid a sea of people. Bewildered and utterly exhausted, we let ourselves get swept up in the crowd and ended up in the line for passport control. The irrational fear of being denied entry into a new country caused my hands to begin trembling. Adding to the stress, the immigration clerk kept a stony face as he intently studied our passports. Eventually he stamped everything and allowed us through.

Getting through the dreaded customs gate was easier than we expected. We had thirteen pieces of luggage, which would usually be a red flag, but amazingly, they waved us on and did not touch anything. We found two porters to carry our luggage out to the curb, where we waited for the van that would take us to our hotel.

On our ride from the airport to the hotel, we were overwhelmed by the barrage of unfamiliar sights and smells, chaotic traffic, and wild driving. I became nauseated, while Amanda lay sleeping with her head in my lap. Ben's face was set with grim determination as if he were just on the edge of carsickness. We are accustomed to the measured pace and politeness of small-town drivers, and this experience was a jolt into the brutal realities of driving in a big, crowded foreign city. Placing my daughter's life into the hands of a reckless driver with whom I could not communicate stretched my nerves to the limit.

Arriving in an exhausted daze, we checked into the hotel and rode the elevator up to the twentieth floor. We dragged our enormous array of luggage into the room, hoping to fall into a luxurious bed and sleep for days. However, there we had another jolt of Chinese reality. We were dismayed to find one small bed that would be impossible for three to share. Frustrated beyond description, we spent close to half an hour trying to obtain a bigger room. After twenty-two hours of traveling, all we wanted was to close our eyes. Finally conceding defeat, we came back and squeezed into the tiny bed. We immediately fell into a restless slumber.

The next morning, we showered, ate a disappointing Western breakfast, then quickly packed up and checked out. We headed to Shengxi and our new hotel, ready for a battle with the concierge, if necessary. We were determined not to be squeezed into a single bed for the upcoming weeks.

Much to our surprise and relief, we entered a lovely room with not one but three large beds with fluffy white quilts. We were amazed to discover a separate sitting room and an extra bathroom. What luxury! And a sharp introduction into the disparities of life in China. But as soon as we landed on the beds, we discovered they were like solid planks covered by deceptively lush bedding. By this time, however, we were so tired that we were beyond caring; at least we could stretch out. We felt as though we could sleep through an entire week.

2

We have been in China for one month. Settling in was difficult, and the SARS situation has begun to cause us some worry. We cannot access news about it on television, due to the Chinese government's frequent blocking of CNN, but our families and the Internet keep us informed. So far the virus has not reached our area, but we are keeping a close watch.

We have decided not to enroll Amanda in school to finish the year. I am giving her math lessons and writing exercises until next fall. She was already well ahead in her class at home, so using this time to become accustomed to our new life instead of immediately throwing her into school feels like a far better choice.

While Ben is busy at work all day, I sometimes find myself bored. Homeschooling helps fill the hours, even though getting my dear daughter to do math is difficult. I threaten her every day that I am going to enroll her in the international school, but she knows I am all talk. However, she does understand that come September she will be boarding the school bus just like all the other kids. I will not tell her, but I really do not look forward to losing my daily companion. I will have to find more to do to keep busy.

I have not yet met anyone who can grant me access to the

orphanage. One woman knows where it is but has only dropped clothes off at the gate. The guards there apparently do not speak English, and she could not extract any information from them. I need to do some further investigating and find someone who knows the system. I am more determined than ever to do this, and I am not giving up on my dream.

* * *

Choosing a house last week meant arduous rounds with our relocation company to three expatriate compounds. We were not expecting to live in anything better than our modest home in South Carolina, but the choices here are very slim. Because nothing smaller was shown to us, the house we decided upon was twice the size of our house back home. When we learned the monthly rent, we understood why foreigners are so welcome here. Ben's company had to pay an exorbitant amount to get us into a secure area. Fortunately, only a percentage of the rent will have to come from our own budget, but we are responsible for the cost of our vehicle, gas, and any household help. One exception: because the company has a strict policy forbidding their employees to drive in China, they also cover the salary of our driver.

Living in a huge house in a gated community and having a housekeeper and driver does not represent the luxurious life you might imagine. The high walls and security guards don't seem necessary, but having them is a common practice in expatriate neighborhoods.

Our housekeeper, called an *ayi* (literally "auntie"), speaks only Chinese in the Sichuan dialect, and I find it awkward having her flutter around me during the day. Most times I try to disappear when she's around. However, she's invaluable to have for dealing with management on the many household repairs and problems, and once I feel comfortable on my own, I can easily find a way to cut down her hours to two or three days a week. Unlike many of the expatriates here, I prefer to cook our meals and even enjoy doing the laundry. However, because of my long history with back pain, I will admit that ironing and mopping the floors are chores I gladly turn over to the *ayi*.

Our driver, like many Chinese men, has little respect for women, and I battle with him incessantly over the temperature, the radio, and his erratic driving. While Ben is in the car, the driver behaves perfectly, even going as far as opening my door for me. However, most of the time, it is just me and him in a silent power struggle that charges the air. Those are the times I long to be back behind the wheel of my own minivan and queen of my own house. Some of my expatriate friends take to their new, pampered lives with glee, but for me the lack of independence and privacy is a difficult sacrifice.

* * *

JUNE 17, 2003

Amanda and I have just returned to China after a four-week stay in the States. Ben's company had promised that if the SARS situation got serious enough for the international schools in our area to close, they would get us out of there. Though Amanda is not in school, the schools' closings were our signal to leave. On May 16, we saw a news report stating that Beijing had more than 16,000 people in quarantine. That frightened me and jump-started our corporate office personnel to arrange our flights.

There were never any cases, that we know of, found in our city, but most of the restaurants and hotels had shut their doors just to be safe. Keeping our promise to let our driver off on the weekends was hard, considering how difficult it was to find a taxi during the quarantine. Even locating an open grocery store became increasingly frustrating. Ben wasn't permitted to return home with us because the company was in a critical stage of their start-up process. Amanda and I cried at the airport to think of him having to stay in our big house all alone. We had only been in China for a few months and I was miserable, but I did not want to return to "civilization" without my husband.

On our flight to the U.S., every person on the plane voluntarily wore a face mask. Amanda resisted wearing hers, but after I put one on her stuffed bear, she agreed. When we arrived home, we stayed with my sister Lisa, but could not really enjoy the visit because we were too worried about Ben. Getting on the plane to return to China should have been difficult, but knowing that it would take us back to Daddy made it extremely easy. Once we had assurance from Ben's company that the SARS epidemic had passed, I was ready to return and try it again, this time with a better attitude.

3

Today I started work in one of the larger orphanages in Shengxi, which houses about one hundred and fifty children. A few days ago, Ben met the husband of Ann, the only volunteer currently working with the children. He arranged for me to meet Ann at the orphanage at nine this morning.

When I arrived, Ann was not there, so I sat in the office area. For an hour I waited in a hot little room with three Chinese women staring, laughing, and talking as if I could not understand I was the topic of conversation! It was very uncomfortable, but I was determined not to show any loss of composure.

Director Yao, one of four directors at this institute, appeared and proceeded to ask for many pieces of identification: passport, extra picture, resident permit, home card. She spoke only a little English, so my driver, Mr. Li, stayed on to translate. Finally, Director Yao sat down beside me and put her arm around me.

She said condescendingly, "You are too young. What qualifications do you have?" To be so desperate for help, they certainly tried to put up barriers for volunteers. Undaunted, I told her I was not young; I was in my thirties and had two children myself. I tried not to sound offended as I said, "Look, I just want to help with the children. I want to do what Ann does here." I dangled

Ann's name shamelessly; because of her husband's frequent donations to the institute, she is graciously accepted.

Director Yao gave me application forms written in Chinese characters, so I had no idea what I was signing. When Ann finally arrived and explained that I would be coming regularly, Director Yao processed my application. That was my first experience with the unpredictability and seemingly arbitrary decision making of Chinese charitable institutions.

We proceeded to the children's ward, passing through a gated area that included a kitchen, an entertaining hall, and nursing-home buildings for the elderly. Several very old men in wheelchairs watched with rapt curiosity as we walked by. On the other side of the buildings, we passed through two unlocked gates that took us into the children's area, which comprised two ancient three-story buildings.

On our way upstairs to the baby room, we encountered three classroom/living areas filled with approximately thirty to forty elementary-age children. I wanted to stop and visit, but we could not take the time—Ann said the staff needed us to assist in the morning feeding.

As we entered the nursery, the tragedy of it all struck me. The room was actually two open rooms adjoined by a half-wall. On one side were twenty metal cradles lined up for the bed babies— the ones who could not sit up—and on the other side were fifteen little wooden toddler beds for the babies seven months and up— those who could not walk. As soon as they could toddle, they were moved to the next room, called the Kindergarten Room. As I looked over the babies, I was shocked at the birth defects, disabilities, and lack of human contact apparent in their listless eyes.

Eight babies were lying on the floor's hard wooden planks, crying, and Ann scooped one up. The room held approximately twenty-five babies, and nowhere could I see any toys or diversions to entertain them; nor were there any coverings or soft padding to make them more comfortable. They just lay in their cribs crying or stared vacantly at the water-damaged ceiling and filthy walls.

Ann is a registered nurse and immediately began rotating the hip of a baby girl named Jia Jia. Most of the babies had bedsores on the backs of their heads from lying in the hard cribs all day. Because of the lack of mobility, they had not developed muscle tone and most could not sit up, roll over, or lift their heads. I sat down and played with a few babies on the floor before moving on to the younger infants in the cradles. The lifeless expressions on their faces wrenched at my heart. Looking at these children, I felt engulfed by a sense of hopelessness. Ann reminded me that I had to be tough, that it was not about me. It was about giving them a measure of unconditional love before we had to leave.

My resolve not to cry dissolved when I spotted two baby girls sharing a crib. They were not twins, but only placed together for lack of a free bed. One of them had a cleft lip, the other was a preemie. They were trembling from head to toe, one crying silent tears, the other just staring blankly at nothing. I was too afraid to pick them up—they looked so fragile—so I started gently rubbing their little legs and tiny fingers. I tried to hum soothingly, but it frightened them, so I stopped.

At feeding time, two workers brought out a huge bucket of bottles and placed rolled-up sheets next to the babies in order to prop the bottles up. Ann and I moved from baby to baby, holding them with a bottle for a few minutes each. Frequently in their frenzy to suck the milk, the babies would knock the bottles out of their mouths. Ann said it was important we get around quickly and reposition those bottles; the babies could not do it themselves and the *ayis* did not have time.

I came to another cleft baby, who could not get anything out of his bottle. I spent the next fifteen minutes squeezing drink after drink into his mouth until a worker came and snatched the bottle out of my hand. The *ayis* did not appear to understand why we gravitated toward the handicapped. It was obvious that they ignored the children in need and gave all their attention to the pretty ones who did not have disabilities.

Soon, the room nannies waved us over to help feed the toddlers. We sat on the floor, with two or three toddlers lying or sitting in front of us. Each of us took a bowl of rice and began feeding the closest children.

With feeding time over, it was time to ready them for their nap. We stripped down children one after the other, and two workers came to pick them up and take them to the other room where the industrial-size sink was located. The children were rinsed off from head to toe and dropped back on a bed or crib with a clean shirt. It was like an assembly line, with as much coldness and impersonality as that implies.

We moved around frequently because they do not like volunteers showing too much attention to one baby. The assembly line began again; dressing thirty-plus babies takes a while! For diapers, we wrapped a thin piece of cloth around the genitals. An added rectangle of plastic with a rope tied around it supposedly kept the cloth from leaking.

While Ann and I worked, we attempted playing with the babies and teasing them, to give them positive attention and stimulation. The workers, on the other hand, were in such a hurry to get through their tasks that how they handled the babies was nothing short of alarming. To pick up a baby, the *ayis* grabbed one arm and one leg and held the child away from them like a sideways rag doll. Even the smallest ones received this treatment!

The morning was exhausting, both physically and emotionally. As Ann and I walked out together, she asked me if I was planning to come back. Even though the work was hard on my heart, there was no doubt at all in my mind about my answer.

I was hooked—I absolutely loved it. Perhaps I couldn't change their circumstances, but I felt I had an abundance of love to give these deprived children. Ann was thrilled—she was leaving to go Stateside for a month, and she's relieved I have promised to be there every Tuesday.

As I reflect on the morning, it occurs to me that the two workers in the baby room had an extremely negative attitude toward us. At the end of our allowed time, one of the workers had impatiently tapped her watch as if to say, "It's time for you to go now." They had stomped around us and taken every opportunity to act as if what we did and said to the babies was ridiculous. I know that we have to keep our own attitudes cheerful and realize we are not there to change everything at once, only to do what we can to make the children's days brighter. If we try to change things too fast, they will not let us return. Ann said that has happened with bossy volunteers in the past, so I will have to be very careful about what I say and do.

* * *

Before I arrived in China, Ann was the only foreigner allowed into the orphanage to visit the children. The company her husband works for contributes regular donations of money and goods, making a close relationship with the directors possible. Ann sponsors two children who occasionally come home with her for weekend visits. She told me that years ago a volunteer group was dismissed for becoming too aggressive and opinionated on how the orphanage should be run. Since that time, Ann has been visiting the children solo each week to do what she can for them. I was fortunate she risked her own position and brought me in under her recommendation.

* * *

JULY 9, 2003

Amanda and I went to KFC for lunch today. The fast food we take for granted in America is a real treat here, but the outing was overwhelming without Ben. When he is with me, the Chinese men do not stare and follow as much. I know they are curious, but it will take me a while to adjust to such blatant disregard for personal space. Ordering at the register was not an easy feat. I was given a picture menu, but even when I pointed at what we wanted, the cashier kept asking questions I could not understand. Why do they assume a blond, blue-eyed, tall foreign woman can understand their rapid Chinese? I just stared back in utter confusion.

We were finally successful in getting food and even found a seat in the busy dining area. It is amusing how such an insignificant event in our home country becomes such a complicated affair here.

Ben, on the other hand, is adjusting well at work. He seems to be learning how to deal with the total chaos that is big-city China. I still worry about the stress he is under, but I can offer him only limited help. It has made a big difference getting settled in our new house and having a permanent place. I know now that I have to get down to business and make this house a home for my family. I also know that how I adjust will affect Amanda and Ben. Everyone always looks to Mom to see what is going to happen next, so I have to shape up and make this work, for all of our sakes.

4

JULY 11, 2003

Ann asked me to initiate a new volunteer. She warned me that Yolanda was very outspoken and flamboyant, and asked if I would caution her about making derogatory remarks to the staff about the care and treatment of the children. She is worried we might be banned from our volunteer work if anyone is too judgmental.

I met Yolanda at the coffee shop near the orphanage, and as soon as I saw her, I knew there was going to be trouble. For one thing, the temperature was supposed to hit about 105 degrees. I was dressed for it in thin khakis, white T-shirt, and hair up, but not Yolanda. She was Spanish, forty-one years old, and a fitness fanatic with a body that bespoke long workouts over many years. Yoli (as she instructed me to call her) was wearing two shirts and a pair of tight silk pants with stiletto heels, her dark hair a wild mess of curls around her face.

Yoli was a fast talker and rapidly took me through her life story and what had brought her to China. Based on her many anti-American comments, I figured she was probably disappointed that I was going to be her volunteer partner.

Jumping in when she finally paused for air, I quickly shifted the conversation over to expectations of us at the orphanage. I tried to convey to her the seriousness of not making a bad impression and not criticizing the care of the children. I thought I was getting my point across, but I was about to find out that not much gets through to Yoli.

After going through the proper administrative channels, we made our way to the baby area. As soon as she took one look, she started in with disdain and attitude. I told her she had to remove her shoes and wear the ones provided, but it was obvious she resented parting with her deadly weapons. She did so, though, and grudgingly put on the ragged slippers we all have to wear. The slipper policy is one of the few rules put in place to stop the spread of outside disease, and one we all strictly obey.

For a short while, we enjoyed playing with the babies, but soon it was feeding time. It was the usual routine; the workers prop the bottles on sheets and allow the babies to suck for about five minutes, then come and snatch the bottles away. The babies still appear hungry, so I am not sure why they are not allowed more milk.

Yoli and I took the bottles we were able to hang on to and tried to move around to the babies who had yet to be fed. One little preemie boy looks like a shriveled-up old man. They never move him and his head is completely flat on the back from always lying in the same position. He is so skinny; he looks to weigh not more than four pounds. They had not bothered to give him a bottle, so I grabbed one and rushed over. I realized why they hadn't bothered; he was so weak he did not have the strength to suckle. I spent the next few minutes giving him drinks in small bursts by squeezing the nipple directly into his mouth.

When it came time to undress the children for their baths, Yoli asked me to take care of the premature boy because she was afraid of hurting him. I picked him up and laid him on my left arm with his face in my hand. I was amazed at the way his little body fit on my arm. I massaged his shoulders and neck to help with the stiffness. I rubbed his tiny eyebrows because I remembered my baby girls both used to like that, and I was looking for a way to make him feel loved and comforted without causing more pain.

A worker took him from me and held him with one hand under his head and one hand holding his ankles. He was so stiff that he looked like a doll. She held him under the cold water, and Yoli wept. I was trying to hold it together because Yoli had already made the *ayis* angry by her outburst of emotion.

I had tried to prepare Yoli for the cold, brusque way in which the *ayis* behaved toward the babies, but my words apparently had not registered. Under her breath, Yoli was calling the *ayis* dirty names; she thought they could not understand. They knew enough to know she was talking about them, so I kept my head down and did not respond. I know Yoli thinks I am a wimp, but I do not want to make things worse for the children.

The disgusted looks Yoli kept throwing their way did nothing but infuriate the women more. The workers passed the babies under the stream of water and then dumped them into their cribs with a piece of clothing. Most of the time, the *ayis* threw the clothes over the babies' faces, causing them to struggle for breath. Yoli and I rushed around dressing them and trying to calm them after the shock of the cold shower. What Yoli does not understand is the more compassion, pity, and outrage we show on our faces, the rougher the staff is with the children. Two of the infants had bruises that were not there last week; based on their limited mobility, I can only imagine how they got them.

I hope Yoli's attitude will not get us thrown out. Even though we cannot change the situation, at least we can give the babies a little love and care while we are there. What I learned from Ann is that we simply have to keep silent and do what we can. Histrionics only make it worse.

The preemie boy is really struggling and I can't get him out of my thoughts. I want him to prove to the workers that he can survive. It is obvious in the disapproving looks they give us that they think it is a waste of time to nurture him. If nothing else, this orphanage runs a flawless model of survival of the fittest. One final thought for the day—I hope that Yoli will not want to come back. To lose a new volunteer is sad, but it will be better for the children.

* * *

JULY 14, 2003

Amanda and I just returned home from the pet market. It will take a while to recover from this latest excursion. On the ride back, Amanda hung her head and let the tears flow. I held her hand and tried to keep myself composed.

The memory of the confusing maze of open flea-market-type stalls will stay with us for quite some time. The chaos and clutter of animals, pots, plants, and flowers was overwhelming. The Chinese who were not lounging around, eating, or sleeping were hawking their wares, calling, "Lookie, lookie," to the passing customers.

The first animals we encountered were caged birds and cats. The emaciated cats were wet with perspiration and looked to be near the edge of death; some of them made pitiful screeching noises. One mother cat lay lifeless on her back with her kittens suckling on her deflated nipples. Though the weather was extremely hot, the animals had neither water nor food. The cages of rusted old metal or ragged bamboo were small, with too many animals packed inside.

It was like entering a scene from the movie *Mulan* as we passed by crickets in small bamboo cages resembling miniature palaces. The insects are ruby or purple in color and treated like royalty, especially by the lonely old men who buy them as companions. In many parts of China, cricket fighting is a popular sport and gambling on it is common.

In one of the dog stalls, a shopkeeper was preparing to feed his pups. He set down one small bowl of rice, picked up two puppies, and then roughly dropped them in front of the bowl, where they frantically tried to eat. The pups got only about three or four quick bites before the man yanked them up and threw them back in the cage. All the dogs were eyeing the bowl and whining with hunger. To see the desperation to reach the food so visible in the dogs' eyes was more than I could stand.

We spotted a huge dog that was possibly a mastiff in a monstrous cage. The locals were amazed at his size and kept sticking a broom into the cage. They kept poking him with it until he would wearily stand up and give a defeated bark. He had bald spots all around his backside and only stood with difficulty. I am sure they have no intention to sell him—he is just a means of entertainment.

It was too much for Amanda's soft heart to see these poor animals suffering so much. We will never go there again.

5

JULY 18, 2003

My clock alarm went off at eight o'clock this morning. Contemplating what I would do to fill up another long day, a wave of homesickness settled over me. Knowing I needed to get out of the house, I searched my brain for ideas. The expatriate association I'd joined had provided me with English taxi cards to help get around Shengxi, so after settling on the front porch with my mandatory morning tea, I pulled one out that read "Plant Street." I thought it might be fun for Amanda, and since it wasn't raining for the first time in a week, we decided to try it. We left our house and walked out the front gate to find a taxi.

After a harrowing ride from the reckless driver, we were dropped off on a cluttered side street. Dodging the many beggars and vagrants along the sidewalk, we saw cages of pigeons and tanks of fish inside small shop windows. I decided we must be in the wrong place and immediately hailed another taxi. I handed him the "Friendship Store" card, hoping it might be a pleasant environment. It turned out to be a mini-mall. We browsed around on every floor but did not buy a thing.

We left the building empty-handed, hailed another taxi, and presented the "McDonald's" card. After being dropped at Walking

Street, walking the three or so blocks to the restaurant, and climbing the stairs to the dining area, we ordered two hamburgers.

In impeccable English, the cashier told us, "I am sorry, but we
don't have hamburgers. We only have cheeseburgers."

Trying to hide my amusement, I said, "Hmmm, just take off
the cheese."

The cashier repeated she was sorry, but they could only make
double cheeseburgers. We settled for cheeseburgers and enjoyed
them immensely. Even though it was just McDonald's, it was a
taste of home.

I was interested to see that the Chinese McDonald's was
almost exactly like an American McDonald's, except for some of
the strange food items offered, Asian music blasting over the inter-
com and the carnival-like atmosphere.

There is little question that China is quickly joining the rest
of the world in becoming a fast-food nation. While you can still
find most elders at the local Chinese noodle shop eating their on-
the-go meals, the younger generation packs into McDonald's and
Kentucky Fried Chicken just as American teens do. Fast-food
prices are much cheaper here than in America, but it still surprises
us to see the usually frugal locals splurging on fried chicken and
cheeseburgers.

* * *

AUGUST 6, 2003

I just returned from the orphanage—the one place in this dream-
like existence where I feel useful. A few days ago, Regina, an
expat from Germany, called to tell me she wanted to join us in
our volunteer work. I arranged to pick her and Yoli up at the coffee shop.

I was feeling sluggish and weak from the unrelenting heat, but if I didn't go, they wouldn't either. I went and I made it through the morning just fine. This is a life full of contradictions; being at the orphanage is the worst and best thing about being in China, and I am thankful to have something to take my mind off my near-continual homesickness.

Today I took fresh-baked Chinese cookies for the administrator and the nursery workers; the gesture improved their dispositions considerably. With three of us helping, there was more time to play and not simply work.

I got some delightful, rare giggles out of several of the toddlers, and that made the visit thoroughly worthwhile. They loved it when I tapped my nails on the hardwood floor and then ran my nails up their necks and around their ears. (Most of the toddlers now lie on the floor until feeding time.) The more I tapped and tickled, the more they giggled.

Regina is going to be a good addition to our team. She is tough and has Yoli easily under control. I do not say much when I am there; I devote my energy to the babies. I don't want to take up valuable time by analyzing everything that goes on and discussing how it could be better—that can be done on our own time. I have plans, but now isn't the time to attempt to expand our limited access to the children. First, we have to earn the trust of the staff.

The boy preemie was removed a few weeks ago and is still not back. They say he is in the hospital, but I suspect they're keeping something from us. I can tell by the way they won't look in our eyes when we question them about him. Yoli and I think he may have died. I really don't need or want to know—at least right now I can imagine there is a chance he is still alive. I don't know how I would deal with the confirmation of my suspicions.

There is one special baby I call Squirt. Every time I walk away from her, she cries such a small, pitiful wail. Because they can already see the attachment, the *ayis* are calling her *my* baby. They pass her to me after each bath so that I may dress her. She appears to be about six months old and is so tiny, with dainty hands and feet. I'm reluctant to admit it, but I already love her so much. She reminds me of a little Kewpie doll. The minute I touch her she ceases crying and watches me silently with big, almond-shaped eyes and a serious expression. If we were in another place and time, I would be content just to spend hours rocking her and whispering softly to her.

Today I took her to the window and showed her around. Even when I am with another baby, each time I pass her, I touch her leg or cheek and talk to her. I have learned many times over in the past few weeks that human touch is a wonderful thing, especially to these abandoned babies who are bereft of it.

I have almost gotten a smile from Squirt a couple of times. Today she lifted the corner of her mouth for a split second. She is a very serious little person. The day I make her grin will be cause for celebration, but I will be careful not to overly favor Squirt at the expense of so many others in need of loving attention. I enjoy them all, though for some inexplicable reason she is just a tad more special to me.

The baby who was so sick last week still has a fever this week. I took extra time feeding him today and massaging his body. I'm hoping desperately that he will get better soon. Ben is worried that the babies are making me ill, but I just have to take that chance. When I leave the room, I scrub all the way up to my shoulders. When I get home, I shower and wash my hair. I take all the precautions I can, but because of the stifling summer heat, there is no way I can wear a mask.

* * *

Many good things are happening at the orphanage, which should help lift my homesickness. We now have three volunteers coming, the workers are gradually becoming nicer and more accepting of us, and some of the babies are improving—they're more animated and their fevers have dropped some.

At the next expatriate meeting, Regina is planning to announce that anyone who is interested in volunteering on other days should see me. Without being aware it was happening, I've been named the official leader of our small but growing group. Now I have the responsibility of keeping this group organized; with more effort, perhaps we can work toward getting volunteers for every day of the week! That's my dream right now: for these children to receive affection and love each day. The workers have too many babies and not enough hands, and it appears that if we help without judging them or having a negative attitude toward their practices, they in turn treat the babies better.

6

Spirits have risen a good deal in our house this week. Today we found some Western-style groceries, so tomorrow morning I am going to make pancakes and bacon. Tonight, however, we went to a fancy Chinese restaurant, where we were shown to a private room with a large round table in the middle. In China, people believe all tables should be round, with a turntable for easy access to food.

The table was dressed in fine linen, with several plates, glasses, and chopsticks at each setting. We sat down with a little foreboding, and I timidly asked for forks for Amanda and me. The waiter eyed me strangely but brought them anyway. We hadn't any idea what to order; there were so many plates and bowls—what were they for? We selected a few different dishes just to experiment and we surprised ourselves by enjoying many of them.

* * *

Since things are heating up in Iraq, security around our compound has been tightened. Though I think the five-foot metal wall around the area should discourage any unwanted visitors, we now have a security fellow walking around in army fatigues with a walkie-talkie and acting as though he is G.I. Joe. He is alarmingly young, making me feel about as safe with him on patrol as I might with a child.

Yesterday he stayed around our home for the entire day, staring into our windows and acting strange. His behavior unnerved me so much, I finally pulled the curtains shut. The company also distributed an email instructing us not to wear or fly the American flag until further notice. Later today, a customer service representative was here with a repair person. I asked her what she thought about the situation in general, and she didn't even know who Saddam Hussein was!

When I expressed confusion, she told me the average Chinese person doesn't get the news like we expats do—they get only whatever news their government deems appropriate. Call me naïve, but I was stunned. I had known I was coming to a Communist country, but never really thought through the implications of living under a Communist regime. This was yet another reminder among many that I'm living far from home, where this war is big news every day.

One of the woman's responsibilities is to chaperone workers in our house, so she watched Iraq War news clips on our TV while waiting for the maintenance work to be completed.

On Monday, we must get to the American embassy to register so they will know we are here, just in case the political unrest affects expatriates in China. In truth, I don't feel we are in jeopardy; I worry more about what is happening at home. I feel so very far away.

* * *

AUGUST 10, 2003

We had a marvelous day today: delicious pancakes and bacon this morning, and then a shopping trip to the major department store.

We bought two bicycles and rode them home, with Amanda taking turns riding on the back racks with Ben or me, looking just like a family of locals.

It is common for people here to get around on bikes, but it was quite a sight for some of them to see three Caucasians riding alongside all the traffic. We got many stares and even more laughs. Halfway home, we were so pitifully tired that we stopped at Simon's coffee shop and sat down for a sandwich and a drink.

While inside, we looked out and saw a man making off with Ben's new bike! We both dashed out, yelling, "Hey, that's our bike!" The man didn't understand English, but the restaurant owner ran out with us. He screamed something in Chinese, and the thief dropped the bike and ran off. We were fortunate, because bike theft is a common occurrence here.

When we arrived home, we were completely exhausted. I stretched out for a catnap, while Ben watched our "reality" TV, which is CNN. When he finally pried me off the couch, the three of us went for a walk to the lake beside our compound. We took along the little Singaporean girl who lives next door. Judging by the suspicious looks we received, I think people thought we had kidnapped her. The vast park surrounding the lake was swarming with people flying kites and having picnics. The girls and I splurged on ice cream and it was good—surprisingly so—just like American ice cream.

Later we came home, ate dinner, and watched a movie. I think we are at last settling in, because it no longer bothered us when all the way home the locals ridiculed us; we just laughed right along with them. It wasn't a perfect weekend, but for a weekend here, it was about as good as things get. Our attitudes are becoming more positive. I do believe we're going to make it!

* * *

AUGUST 16, 2003

The bicycles were fun, until they turned into lethal weapons. Today I'm in pain from my head to my toes. My hand is bandaged and my knee is swollen. My legs and the back of my arm are a patchwork of bruises. My whole body is throbbing, and walking takes far too much effort. I look and feel as if a gang of thugs had attacked me.

I confess, I am not the most coordinated person in the world, and my brilliant idea of riding close beside Ben and grabbing his handlebars to pull myself along was not the best idea I've ever had, especially when we ended up flat on the pavement because of it. The locals first heard a scream and then witnessed a big tangle of arms, legs, and bicycles. And me—I was howling like a banshee over the gravel embedded in my bloody palms.

As we were lying in the street, many people passed by, gawking and smirking and likely thinking, *Serves those idiots right, trying to act like one of us!* Amanda was banged up a little, Ben too. I got the worst of it because I was on the bottom. I lay sprawled in the dirty street, crying like a child; Ben attempted to get me to stand up, but I ached so badly I couldn't move for some time.

Amanda and Ben performed first aid on me when we arrived home—if not for my discomfort, it would have been entertaining to see the role reversal. Amanda brought me a blanket and pillow and kissed my hand, sweet daughter that she is. Ben's bike was a wreck, and between moments of feeling compassion for me, he made it clear that I was to blame. The hand brake is history and the pedal is bent; it is a good thing it was inexpensive. In retrospect, even though every muscle is screaming at me, I think I probably got off lightly. Sometimes I just have to learn my lessons the hard way.

7

My time at the orphanage today has left me stunned and in a fog that I think is partially shock. It's taking all my energy just to lift my fingers to this keyboard, but I know letting it out will ease the strain that today's events have placed upon my heart. As I've done all my life, I need to write it out to let it go. Arriving home, I dragged myself up the stairs and climbed into the shower. After a good twenty minutes of hot water, I feel ready for my daily release of writing.

* * *

Yoli and I entered the baby room this morning at nine and the first thing I noticed was the lack of *ayis*. Usually at this time there are two or three of them sitting around the TV watching their soap operas while supposedly paying attention to the babies. Today there was only one. I gave her the supplies I had brought for today—baby soap, powder, and wipes—and entered the other half of the room to see my babies.

The room had a stifling, pervasive odor of urine and sweat, a combination I haven't yet adjusted to. I told myself it didn't matter and tried to put it out of my mind, but I couldn't shut it out. Some of the babies were mewling loudly; others were quiet and motionless. I walked through the middle rows and worked my way down one aisle, adjusting the babies while talking to them softly. Many had legs or feet caught in the metal bars of their cribs, causing them distress. Most had heat rashes from the soaring temperatures and lack of flowing air. When their shirts rode up, their already irritated skin rubbed against the straw mats they were lying on, adding to their misery. I continued down the aisle, releasing feet and straightening shirts as I went.

A baby girl covered to the neck with a towel instead of the usual sheet caught my eye. Most of the babies were sick today, many with fever, runny noses, and coughs. This baby looked as though she had cried herself into exhaustion, but her eyes were open. Bending down to speak to her, I noticed her eyes were not following me. I looked closer and saw that her eyes had a white, nearly opaque, film over them, so I could hardly see her pupils. The towel over her tiny chest was not moving up and down and she wasn't blinking. My mind reeled as the thought struck me, Oh my God, she is dead.

I could scarcely believe what I'd found. My heart plummeted and for a moment seemed to stop. I shuddered and involuntarily recoiled from the crib. By this time a few more workers had arrived; I called one over while pointing to the baby. She peered into the cot, and beckoned a few other staff workers to come look. Nonchalantly, they sauntered over and one of them shoved the crib roughly, trying to make the baby move. The child's body rocked violently from the force of the shove.

As I watched in horror, the worker repeated her action and then said something to another worker, obviously confirming that the baby was dead. They didn't touch her in any way or listen for breathing. Making no attempts at resuscitation, they dismissed her and walked off to continue their interrupted conversation.

I backed away, struck by their indifference. I was in shock

because of the dead child herself, and then again because of her unemotional treatment by the workers. I tried to compose myself, still feeling faint as I watched the workers chatting together, laughing and acting quite plainly as if the little girl's life meant nothing. I realized I wasn't inhaling and took a sobbing breath, but it didn't calm me. The tears broke free of my eyes as I contemplated what a brief and tragic life this baby had lived.

One of the *ayis* left the room, and a few minutes later, a nurse came to check the baby with a stethoscope. When she heard nothing, she covered the baby's face with the towel and walked out of the room. Alone with the little girl, I returned to her side and thought, say a prayer, just for her. It took some time for me to gather the words. Finally, I asked God to take her in His arms and comfort her.

While standing there, I saw Yoli on the other side of the room, with the toddlers and unaware of what had happened. I drew her near and told her one of the babies had died; she didn't handle the news well, becoming agitated and upset. She wouldn't go near the baby; instead, from across the room she gaped at the cradle, wide-eyed.

An old Chinese man with a significant stoop entered the room. Although I've been working here for weeks, I'd never seen him before. He was small in stature and his face held lines of wisdom, or perhaps sadness. He approached the little girl's body, slowly removed the towel, and asked a worker to provide a pair of pants for her. He gently dressed her and placed a sheet on the floor. Lifting her out of the cradle, he ever so softly laid her on the sheet. Bundling her neatly, he lifted her small body close to him and took her from the room.

He didn't make eye contact with me, but I know he was aware I was watching. For my own sanity, I forced myself not to think about what would happen to her next.

Eventually, one of the *ayis* who had been laughing and chatting minutes before came and brusquely removed the baby's scant comfort—her straw mat and towel. Outwardly, the *ayi* showed no compassion whatsoever for this child who had been in the care of the orphanage for such a short time. I wanted to believe she would make time for that later, as I know that Chinese people carefully guard their feelings.

I wished to leave immediately so I could cry openly, but I knew many of the babies were terribly sick and needed me. Somehow, I kept going; I took temperatures, fed rice, gave bottles, and dressed their little bodies after their baths. Mechanically I followed all instructions, washed up, and started down the stairs.

In my distracted state of mind, I had forgotten Yoli and had to return for her. I found her, helped her gather her things, and we both left.

I waited in the car while she went to the office to drop off papers. As soon as the car door closed, I dialed Ben's mobile. When I heard his familiar, comforting voice, I lost all composure and the dam burst wide open. I'm sure my driver was wondering what could possibly be so wrong, but he chose to ignore my tears and ranting on the phone. Ben assured me that he was leaving work early and would be home as soon as possible.

When Yoli returned to the car, her amiable, easygoing nature had returned. She looked at my tears and said, "Cheer up." Stunned at her ability to switch between emotions so quickly, I couldn't answer her and turned the other way to stare out the window.

Arriving home, I went directly upstairs to shower. Surrounded by the heat and soothing rush of the water, I scrubbed until it ran cold.

Sitting here now, I don't know what I'm supposed to be doing. I can't stop thinking about the baby. Shouldn't I be part of a grieving process or a funeral? There has to be something to mark this child's passing.

I'm going to make Amanda some lunch and afterward I think

I will sleep for a while, if I can. I keep seeing the look on that little girl's face, her milky, lifeless eyes wide open and her arms outstretched stiffly. She was only about five months old and so very tiny and helpless.

I can see now why previous volunteers stay with the orphanage for only a short time and never return, but I will continue to go until they say I can't. I know the *ayis* resent my presence. Even if I can't understand their words, I can see the animosity and disapproval in their expressions and feel the friction crackling in the air. I don't care. I will bear the feelings of not being wanted by the staff. I will not give up on these children.

* * *

AUGUST 20, 2003

Yesterday at the orphanage when I discovered the lifeless baby girl, something in me was irrevocably shattered. Whatever naïveté and innocence I may have harbored about that place disappeared forever. The rest of the day was a blur, and last night was one of the worst I've ever had. I couldn't sleep because my brain kept churning with a reenactment of finding the baby dead in her crib. Every time I thought I might drift off, my eyes flew open with a clear image of her vacant face. Sometime in the middle of the night, I found myself in tears again, and soon I was sobbing with great, heaving shudders. And I was not only sad—I was angry and becoming outraged the more I thought about it. I went downstairs so I wouldn't awaken Ben, and lay on the couch ranting and raving at God while the tears streamed.

I just cannot understand how those babies could live—and die—in such misery. As things are now, they do not have a real life, only a pathetic, tragic semblance of existence. Currently, most of them come out of their beds only once a day for a five-minute cold spray under the sink's tap. Soon after I started at the orphanage, the workers allowed a few children to be out and on the floor, but now they don't want us putting them there. The poor babies lie on their backs on those itchy straw mats twenty-four hours a day! Their little heads are flat at the back and some are covered in sores. It is infinitely depressing.

After my emotional outburst subsided, I got back to bed around 3 a.m. I am still so tired and discouraged. I am struggling with the question of my purpose here and whether I am doing any good at the orphanage at all.

* * *

SEPTEMBER 1, 2003

Today, at last, Amanda has recovered after a swimming pool accident she had last week. My silly little girl decided going down a waterslide upside down with her eyes closed was perfectly acceptable. When she rounded a bend, her head hit the side and she was knocked unconscious. I was engrossed in a book and, because of the roaring of the waterfalls behind me, wasn't even aware of what had happened until I happened to look up to check on her. Imagine my shock to see two Singaporean girls holding Amanda out of the water until she could regain consciousness! I am afraid to think of what might have happened if those little angels had not been at the end of that slide and willing to help.

When Amanda came to, she was asking strange questions— more so than normal. I got her home and called a friend who is a registered nurse. She told us the warning signs of a concussion to watch for, which both Ben and I did every second for the following twelve hours.

Between rounds of searching Amanda's pupils for signs of change, came the constant accusing questions: "Why weren't you watching her swim?" "What were you doing?" "Don't you know what could have happened?" Yes, I decidedly didn't win any Mother of the Year nominations that day. My hard-learned lesson was: No more books allowed poolside.

Amanda had a knot on her head but was otherwise fine, though she gave both of us a few gray hairs from worrying. It is terrifying to fathom your child needing emergency care in this country. I've seen the hospitals here, and the thought of an emergency making a visit there necessary for my family is one I cannot bear.

* * *

On Wednesday, we drove to the U.S. Embassy and registered officially as expatriates living in China. We thought we would see some Americans, but there was only one among several Chinese. Many local people were busy trying to get through the mounds of paperwork that would bring closer their dream of going to America. It was a chaotic frenzy, but at least now we're accounted for and we will receive important emails and travel warnings from the embassy.

On the way, our driver tortured us with a cassette of John Denver singing "Country Roads." After listening to Chinese radio for months, it was nice at first, but we should have never joined in. When he found out we knew the words, he wanted to play it repeatedly. Amanda and I started laughing at what a strange sight we must be—all of us singing "Country Roads" at the top of our lungs, even the driver. After the same tune all the way there for an hour and all the way back for an hour, we never wanted to hear—or sing—another John Denver song again. Upon arriving home, Ben looked at me and said, "I wonder how long it will take to get that out of our heads?" It could be worse, I suppose.

* * *

SEPTEMBER 17, 2003

The past few weeks of high fevers and sickness among the children at the orphanage finally drew the attention of the staff, causing subdued moods and more attention to be paid to the severity of the situation. Two toddlers were hooked up to drips and another baby was given a powder substance as treatment against infection. All the babies are so dehydrated—I've never seen them given water or anything except the rations of milk. Two babies were inexplicably missing; they were very sick last week and we are not sure what has happened to them.

However, the good news is we have a new worker who genuinely cares for the babies. She was attending to the ones who were crying. Instead of yelling at them she would pick them up and show them affection. Just watching her interact with such tenderness moved me deeply. This is a welcome blessing; I hope she was hired for the baby room and not just borrowed from another area. Even if she is only here temporarily, at least it means a few days of love for these affection-starved children. She is Chinese, which means the other workers are more likely to be influenced by her good example.

One of the *ayis* was leaning against a bed's wooden headboard with a toddler propped between her knees. The little boy had a drip pole attached, so the *ayi* was sitting with him to make sure it didn't become disengaged. I knew she must have been stiff and uncomfortable from sitting there for so long, so before I left I slipped a soft bed wedge behind her back. I wanted her to know that we are concerned for the staff as well as the children.

With the new worker and the two nurses present, it was a better day for the children. However, I did see Tilly, the unruly and dispassionate *ayi*, smack a few toddlers because they were crying. Everything had been calm in the room until she entered and began talking. Then, one by one, most of the babies and toddlers heard her voice and started whimpering or crying silently. It is evident whenever she comes around that the children are terrified of her.

Tilly is a big, menacing woman who looks as though she could play football if she chose. I dubbed her "Tilly" after Attila the Hun, and now that's what all the volunteers call her. Tilly has a large head and a butchered hairstyle and she sweats all the time. Her eyes remind me of a snake's, and she looks so mean she scares even me. When she returns the babies from their baths, she dumps them from about five inches in the air so their little heads thump on impact. It appears at though she takes pleasure from this, smirking as she abruptly turns and stomps away.

I can only hope for her transfer to another part of the orphanage where she will not have contact with such innocent and helpless little children.

* * *

SEPTEMBER 18, 2003

Cute, cuddly, and lots of fun, Max and Milo are our tiny Chinese pug puppies. At times, I feel as if I may have lost my mind, but when I saw them, I fell in love instantly and had to rescue them from doggy hell. Our favorite, Max, knew just how to win our hearts. At the street shop, when I returned him to his cage, he looked up at us with his deep brown eyes and whined plaintively. I had no choice but to bargain for him.

The second one, Milo, I bought on a whim because I didn't want Max to be lonely while we're away on our annual home visits. It hardly makes sense to me, but I felt compelled to buy them both.

I worried about Ben's reaction, but he's not too upset, just surprised we have been here six months and I hadn't done it by now. I don't know what will happen when we try to get them out of

China, but I'm not going to worry about that now. Amanda favors Max because he is short, fat, and wobbly with a tan face. Milo is also cute—he has a black face and is a little taller and less puppyish.

This may have been a rash thing to do, but it will at least ward off my inevitable loneliness next week when Amanda starts school. The pups are sure to keep me busy—I am already working on house-training, and that is a much bigger job than I anticipated.

* * *

SEPTEMBER 21, 2003

Amanda has taken to the new international school with real enthusiasm. Every morning she climbs on the bus, the only non-Asian child in the entire neighborhood, as if it is just a normal day in the life of any third-grader.

When she arrives home, I am always waiting with a hug and a snack—a hint that I am going to quiz her eagerly about her day.

"What did you do today?" (How can one child do so much "nothing"?)

"Who did you talk to?" ("Gosh, Mom, why do you want to know?")

"What did you have for lunch?" (Rice and ketchup?! Ugh!)

I miss her so much but am relieved she is adjusting. I think starting a daily routine has been instrumental in improving her attitude from her previous doldrums and restlessness. Too much time wandering around listlessly with nothing to do can make a person go a little crazy—too bad *I* can't go to elementary school.

I've met Amanda's two new friends. Madison is a petite but dynamic little girl from Canada; I've never seen so much energy packed into one tiny person. Salla is a beautiful, quiet girl from Finland. They have accepted Amanda into their tight-knit group and since then I've begun to see more of the child I used to know. There are now more smiles and giggling and fewer "I want to move back home" conversations. The relief for Ben and me is enormous; it was a gut-wrenching feeling of anguish to think that the move we'd thought was going to be such an exciting adventure turned out to be the cause of our child's misery.

Even though I still often feel the gamut of emotions from depression to elation, we are finally starting to adjust to life in China. We have made some expat friends and at least once a week we meet up for dinner and conversation. It's comforting to know people who are going through the same things we are, and together we are learning to cope in this sometimes frustratingly alien culture.

8

SEPTEMBER 23, 2003

Last night the plight of the babies at the orphanage got to me so much that I couldn't imagine ever going back there. I couldn't sleep; I tossed and turned for hours. I was torn and miserable. I wanted desperately to see my babies, but I dreaded returning to that dismal and depressing environment. I even imagined I was ill, feeling mysterious pains all over my body. My mind invented one reason after another to excuse me from returning. The recent sickness in the room and bad attitudes of the *ayis* had left me profoundly affected. I have never been the confrontational type, and the tension-filled atmosphere in the nursery makes me want to hide.

However, I woke up this morning and felt my old initiative kick in. I got my bum in gear and headed out the door.

After dropping off muffins in the office, I walked through the orphanage's courtyard to get to the children's area. I passed several elderly people sitting outside in their wheelchairs, taking in fresh air. As I passed them, their faces remained solemn until I said good morning, and then they lit up. They are so lonely; I only wish I could converse with them in their dialect. If the Mandarin language classes I am taking would just focus more on the local language, I could put it to great use in my daily life.

I climbed the three flights of stairs, came into the *ayi* room, and removed my outside shoes. I put on my slippers and quietly slid into the baby room. I think the *ayis* were surprised to see me—so many volunteers don't return after going through a tough phase in the baby room. Even though we only visit once a week, I know these babies look forward to seeing us, and to quit would remove the sole scrap of love and affection they receive. Not to mention I am originally a Kansas girl, and they grow them strong, so I won't be giving up easily.

Regina and Yoli were already holding babies, so I went directly to the bed where Squirt sleeps. She was gone! My heart began thumping as I looked around frantically. Then Regina turned around with Squirt in her arms.

"You scared me," I said. "I thought she was gone!"

We got a hearty laugh out of that. It wasn't even funny, but we often find ourselves cracking up at the strangest things—it must be a coping mechanism. A little later, as I held her on my lap, I had a talk with Squirt. I said I was expecting her to make it because many people were praying for her. I told her to try to eat as much as possible every day before the *ayis* take the bottle away. As I was giving her these instructions in a very serious voice, her mouth tilted up on one side and I got a smile.

I jumped to my feet, held her high, and said, "Did you all see her? She smiled!"

Thankfully, Yoli had been watching our little exchange and had witnessed the smile, proving I was not hallucinating. This is one serious little munchkin and that smile was worth a ton in gold. When Squirt got her bottle today, she drank almost half of it before the *ayis* snatched it away. It seemed as though she'd understood exactly what I was saying. I gave her a kiss on her cheek before I left, and she stared at me with a perplexed expression. (Perhaps she has never been kissed? I am going to make certain she gets accustomed to feeling that little lip pat of love.)

Next week I intend to bring a soap dish and some soap. I watched as the *ayis* carried the same bar of soap from room to room—apparently it was the only bar available on the entire floor. Of course, I'll bring other things, too, but I'll be sure to bring soap so each room will have its own supply. Such little things do much to ease the *ayis*' heavy workload.

The hot, fresh-baked muffins were a hit in the *ayi* lounge. I am getting much better at learning how to make a good impression, evident from a positive sign when I prepared to leave. As I was putting my slippers in a bag as usual to take them home, the *ayis* pointed at their shoe rack and indicated I could leave mine there too. Her gesture brought tears to my eyes. I know it is silly but I take it as a sign that they know I'll be returning. I can't say they like me yet, but I'm content to take it one step at a time.

When I got home, I happened to talk to a neighbor who had volunteered at the orphanage a year or so ago. Although she had not been there in a long time, she agreed to consider starting again. We now have four regular volunteers, but my goal is eventually to have enough people so we can be there every day of the week. Ann is going to be so proud when she returns; she was the only volunteer at the time she initiated me. Now that we have more than one person, we can proudly call ourselves the Shengxi Volunteer Group.

* * *

SEPTEMBER 24, 2003

The puppies that had been so much fun and so playful upon coming to our home began showing signs of illness after only one day. This sluggishness prompted me to decide a veterinarian visit was necessary. After an hour in jammed and chaotic traffic, my driver and I arrived at a small clinic.

By China standards, it wasn't as bad as I'd expected. The

doctor spoke a little English, and after a thorough examination, he confirmed that Milo was very sick and Max was in the early stages of illness. He said he would need to see them daily for at least the next three days.

When I asked how much the treatment would cost, he smiled and said, "Very much money."

Impatiently, I asked him how much "very much" was, but all he did was repeat, "Very much money."

At that moment, the feeling that Ben was going to want to wring my neck overtook me. It looked as if my inability to turn down a sad face had gotten me into a heap of trouble.

The doctor gave me an injection to administer to Milo in the evening. As he handed it to me, he said, "Now you are a doctor."

I told him if I was the doctor, I wanted his white coat. He laughed and gave me two containers to gather urine and bowel movement specimens. I could see I was becoming inextricably involved in an expensive and complicated procedure. If only I wasn't such a soft touch—for sick little babies *and* puppies!

9

SEPTEMBER 25, 2003

Today Regina and I were the only volunteers at the orphanage. Yoli leaves tomorrow to return to the States permanently. I recall how at first I had wished fervently for Yoli to stop coming because I'd been afraid she was going to get us thrown out with her outrageous antics, but I admit I really missed her today. Her energy alone seemed to brighten the room; not only that, she was surprisingly industrious. It was a hectic morning with just Regina and me trying to attend to all the babies.

We were thrilled to learn that two babies were adopted last week by American families. The negative side to these adoptions is that only last week, these same two children were tethered to intravenous drips. It seems the orphanage willingly provides medical help when the children are about to be seen by foreigners. Before the babies' departure from the orphanage and their memorable day of adoption, called "Gotcha Day," the nurses were sent in to pep the children up.

Several others are also in dire need of nourishment. One little boy, about one year old, has been very ill with fever for three weeks. He is so dehydrated that his muscles don't work; he is completely limp. When I lift his arm or leg and then release it, the limb flops down lifelessly. His lips are entirely scabbed over from being so dry, but the *ayis* won't allow us to give him water or milk. When I ask politely, they simply shake their heads solemnly. I fail to understand this way of doing things and find it exceedingly frustrating.

When I left today, I went on a hunt for Vaseline for the child's cracked lips but could not find any. I intend to call every foreigner on my list tonight until I find someone with an extra bottle of Vaseline.

Disappointingly, the new worker who treated the babies with such care last week was nowhere to be seen today. For some reason, the rest of the workers all seemed to be in dark moods. I brought in more fresh-baked cookies, which they usually enjoy; I also brought four bars of antibacterial soap and baby wipes. These items are not stocked at the orphanage, but are needed and appreciated.

When we first arrived, we began taking babies out of cribs and lining them up on the donated soft mats on the floor. The *ayis* disapprove of this, but we insist—the babies are on their backs and confined to their cribs day and night. The workers remove them only for a quick bath or cold spray under the tap; most of them have painful head sores from this unnatural confinement. We have one hour to play before feeding, so we make the most of this time and get as many babies active as possible.

I sat on the floor in front of four babies while holding one little girl in my lap. Regina gave her attention to the toddlers tied to the wall in their walkers so that they, too, could benefit from some interaction. Our affection makes a great difference—before we begin they look utterly bored and listless, and afterward they are much more animated and lively.

While we played, we tried to rotate the babies so each would have an opportunity to see the goofy foreigners and get out of their beds for a little activity. At ten o'clock, a cart was wheeled in with ten bottles of milk and six bowls of rice. There are usually about twenty-two babies, so they must always share this meager bit of nutrition. We returned the babies to their cribs and began propping up bottles.

When the bottles had been distributed, Regina and I positioned ourselves between two cribs and used both hands to hold a bottle each in two babies' mouths on either side of us. We let them suck about half the milk and then moved on to feed two others. This takes coordination and is very hard on our backs. Our arms are stretched as far as possible, and we're trying to aim for two anxious mouths—not easy targets!

After a few minutes the workers started taking away the bottles, so we moved on to the toddlers and bowls of rice. We sat down and pulled two or three walkers in front of us. Not surprisingly, these children all eat from the same bottles, spoons, and bowls. Is it any wonder they all become sick together?

When we finished the feedings, we were instructed to pull off all their clothes so they could be taken one by one to a bath. The babies are all washed in the same bathwater—how hygienic can this be? Then they are dumped back into their cribs along with a clean shirt or clothes for us to dress them in. After that, their marathon naptime begins all over again.

Squirt is still stubbornly hanging on to life. She was sleeping deeply when I arrived, so I left her slumbering until the bottles came. I like to gaze down at her while she's asleep because her face is soft and free of the worried look she ordinarily harbors while awake.

At feeding time she was awakened, and the *ayi* gave her perhaps three small gulps before removing the bottle. After the worker had moved away, I quickly grabbed another bottle and returned to give her more. Squirt sucked it down rapidly. Five minutes later, I checked on her, only to find she had soiled herself and the bed. I ran for the wipes and frantically cleaned it up before the workers could see it and scold her. She observed me the entire time without uttering a sound, just staring up at me with those solemn eyes.

Now I know the reason they don't want her to eat: she is so sick, too much liquid will cause her to have diarrhea. But the fact is that she needs nourishment or she will not live. Even if it comes right out the other end, she still needs food. If they would give the sick ones juice or water it would help, but they won't. If we become too insistent, they will prevent our visits, so we have no choice but to keep our opinions to ourselves.

Before I left, I took Squirt to the window and showed her off to the people locked up in the building across from us. These are special-needs adults, and they appear to lead a horribly depressing existence. They waved through the bars and I lifted Squirt's tiny, fragile hand to wave back. Showing them the beautiful babies through the glass breaks up the monotony of their days and it is such an easy gesture of kindness to make.

Regina confessed to me today that it is becoming increasingly difficult for her to come and work in this dismal environment. Her husband was complaining about how it is affecting her moods. She admitted that at first it was exciting to know she was helping so much, but now many times she leaves feeling hopeless. I can honestly say I know how she feels. I pray she will continue anyway; it will be terribly rough on me if I have to go alone. We have divided the work up so that two of us come in on two mornings and the other two volunteers (Lucy and Sonya) on two alternate mornings.

When scheduling volunteer time, I keep teams of two together. I've learned we need one another's emotional support even to walk through the doors. Some days are so bad that I don't know how I'll summon the strength to go back, but then I'll wonder if the babies would miss me and think, Heck, yes . . . they would miss me! But at times the decision to return is not an easy one. I love it and hate it at once.

The hardest part is the journey to the orphanage. The image of that cold, unfeeling institution dwells in my mind and urges me to

stay away—I can't think of anyone who would truly enjoy spending time in such depressing surroundings. But when I force myself
to walk through those gloomy doors and I see the faces of all those
children who are so bereft of human touch, I feel a warmth and
peace deep inside my soul. I know this strange "opportunity" is a
once-in-a-lifetime gift to me to make a positive difference in the
world. I continually remind myself not to waste it.

When I return home from the visits, I usually shower and then
fall into a deep sleep—it's my new coping mechanism. Those are
the only days I nap, and napping is the best way for me to deal
with all I see and absorb. I slept only fifty minutes today before
Amanda got home from school, but it felt as though I'd been in
a coma. Once awakened, I was able to jump back into my "mom
routine" and temporarily put aside thoughts of the orphanage.

The seasons are changing and many of the babies remain sick,
with high temperatures, fevers, and colds. I have also been running a fever sporadically for two weeks. Since my arrival in China,
I have lost twenty-one pounds from my already thin frame and I
feel miserable and run-down. I haven't been able to eat anything
except instant potatoes for lunch for the past two days and no
breakfast except for a Coke. I have to get over this low point; I've
too much to do to be ill!

* * *

SEPTEMBER 28, 2003

Milo, our second pup, is sick and refuses to eat or walk. If I attempt
to prop him up, he just stands there, swaying back and forth until
he falls down. It is distressing to see him so frail when just a short
time ago he was a frisky puppy romping happily about.

Today the vet gave him two more injections through the muscle and a bag of fluids by IV. That makes ten injections so far and
he is worse now than before this treatment began.

I became upset and had my driver attempt to interpret for me. I wanted to know when to quit, when to simply be merciful and let him die. I'm not concerned so much about the money, but the shots are painful for Milo. He seems so near death, and I don't want to put him through an ordeal that won't help. The vet was finally forced to admit that if Milo is not better by tomorrow, we should put him to sleep.

Max's health seems to be stable, but I noticed today his nose is getting runny and he is sneezing. The vet said he would probably contract the bacteria that invaded Milo's little body, so it looks as though we may lose him too. I regret having gone to Pet Street; I have no idea how I am going to break the news to Amanda that both of these darling puppies are likely to die.

10

OCTOBER 1, 2003

Beijing is overrun with street urchins. They sneak up behind foreigners to pick their pockets or they beg for money at the side of the street. As we were stopped in traffic, we saw one child, about ten, slip behind a woman and unzip the pocketbook she had thrown over her shoulder. As the child reached in, the woman felt a movement, but as she turned to look, the child expertly moved away.

One way for impoverished families to earn money is to set their handicapped child out in the shopping lanes with a tin can. Sometimes one man or woman has many children that aren't even related out on pickpocket missions; in this way, the children earn their keep and the adult protects them. The children usually have some kind of disability—deformed limbs are most successful in invoking sympathy.

While we were in Beijing today for a day of sightseeing and shopping, we passed such a child. She was a sweet-looking little girl of about seven or so. While people passed her by, she gave them pitiful, pleading stares. Amanda asked me for money, so I slipped her some coins to add to the girl's tin cup. I knew it would go straight to the beggar's sponsor, but the point was that Amanda was expressing compassion. I did not want to squash her impressionable heart by telling her the child would not benefit from the

money. In time, she will learn how the world of street children
works, but for now I wish to nurture her desire to help. After
witnessing sights such as these, I do feel thankful the children at
our orphanage have shelter, food, and a dry bed to sleep in. They
could so easily be homeless, but at least they've been rescued from
that awful fate. I have learned there are much worse places to be
in China than an orphanage.

As we walked along to find a taxi, one old woman followed
us, almost staggering and shaking her can at us while repeating,
"Money, money, money." I found her attitude rude and aggressive,
insinuating that she was entitled to our money. We did not contribute to her tin can and I walked away wondering who taught
her the English word *money.*

Beijing is a vastly different world from where we live, and the
people here are so different from those in Shengxi. The city offers
endless amenities to foreigners to make their lives easier: Western
restaurants, zoos, museums, shopping, and many other forms of
entertainment. When we are there for a day we feel a mite envious, but then we reflect on how lucky we are in Shengxi, our
considerably smaller town, to be seeing the real China and not the
commercialized, metropolitan side of the culture. Visiting for a
day trip is enough, and when we return home to Shengxi, we are
again satisfied with our lives here.

* * *

OCTOBER 6, 2003

On my way to the orphanage, I stopped to pick up a new girl,
Sheila. She is from Hong Kong originally, but just moved here
from a seven-year stay in America. Looking very young for her
age of thirty-something, Sheila bounces along with a playful,
sweet personality. She wants to get involved with the orphanage because her church in the States does a lot of mission-related

work for China. Sheila speaks Cantonese, Mandarin, and English. It will be a tremendous asset to have her communication skills to help us to accomplish more for the children.

We made our way to the office, and with her strong language skills, Sheila breezed through the registration process. On the way to the children's area, I gave her a quick tour.

In the baby room, many of the babies' conditions had improved greatly this past week; there were far fewer sick ones lying about. Only three children were still running fever and several looked fully recovered. Sheila was nervous about handling the babies with disabilities. She did not want to hold the spina bifida babies for fear of hurting them, and she declined to feed the one with a cleft lip and palate. He is difficult to handle because he has no top lip and the roof of his mouth is open to his nasal passages, causing the milk to come right back out again.

Overall, though, Sheila did as well as could be expected for her first day. She was holding one sick girl whose cheeks were burning scarlet with fever, when the toddler started choking. Sheila became alarmed and I made a dash for her, but before I could get there, the girl began projectile vomiting. Sheila held the child away from her body, trying to avoid the vomit, and the scene was horrifying. I have never seen such a little person throw up that much.

I ran to fetch the supervisor, who took the child and settled her in her crib. I went in search of a mop while Sheila was on a mission to find soap and water for her arms. I felt bad for her—what an initiation!

While I had the opportunity, I asked Sheila to read the tags on the cribs for me. She informed me of the dates the babies had arrived, their names, and what their health problems were. I received a huge surprise about my little preemie girl, Squirt. She isn't a girl. She is a little boy!

I stood there in shock for a moment, and then argued, "No . . . that's wrong—look at her dress."

We lifted the dress, opened the diaper, and saw that Squirt was definitely a boy. Just last week I had changed his diaper but was frantically hurrying, so I neglected to see a certain body part in there. Today when I saw the evidence, I had a hearty laugh. I can scarcely believe that all this time I thought I was snuggling a baby girl. I suppose the only preemie clothes they have are girl clothes; I will take care of that problem next week. It just astounded me that she is a he because Squirt has such petite fingers and toes and such luscious little eyelashes—what a gorgeous boy.

He thought all the attention was marvelous, and when we had to move on, he cried, sounding much stronger than last week. He still has some fever, but looks vastly improved. I am so relieved; I know he is winning the battle. Before we left, I gave him more attention and then kissed him goodbye.

After leaving the baby room, we stopped at the five-to-eight-year-olds' room. Peering through the window, I saw the children sitting at little wooden tables, waiting for lunch to be served. The tables were similar to those I've seen in Sunday schools: small and worn, with a haphazard array of old chairs. On each table was a blue-checked paper cloth and a small vase of artificial flowers. Through a doorway I could also see that the adjoining room was fitted with short wooden beds lined up in a row, each with a straw mat folded on top. It appeared to be storybooklike and nice (to the extent that orphanages can be nice), if one could only ignore the sterile feel of the place.

Down the hall was a semifunctional kitchen the size of a bathroom stall, with just a hot plate to heat water and a sink with a faucet that would not work half the time. There is usually only one bar of soap to share between all the rooms. I have heard there is more in storage, but the administration is miserly about supplies. I can never be sure what is true and what is not. Along the wall was a line of four pots cradled in ancient chairs, serving as portable toilets. The children are not allowed personal items such as toys or books, which, to me, is strange for an orphanage. Clothes are kept in one location, and every morning the *ayis* lay out an outfit for each child to wear.

The children were excited to see me. I smiled and said hello, and they began jumping around and trying to talk to me all at once. When I asked what they were doing, they told me in Chinese that they were waiting to eat and then would take a nap. I leaned in through the window, poking as many as I could in the belly buttons or pulling at their ears to make them giggle. They looked downcast when Sheila and I started to leave, but I tried to remain cheerful, saying something comforting to each of them. There must have been thirty children in that room, and every one of them was starved for attention and affection.

Several of the children have something wrong with their ears—it looks as if they have been sewn shut. Many of them have deformed limbs. I researched this recently and found that two reasons for the high number of birth defects are unhealthy diets and the lack of clean water. Another reason is poverty—many women can't afford or don't have access to nutritional supplements such as folic acid, which is important for a healthy fetus. Xiao Feng, a small girl with a beautiful smile, is missing a hand. When she saw me look at her arm, she quickly hid it behind her back. I find it difficult to believe this small problem was the cause of her separation from her family, yet when I ask, there is no other explanation.[2]

One little boy with the face of an angel has albinism. His skin and hair are white; his eyes stand out vividly against the paleness. The other children call him Le Bai, which translates to "Little White." He has such a sweet and gentle disposition. I can't imagine that just because of this skin difference, his parents abandoned him. He is still Chinese on the inside!

---

2 Xiao Feng was adopted by a family in the U.S. in early 2007.

When I first started working at the orphanage, the children observed me with intense curiosity, but only a few would venture close. Now they know my face, and it gives me an incredible, almost indescribable, feeling of joy to have them run to me for hugs as I pass by their doors. In the process, I am also breaking down the walls the *ayis* have erected.

Sometimes I am able to make the *ayis* laugh, usually by my butchered attempts at speaking the local language. Today I wore the cross Dad gave me and they all clamored to see it. The toddlers loved it so much that I had to resort to playing defense to keep it safe. Director Yao also wanted to handle it, as if just by touch she could receive some magical power. Gradually, I'm learning how to appeal to these outwardly reserved people.

On the way home, Sheila was in a world of her own. She was silent, except for telling me that she could still smell the sick babies on her. I warned her that she probably would continue to smell them all night, too, even after a shower. I think it is partially psychological, a trick of the mind, because no matter what hygienic measures I take after each visit, the smell lingers with me for some time. I asked if she wanted to join me next week, but she was hesitant to commit. I hope she can summon the strength to return. It is overwhelming at first for anyone—I'll never forget how I felt—but especially for someone with as gentle and kind a heart as Sheila.

* * *

OCTOBER 11, 2003

I came home today from the orphanage to find Milo in the worst condition yet. I was on the floor, sitting beside him, when he suddenly began having violent convulsions and foaming at the mouth and nose. When this finally ceased, his breathing became erratic and raspy. Mr. Li, our driver, arrived, and we wrapped Milo in a towel. We took both the pups downtown to the vet's office, where Mr. Li acted as translator again. He explained what had happened, and the doctor decided it was time to let Milo go. Before I could comprehend or absorb what was being said, two workers had snatched our little puppy and whisked him away.

Now completely frustrated, I yelled, "No, not yet! I want to hold him while he dies!" After he was given the injection, I walked around with him snuggled in my arms, whispering to him until I was overcome by the oddest feeling. You hear people say they can feel the life go out of someone; after today, I can attest that description is accurate. When Milo's eyes became still and his body ceased to be pliant, I handed him to the one compassionate worker, who laid him on the corner of the desk while he assisted with Max. After some prodding and poking, it was confirmed that he, too, might die. As we headed out the door, I turned and saw that Milo's body was still lying, forgotten, on the corner of the desk. What a dreadful last picture to have imprinted on my mind.

* * *

OCTOBER 13, 2003

I've just returned from standing with Amanda at the bus stop. The wind is high this morning, but the temperature is mild. It was a perfect time for Amanda, Max, and me to enjoy a few quiet minutes together.

My gaze rested upon a construction crew at work across the road. I watched as a man squatted on the street, using water from a hose to brush his teeth. Behind him there were five men carrying a massive tree with a trunk and root ball the size of a small utility building. Astonishingly, they plant these gigantic trees at new housing sites. At the construction area, an old man caught my eye because his body was permanently distorted, likely from carrying bricks most of his life. He methodically placed the bricks in two canvas bags, knotted them on both ends of a bamboo pole, and then carried the pole across his shoulders to the partially constructed building. It was nothing short of amazing that he was able to lift it. On the sidewalk in front of the site, an ancient couple hobbled around, selling baskets of steaming rice and fresh fruit.

A few minutes later, I directed Amanda's attention to a passing motorcycle carrying not two, not three, but four men! They are small men, but men all the same.

Last night I stood mesmerized as I watched six men descend, using the Chinese method, the outside of a high-rise building. They wrapped their legs around a rope while sitting on the paint bucket attached, and one of their trusted colleagues lowered them the fifteen or twenty floors to the ground. Five or six men were coming down simultaneously but at different levels. They reminded me of spiders lowering themselves on their silken threads.

Here, building developers or owners allow their construction workers to live in the apartments or homes right up until the floors are installed. Then they must move to tents or buildings quickly erected for temporary use. Every night, from my vantage point, I can see some of the workers playing cards. Others are squatted on their haunches in front of big bowls of water, washing their clothes for morning. At the building's rear, still others have the hose out to take showers with.

Sometimes, when I'm out walking Max, I can hear them singing, but most times, it's fairly quiet—they're likely tired from working so late. It is much like a camp, with small children running about and playing games. If one of them happens to glance out and see me with Max under the streetlamp, he immediately notifies the others that an American woman is outside, and soon I have an audience watching Max do his business. Sometimes I'll return their stares and say hello in Mandarin, and boy, do they scatter!

As long as you remain behind the tall walls of our housing development, you might believe you are in any upper-middle-class American neighborhood, but step out or look beyond the wall and you'll get a shock, a jolt of reality. You quickly remember that you are halfway around the world in a country that you would have never chosen, given other options. Now that we are here, it is beginning to grow on all of us.

* * *

Heather called this morning, and she was furious with me. I had to tell her we are not moving back home until next summer. She doesn't understand why we can't simply pack up and go wherever we want to, whenever we want to. I know I promised her we'd be away for only eighteen months, but it's now clear that Ben's assignment is not going to be finished within that time. Not only that, but I feel my work at the orphanage is just beginning, and I have many more plans and improvements to implement. I am torn between wanting to please Heather and needing to stay here. I can only hope she'll get over her anger, and perhaps one day understand what an enormous sacrifice remaining in China is for me.

11

OCTOBER 14, 2003

This morning I broke the news to Amanda that we couldn't torture Max with further vet treatments. He has been extremely sick all weekend and has not eaten since Friday. Amanda said her goodbyes before leaving for school. She tried her best to be a big girl and I was proud of her. She would rather lose her puppy than see him suffer any longer.

At the veterinarian's office for the last time, I held Max in my lap while they gave him the injections to euthanize him. For unknown reasons, the vet used a different medication that required two shots. His assistant asked me to leave after the first one, but I refused and, of course, that made her angry. I insisted that Mr. Li inform her that Max wasn't leaving my lap until his heart stopped beating, and only then would I leave. Mr. Li didn't quite understand, but everyone got the picture that I wasn't moving. The assistant kept lifting Max's head up by his ear to look at his eyes and then dropping it, until I scolded her to be gentler. The second injection was finally given, and I'm just glad our second little puppy is now at peace.

* * *

OCTOBER 20, 2003

I thought I would be going alone to the orphanage today, but I saw Regina yesterday at a luncheon and was happy to hear she wanted to join me. This morning, just as I was heading out the door, Sheila called and asked if I could pick her up, too. Soon the three of us were headed toward our babies and two hours of smiles and sadness—a little of the first and probably a great deal of the latter.

Sheila asked about the little girl who had vomited on her two weeks ago, and was told the child had died. That put a damper on the morning, but we brightened when we saw that almost every one of the other babies appeared to be well. However, I held one little girl who felt feverish. A worker argued with me, producing a thermometer, and when we took the child's temperature, she was humbled to see that I was right.

Moving along, we got out the bottles and began feeding the babies. There were two new ones this week. One can sit up in her crib, which is highly unusual. Achieving normal milestones takes these kids a lot longer than the average child because they spend so much time each day on their backs. When they reach about nine months old, they're finally able to sit in a walker for part of the day. Tragically, although they are out of their cribs and sitting up, they can't move about or "walk" because the walkers are usually tied to the wall.

This particular little girl sat up in her bed and, with a grave expression, watched our every move. Since she was quiet, the workers left her alone. She had beautiful eyes and oddly dark skin. Regina and I agreed she somehow looks like a Bella, so that is what we decided to call her. I fed her breakfast and she remained solemn throughout, despite my trying every antic in my repertoire to make her smile. As I fed her, I pondered what could make a mother or father leave such a precious thing to grow up alone. I felt certain that somewhere there was a mother grieving over her abandoned baby.

The babies' diet is appalling, and that of the other orphanage children is equally atrocious. For breakfast, the toddlers and older children have rice with greens mixed in. For lunch, they have greens with rice mixed in. For supper, it's rice and greens. It doesn't look that bad, but no one would want it for every meal! Clearly they get sick of it because there are a few who spit it back out even though their hunger is evident. It appears to be an act of defiance, so we simply keep shoveling it in because we know they won't be allowed to eat again for several hours.

Squirt was waiting for me to visit him today. I know this because he was just tickled to see me! When I approached his bed, he recognized me and kicked his skinny little legs in excitement. I picked him up and held him close. I was saddened all over again to feel how small he still was; he felt like a bag of bones. Each time I feed him, I whisper to him that he really needs to fatten up. Eventually I had to give the other babies some attention, but before I left Squirt, I gave him a special rocking session on my lap while I sang "Itsy Bitsy Spider." I hope none of the others notice how I spoil him; they may become a little jealous.

The workers were unusually pleasant today; we had only one incident this morning during bath time. After one of the toddlers was dressed and laid down, she stood up on her bed. We were all busy dressing other babies and didn't see her as she fell onto the floor, landing on her head.

Tilly ran for her, fussing and looking like she was going to blow a fuse, but I made sure I reached the screaming child first. I pulled her into my arms, cradling her head against me and calming her down. Tilly retreated, but only after pointing her finger in the child's face as if to say, "I'll get you later!" The girl became quiet, staring into my eyes as if surprised at my attempt to comfort her. After I laid her down again, she silently held her arms out with a pleading look that melted my heart. A nasty goose egg was already rising over her eyes. I scooped her into my arms one more time and hugged her gently before moving on to dress more children.

I'm optimistic today. Most of the children are well again, the workers are getting kinder, and we volunteers are feeling stronger. More expat women are becoming curious about the work we do and are considering joining us.

* * *

OCTOBER 24, 2003

On my way to the orphanage today, I picked up Sheila and Regina. Ann met us there, making a group of four women anxious to hug some children.

We discovered that another little girl has been approved for adoption. She is a two-year-old named Jin Ji, and she's full of trouble. She likes to stand up in her crib and peer over the side to watch us feed the babies. Jin Ji is the room mascot, and the workers treat her much better than the other children. I know she has adventured around the orphanage, because she constantly grabs my hand and tries to lead me out the door.

While we were working, a baby arrived who had just been discovered abandoned. She'd been found with a note in Chinese that gave her first name and her age; an *ayi* translated and told me the baby was four weeks old. She looked perfect! I'm certain her family abandoned her because she was a girl—under the one-child policy in China, most families want a boy, to carry on the lineage.

The tiny girl cried incessantly. I kept picking her up and rocking her, but she clearly wanted milk. When the workers finally produced the bottles, we all dove at them. I raced back to get the new baby a bottle of her own, but there were none left. Several other babies were screaming because they were hungry, but there were just not enough bottles to go around.

I waited until a bottle with leftover milk finally became free, took the new baby onto my lap, and fed her. She ate ravenously, but after she'd filled her little tummy, I still couldn't get her to calm down. Ann guessed she was probably still used to being swaddled, so we bundled her in a towel, which instantly stopped her crying. I'm sure it was a traumatic day for her and she still yearns for her mother. She will have to get used to the life of an orphan, which means no more hugs, kisses, or cuddling except from the crazy expat women who come in a few times a week. I felt so sorry for her and hated to leave.

I'd brought candy for the older ones, but I must have miscounted them last week. Outside their room, I counted them again to find I was four short. I couldn't possibly give the candy out and leave four children with nothing, so I left silently. Next week I'll have to remember to pack extra.

I padded downstairs to the deaf children's living area and gave the candy to them instead. One girl who looked about seven years old kept blowing me kisses—wherever did she learn that? After I gave her candy, she put her arms around a little boy standing behind her and gently guided him to me to make sure he got some too. I was touched by this gesture of caring and affection, so rare among the children in this bleak institution. On my way down the stairs, I looked up and saw that the little deaf girl was still there, blowing kisses with a forlorn look. She wore a hearing aid, but I don't think she could speak.

Before leaving, I took some time to look around and found what appeared to be an indoor playroom. Several wheelchairs were crowded in a corner and a few toys were strewn about. Although it was lunchtime, no children were to be seen. A woman carried a large pan of rice up the stairs; she was followed by another woman balancing a cookie sheet spread with sautéed mushrooms, which is the first sign of variety I've seen for lunch.

I also found a schoolroom equipped with desks and a chalkboard. On the walls were taped a variety of children's posters just like at my children's schools at home. I've passed by that room many times but have never seen anyone in it. Do they have classes at all? I dearly hope they do, but this remains a mystery.

* * *

OCTOBER 30, 2003

Today we had no choice but to dress the babies in wet diapers after their baths. Perhaps the laundry is taking longer to dry now that the weather has cooled. Next week they will likely all be sick from wearing wet diapers. I desperately want to show the *ayis* better ways of doing things, but if I do, I'll be denied any chance of returning. I just have to be meek—which isn't like me at all—and do things their way.

When I go home to South Carolina next summer, I plan to buy cloth diapers in all sizes for the babies. Ben is going to speak with someone at his company to see if they might be interested in sponsoring the shipping if we buy the needed items or get donations. We also plan to collect donations of other items such as wipes and diaper-rash medications. I'd like to be able to start a supply cabinet and keep it stocked with everyday necessities.

Two toddlers were particularly overjoyed by our visit. One of them, Yue Hua, is the child whom I taught to walk. She was desperately attached to Yoli and now has transferred her affection to me. She loves it when I pick her up, but when I try to put her down, she clings to me, wrapping her little arms around my legs and staring up at me wistfully. Yue Hua has adopted the American way of hugging, and any time I sit down she flies into my arms. Fine with me—she is so huggably sweet. Yue Hua is supposedly in the process of adoption to America, but I don't know where we stand on that. She has the most solemn eyes I've ever seen on a child; they're so full of a sadness that I can't reach. She rarely smiles, but when she does, she makes it worth the wait. I pray the paperwork will be hurried along so she can get to her new family as soon as possible.

* * *

NOVEMBER 4, 2003

When I arrived today and headed for my special baby, Squirt, I found his little bed empty and all his blankets gone. A feeling of dread washed over me. I didn't want to ask; I was afraid to know and I was afraid not to know. My hands began to shake. I glanced around and caught the workers turning from me. I could tell from their downcast, guilty expressions that it was bad news. My eyes finally met Xiao Annie's, the only *ayi* who would look at me, and then I knew. She passed a palm over her eyes—the sign that someone had died.

I stumbled to the small stools we sit on while holding the babies. My legs lost all strength as I lowered myself and covered my face with my hands. Mercifully, no one patronized me by attempting words of comfort.

I was in shock. I couldn't understand. Three days ago, Squirt had been fine; he was not sick, and he was eating with a hearty appetite. I was certain he was going to make it. Every time I fed him, I stared into his eyes and willed him to survive. Sure, he still looked like a shriveled-up old man, but it seemed his hunger to live was sustaining him and helping him to become stronger each week.

Squirt is gone. He never had the chance to get well and to have a family. I can't stop thinking of his last moments. I wasn't there for him.

I wasn't there.

I did not get to hold him as he left this world. He had to die alone. I wasn't there.

I can't do this anymore.

12

I pulled myself out of the black cloud that was threatening to envelop me. I am reluctant to admit that all my life I've had times of trial where I've struggled with bouts of depression. I haven't had an easy road to adulthood, but I've always strived to overcome the many obstacles. My experiences here in China, and particularly at the orphanage, are teaching me that if I remain strong, I am capable of not allowing the depression to take control. I refuse to let it suck any more of my life from me.

I made it to the orphanage this morning.

It was interesting but discouraging to observe haircut day unfolding. As we walked down the hall to the baby room, we could hear crying and wailing at a higher pitch than usual. Inside, we found four *ayis* clustered around a round wooden table with a toddler pinned on it. He was lying on his belly, screaming uncontrollably, while each worker secured an arm or leg and the female barber used electric shears to shave his head. They continued in this fashion, first with the toddlers and then the babies, turning most of them into miniature Chinese monks.

Once the shaving was completed, the babies were swaddled in towels and laid side by side on a floor mat. It was comical to see them all in a row—we could no longer recognize them. At first glance and without their individual hairdos, they looked identical. Even the girl toddlers had been relieved of their locks.

The house barber really needs some lessons. We had to apply makeshift Band-Aids, which consisted of a wad of toilet paper pressed firmly on the ears. I think the grating buzz of the shears was the real source of terror for most of the kids, for as soon as the shears were brought near, the children became extremely frightened, even before the instrument touched them.

The room's supervisor, Xiao May, informed us that she is being transferred next week to a downstairs room. We are worried that whoever takes her place may resent us foreigners intruding on her territory. I can only hope she will accept us, as May finally has. I recall my first visits to the orphanage, when the staff acted as if they did not relish my presence. When our time was up, May would frown and point to her watch and the door.

By now I believe we have proved we are not there to criticize but to help. We break a sweat just as they do and try to lighten their load as much as possible. I think we are gradually working our way into their routine and that, despite their initial resistance, they just may be starting to like us. Lately I sense a certain degree of respect from the *ayis*, as if they have crossed an invisible line of resentment into acceptance.

Squirt's bed constantly taunted me today. When my eyes wandered over there, I'd see the new baby who has taken his spot, which made me sad all over again.

Since it was bath day, the morning flew by and before we knew it, we were making the rounds with goodbye hugs. It was a cold day, and as I strode down the stairs and to the car, my only thoughts were of a warm bath and a cup of hot tea. I managed to get both, along with a catnap, before Amanda arrived home from school. A few hours at the orphanage exhausts all of us. I can't imagine pulling an eight-hour day there as the *ayis* do. I'm developing a new admiration for them.

* * *

NOVEMBER 26, 2003

Today is Thanksgiving. Yesterday I was wallowing in sadness because we won't be spending the holiday with our families in the States. Ben went to a company lunch, but I declined; I just wanted to stay home and indulge myself in a state of melancholy. I secretly pored over the letter Heather had written me on my last night at home and cried fresh tears all over it. Then something amazing happened.

I helped Amanda with her homework; afterward, we put on some music. The next thing we knew, Amanda and I were dancing up a storm and laughing all the while. After the first song, Amanda wanted my silk shirt so we would match (I wore the pajama bottoms and a T-shirt) and we danced for more than an hour, singing the entire time. I could feel the sadness lifting and began thinking of all the things I could still be thankful for even though we are far from home.

I desperately miss one daughter, but I still have Amanda to keep me smiling. The most wonderful husband of anyone I know is mine, and he treats me like a princess. I haven't had to pump gas since April. I can drink as much bottled water as I want and it costs less than four cents a bottle! I am not tied down to a miserable job I have to drag myself to every day. When we get lost, we can deny responsibility and blame it on the driver. I am gaining confidence by learning a language that is considered one of the most difficult in the world. When I do something outrageously silly here, it is not attributed to the fact that I'm blond; they think it is because I am American!

Most of all, I was struck in a new way last night with the realization that I am at last doing something meaningful, and that is what I've always wanted to do. So how can I complain?

Ben returned home to find me in much improved spirits. Tonight we are going to dinner with his friends from work. They want to spend the holiday with us, and I don't feel like struggling to find the ingredients for a meal. The Chinese woman who owns the Mexican restaurant will cook our turkey—it should be interesting to see how a Mexican-Asian turkey for an American celebration turns out. However, I've said it before: it's not the food that makes the day, it's the family and friends.

* * *

DECEMBER 1, 2003

The babies hate bath day—it is so cold for them. The rooms are already freezing, and then the babies are undressed and put through the washing process. As soon as we begin removing their three layers of smelly clothing, they know something is up. The toddlers scream and hide under their covers. Today I kept lifting one blanket and teasing the little girl beneath it, trying to calm her, but I was unsuccessful because she was so frightened.

When they come out of the washroom, they are shaking with cold. We hug and cuddle them, attempting to offer comfort before we begin the struggle of dressing them in their fresh three layers of clothing. We have to be quick—they're brought from the washroom so fast we can hardly keep up.

When we entered the room today, the workers had the doors and windows open. This made no sense; it is winter and the wind causes a bitter draft. About an hour later, the *ayis* closed everything so the rooms would start warming up. I fail to comprehend their thinking. Perhaps they cannot afford the electricity needed to warm the rooms. . . . Even so, why not dress the children warmly when the room needs airing, and save bath time and struggles with the clothes for when the windows are closed and the room has heated up? However, there is little I can say without a backlash; I must resign myself to their way of doing things.

Xiao Yan is our new room supervisor. I really like her; she has a sweeter disposition than some we have dealt with. She smiles a good deal and shows concern for the children. I cannot imagine her hurting one of them. I tried to interact with her a little, but she is very shy around foreigners. It will take some time to build a relationship, but I think we'll be all right with her.

I brought snacks for the special-needs children on the second floor. Whenever I enter their room, chaos ensues—the kids become so excited they can hardly form a proper line. Being an older group of children, they are good at improvising ways to sneak more food. Some get their snack, quickly eat it, and rush to the back to line up for another one. I try to scan for crumbs around their mouths before handing out the snacks—I don't want some to get more than their share and leave the others upset. If I were not trying to be serious and teach manners, it would be quite funny. One little boy, about six years old, is always begging me to hold him. I can't, though; he's just too big for me. Instead, I hug him, and he latches onto me like a leech.

Another girl, age approximately thirteen, has Down syndrome and is always especially happy to repeat the few words of English she knows.

"Hello! How are you?!" she bellows at me.

I reply with, "I am fine. And you?" This makes her giggle and stumble to her chair with a huge smile. I can see such kindness and intelligence in her eyes, making me wish she was allowed to be a part of the world outside. Each time I see her, I feel sad for her isolation.

Christmas is nearing, and today we volunteers are meeting to prepare gift bags for the children. We will all go on Friday to sing songs and bring Santa and gifts to the orphanage. Many people will be attending, so perhaps we'll recruit some more volunteers out of it. The kids all know that foreigners have a Santa, and just like at home, they always ask if he is real. Children really are the same everywhere—that's one of the many lessons my experience here is teaching me.

13

I was invited to a Christmas cookie exchange party, which sounded like a good opportunity to meet some of the newer women in our expatriate association. Poring over my cookbooks to find a recipe, I came across several but knew the hard part was going to be tracking down the ingredients. I got on the phone and called the store in Beijing that carries foreign items.

"Do you have vanilla?" No, sold out.

"Do you have raisins?" No, sold out.

"What about slivered almonds?" No, sold out.

"Chocolate chips? Please . . ."

"Yes, we have four bags."

Bingo! I bought all four, though I didn't need them all. Someone in Shengxi will and I'll be the hero who shares.

Next came the search for white sugar, brown sugar, flour, and vanilla. Mixed luck there—yesterday I found caramel syrup for one recipe, but I couldn't find the chopped nuts I needed to finish it. One of my friends found me a bag each of brown sugar and white sugar, and I found her a bag of flour. Lena, my neighbor, is going to loan me a tiny bit of precious vanilla. I needed two boxes of vanilla pudding and a friend had one, so I'll improvise and cut the recipe in half. I'm supposed to have baking soda delivered

today, but the delivery man is two hours late, so I don't know if
that will happen. I'll gather everything and see if it will be enough
to bake a batch of special cookies. They have to be scrumptious
because the recipes will be shared with ten other women. When
I return to the States for a visit, I'm heading for the baking aisle,
where I'll stock up on sprinkles, chocolate chips, baking powder,
vanilla, and anything else I can fit into my luggage that will help
me produce exquisite holiday goodies next year.

* * *

DECEMBER 15, 2003

December fourteenth was Christmas at the orphanage. All the
volunteers arrived and arranged a circle of chairs in the schoolroom. Most of the children whom we see on a weekly basis were
forbidden from attending; only the healthiest and brightest of
them arrived. They were excited to be taken out of their normal
routine, and it was difficult to get them calmed down enough to
stay seated so we could begin singing.

In Mandarin, the volunteers sang "Rudolph the Red-nosed
Reindeer" and a few other Christmas songs. (I sang in English.)
The kids were mostly interested in touching, so hugs were passed
around in abundance. After a few songs, Santa made his grand
appearance and the kids went wild. They know Santa as *Sheng
Dan Lao Ren*, which translates as "the Christmas Old Man."

Santa handed out the gift bags we had assembled earlier in the
week. Each small plastic bag contained a juice box, a candy bar,
cake, and a small stuffed animal—all tied with a ribbon. The children were less interested in the toys than in the food. They could
hardly restrain themselves as we helped them untie the ribbons
so they could eat the candy bar. It was humbling to see them so
happy over something so small.

Some of our own children came with us, including my

Amanda, who was very frightened. She clung to me most of the time, telling me later that she never wanted to go back there. She was overwhelmed by the cold and the squalid appearance of the rooms. I took her upstairs for a look at the babies, who were very surprised to see me at night. I showed Amanda my favorites, and she tiptoed around, tentatively peeking through the rails of the cribs. I think she felt sad for these children. She suddenly became quiet and couldn't wait to get away from the place.

Later, after the director had left for a meeting, we all stole up to the second-floor room of the special-needs children. They were sitting quietly in their usual chairs, staring at the TV. As we crept in with goody bags, the children looked up in alarm, but once they realized treats awaited them, their faces lit up.

We made the rounds, helping them untie the bags and also giving them a hug or squeezing their hands to show we weren't afraid or repulsed. It brings me to tears to see how they are treated like lepers. They weren't allowed to come to the party, though they can walk, talk, and have feelings just like the others. This culture wants nothing to do with them and they are hidden away because of their deformities or disabilities, yet how they would have enjoyed the festivities! At least we were able to share the gifts, and for that, I am thankful.

14

After the rush of the Christmas season and New Year's, I was excited to see everyone at the orphanage. Immediately upon arriving there, however, I received horrible news: two of our baby boys had died. Although they had been looking extremely frail, it was still a shock to me. Every time I looked at their empty beds today, I had to fight back tears. I got home, climbed under the covers, and just now arose, seven hours later. Sleeping is the only way my mind can cope when it overloads with this kind of grief.

The other babies were doing fine. Recently I read that massaging babies can make them healthier, so I gave many body massages today. I concentrated on the ones who were particularly upset, and they calmed down quickly as I gently rubbed them. They crave human touch so badly, and it is such an easy thing to offer.

No baths were given today because the workers said it was too cold. When they stepped out for a break, I went around shutting the windows. It was near freezing in there, yet I'm sure they were flung open again as soon as I left. Common sense has still not arrived here, I'm afraid.

I saw something interesting today—something I wasn't supposed to see. The workers had bribed two of the older, mentally disabled teens to carry the heavy totes of diapers upstairs. After the youngsters were done hauling the diapers up three flights of stairs and setting them in the room, the workers gave each of them a small bag of potato chips. The teens unzipped their coats while the workers helped them hide the treats and then close their zippers. They were tired but clearly happy to have a secret snack.

The other children went wild today when they saw me approaching with my backpack. Slowly they are learning patience and manners; I don't give them a snack until they are properly seated. I enforce this to make sure everyone gets only one snack each and to teach them manners.

I think all of us are feeling discouraged about the two baby boys. Perhaps if we had been there to make sure they'd had enough to eat, they would have lived. I'm sure I am not the only one who is haunted by that thought today.

* * *

JANUARY 19, 2004

I just returned from the orphanage a few hours ago. Regina was back from her hometown, in Germany, where she had been nursing her sick mother for the past few months. Regina is the jolliest person I have ever met, and I was so happy to see her again. She makes time fly with her silly antics and positive attitude, and the children love to hear her German nursery rhymes.

We walked in to see six of the eight toddlers sitting in their walkers, tied to the wall. They had no toys on their trays to keep them occupied and only Chinese soap operas on TV to stare at numbly. Ironically, they were all wearing identical MY DADDY LOVES ME bibs—obviously a donation from one of the volunteers, or someone with a twisted sense of humor. The kids shrieked in excitement to see us, especially when we circled the room and gave each of them a little squeeze.

The other twenty-two babies were snug in their cribs, lying

under their hand-sewn comforters and strapped in for good measure. I recently discovered the straps aren't there for cruelty, as I'd first thought. Rather, they prevent the babies from kicking off their covers and freezing. It is not a pleasant sight to see straps securing these helpless children, but they are a necessity that must be in place during the winter months. Though we have purchased new heaters with donations, the orphanage director is still reluctant to use them because of the cost of energy. I'm relieved the heaters are at least turned on for a while before bath time to knock the chill out of the room.

After feeding time, we rushed through the bath routine in order to visit the older children and give out coloring books and crayons donated by a youth group in the States. However, when we reached their room, they were having their noontime meal and could not be interrupted. We laid the gifts on their beds. They will be pleasantly surprised when they return from their lunch. Each child having his or her very own box of crayons will be a treat they have never known.

I wish I could have stayed to see them looking through their books. Next time I go I'll bring the rest of the coloring books to the special-needs children. With their imposed isolation and lack of anything to do, they will be the most appreciative of all. Every time I see them, they are sitting placidly at a big metal table and staring into space. I know the books and crayons will add a much needed spark of color into their monotonous lives.

I am proud of this youth group for their efforts at collecting money for the orphanage. They set their minds to do it and succeeded. We are meeting tomorrow about ideas for the donations given thus far. While we don't have enough to sponsor an expensive surgery, we now have the ability to buy more items to make day-to-day living easier for the children and staff. On the list of needs are a new heater/air conditioner and a clothes dryer, which I think we can now provide.

Since I started at the orphanage, many answered prayers and blessings have come our way. I have found that making my weekly email updates detailed and personal makes all the difference. The emails are forwarded to new people, causing my list of sponsors to grow each week. The incoming prayers, gifts, and monetary donations are making the lives of these little angels a little better every day.

* * *

JANUARY 22, 2004

I've had some time to reflect and I've realized that without being aware of it, our family has gradually crested the "culture shock" curve we've heard so much about. I think we've at last become accustomed to living in China. After this startling realization, I admit that I am very proud of who we are today compared with the cowardly bunch who first arrived in this strange and fascinating country.

For example, this evening we couldn't find a taxi, so without reservation, we hopped on the unsanitary, overcrowded double-decker bus. We tossed our coins in and shoved through the crowd just like the locals vying to get a good seat. In addition, we are much better at getting what we want with stumbling verbal exchanges rather than with charades.

We can now walk through the meat department at our local grocery store without holding our breath or averting our eyes. We've already seen, smelled, and experienced so many unfamiliar things that it's just routine shopping. When we're there, the people staring at us no longer make us feel like bugs under a microscope. Instead, I am constantly tempted to perform a comedy skit to heighten their entertainment.

Much to my own warped sense of humor, the sight of numerous men lined up on the side of the road taking a leak is no longer

offensive. I find it amusing that bodily functions in China are per-
functorily performed when and where the need arises, no matter
the location or circumstances.

Somewhere along the way, Chinese soft drinks and chocolate started tasting almost like the real thing. Our once-constant
cravings for junk food from home have dwindled to only occasional longings for the taste of my mother's country cooking. We
no longer complain about the bread we have to eat here, though
it goes bad within one day and you could play hopscotch with
the crusts.

We can flip through Chinese TV and not throw the remote in
frustration. Four men arriving to change a lightbulb in our living
room no longer astounds us. With the thirty-foot ceiling presenting a real problem, we just amuse ourselves while they fumble
with the ladder and argue about whose turn it is to go up. Things
that appalled us when we first arrived are now just mild irrita-
tions. Without question, it's a daily test of patience for foreigners
to live in this land of chaos. However, we've far exceeded anyone's
expectations in adjusting to our new lives. I'm looking forward
to seeing what new obstacles we still have to overcome and the
memories we'll collect in the coming months.

* * *

JANUARY 27, 2004

Brrr—what a cold day! I've just returned from the orphanage,
where it is actually warmer outside than inside the building.
I froze in there today even though I was wearing my thermal
underclothes. And I was once again taken aback by the strange
practices of the Chinese.

In the baby room, all the cribs were gone. Apparently, they'd
been removed for repairs, and not just one or two, but all of them
at once. The babies were lying side by side on two long wooden

blocks. They'd been laid head to head, with half of them pointing one way and the other half the other way. The blocks were only about a foot high, so it was backbreaking work dressing the babies after bath time.

Sheila said the cribs have been gone since Friday and will not be back until next week. Those poor babies are obviously uncomfortable, but at least they have the pads from their cribs and are bundled up tight. It's a good thing too, because the room is frigid, especially close to the floor.

(After I left the baby room, I became even more frustrated when I saw all twenty-five cribs in a nearby room with only one man working on them. Why couldn't they have taken them down one at a time?)

We played with the babies and toddlers for the first hour, after which it was feeding time. It took me the entire time to feed one cleft lip baby! I know she's always handed to me because I have a lot of patience and don't give up. I have seen the workers become aggravated and take the bottle away after the baby has sucked out only a few drops. Then she has to be hungry until the next feeding time, when the situation is repeated. The *ayis* can't understand why we always gravitate toward the special-needs babies. We can't understand why the *ayis* ignore them. It must be a deep-rooted cultural stigma to nourish a less than perfectly formed infant.

In the baby room, I handed out cookies to the toddlers. Yue Hua, my little shadow, usually takes her treats politely and eats them in a corner. This time, oddly, she refused to take a treat. Later she wouldn't eat her rice, which was also unusual. The *ayis* decided her problem was constipation and took her to her bed. Next, four of them gathered around her and proceeded to perform the most barbaric so-called medical treatment you could imagine for a small child with obstructed bowels.

Three *ayis* held Yue Hua down while a wiry older woman repeatedly pushed roughly on her abdomen. Yue Hua screamed and cried hysterically—it was excruciating to hear. After seeing what they were doing, I had to avert my eyes; Regina was also upset but continued to watch. I feared they were going to rupture something in the tiny girl's body. After producing no positive results with this treatment, one *ayi* held Yue Hua's arms back as another tried shoveling rice into her mouth. Finally, they gave up. Though they left her alone, Yue Hua kept crying and her teeth were chattering—most likely from the trauma she had just endured.

Chancing being reprimanded, I went to her bed, climbed behind her, and cradled her against me. I discovered she was burning up with fever. I talked to her softly, singing nursery rhymes under my breath while stroking her head and hands. It took a long time to calm her, and all the while, I was silently fuming. To make things worse, one of the workers became aggravated with me and ordered me to put the other toddlers to bed. I was supposed to take off their coats and shoes and lay them under their covers. They wanted me away from Yue Hua; apparently, they expected her to comfort herself, all because they were angry that she wouldn't eat or have a bowel movement.

Too soon, it was time for us to leave. I returned to Yue Hua and told her goodbye, all the while feeling as if her eyes were pleading with me to stay. I could hardly bear to leave her; I knew she'd have a long, miserable night and there would be no one to stroke her head with a damp cloth or attend to her pain and fever, no one to bring her juice, no one to rock her to sleep. I lie in bed and imagine how utterly lonely and sick she must be right now. I can see her sitting alone on her bed and staring at me with those big, tragic eyes, as she had when I left the room. I'm overwhelmed with feelings of conflict: I don't want to witness any more travesties against children, but I can't possibly abandon them, either.

Yue Hua's adoption dossier is being chased by an American family. I pray she'll be able to leave as soon as possible and that she'll lose every memory she may have of this wretched place. It is my hope that she will become part of a family filled with such love and joy that she will be happy forever.

On Friday, Sheila and I will meet with the administrator to find out the details of the three babies needing surgery. We have two infants waiting for reconstructive operations on their cleft birth defects and a baby ready for surgery on his diaphragm. I hope that we'll be able to get the funds to take care of all of them.

Good news! During the holidays, we had some volunteers fall away, but now we have coverage again for every day of the week. That works well for me; I will be starting Mandarin classes at the university soon and won't have as much time available for the orphanage babies, though I'll still be responsible for a multitude of other administrative duties that I can do from home.

I am anxious to improve my language skills; I want my Mandarin to be good enough to communicate with the orphanage staff without a translator. I could do so much more if I could just speak the language. I also plan to start a class teaching the older kids a little English—as soon as I can speak some Chinese. I intend to be the most disciplined student they've encountered; I've already been studying every day for over a year on my own. I've learned a lot but still have a long way to go.

15

JANUARY 29, 2004

In China, many children with cleft palates or cleft lips die because of complications or starvation. If they do survive, they are shunned by society their entire lives. Some are abandoned and brought to one of the many orphanages similar to the one where I work. China has more than its share of these cleft lip and palate babies. Research doesn't have all the answers as to why they are born this way, but there is a great deal of evidence suggesting it is likely the deficiency of folic acid in the pregnant mother's diet. Most Chinese women are too poor to afford prenatal care or even simple vitamins. In addition, for many poor Chinese families, healthful vegetables are a luxury rarely added to their usual meal of rice, causing further deficiencies.

Because of the cleft deformity, these babies have a difficult time sucking. It is heartbreaking to see the effort it takes them to drink milk without it coming out their noses or spilling over their faces. They often go hungry because the workers don't have enough time to spend on properly feeding them. That's where we volunteers can make a difference; we take the pressure off the workers by being there to help care for these special-needs babies.

At our orphanage, we now have four babies currently in need of this surgery. Each surgery is approximately 5,500 renminbi, which is about US$670. They will need to have two surgeries each—the second when they are a few years old.

We also have four babies who will require heart surgery some-time in the next twelve months. The administrator has agreed to let us have photos of each of them. We will try to find corporate sponsors because heart operations are more expensive than the cleft surgeries. If they do not each find a sponsor, they will likely die—it's as simple as that. These babies are adorable, joyful, and affectionate. They want to be loved just as every other baby does. Since I've started volunteering at the orphanage, we have lost at least four babies to different treatable health problems. It is tragic that something so simple to correct goes unattended for lack of funds!

* * *

FEBRUARY 1, 2004

We received a beautiful new baby today. Her name is Hei Mei, which means "black little sister." Hei Mei is about six months old; she was brought here after her family discovered her minor heart problem. It's not something that needs surgery—she is supposed to grow out of it. She is such a cheerful little thing. Usually the new babies cry for days. Not this one—she was grinning broadly today, adorable dimples making her face sparkle. She has a very dark complexion, indicating that she is probably from the countryside. I know she will be on my mind for a few days. I already can't get that smile out of my head. I think she will quickly become a room favorite with the *ayis* as well as the volunteers.

Yue Hua is much better. I came into the room and she was in the huge metal "time-out" crib, which the children despise. She saw me and quietly started whining.

I came over and teasingly said, "Now, what did you do to get put in there?"

I turned to walk away because I normally do not interfere with discipline, but big tears welled up in Yue Hua's eyes and she stared at me beseechingly. I looked around furtively, decided to play dumb, and lifted her out and into my arms. She stayed on my hip until the bottles were wheeled in, at which point I quickly placed her in the crib. I learned that after the episode of barbaric treatment last week, she'd been taken to the infirmary for the next two days. Hearing this started my anger all over again at the incompetence these children have to deal with.

We have now found sponsors for three of the four babies needing cleft palate surgery. Two will have their surgeries next week and the next two, hopefully, in about two months. It will be the first of two surgeries for each baby, and the most important phase. I am so grateful for all the donors who responded to that tug on their hearts and committed so much help, time, and money.

The painting project is over and the babies have their beds back! When the bedding was lifted off the wooden platforms they'd been sleeping on for a week, the platforms were wet—not just damp, but *wet*—from soiled diapers and sweating bodies. I pray the babies don't get sick from their week on soaked, hard boards.

* * *

FEBRUARY 5, 2004

Yesterday at the orphanage, things were in complete disarray. Sheila and I arrived with Macy, a new volunteer from Texas. Sheila took her to the administration office for registration while I proceeded to the baby room. I stopped at the kindergarten room, where all the kids became agitated because they saw my backpack and knew that meant snacks. I insisted they sit down. The chairs are lined up in two facing rows and there are about thirty-five kids, so it took a while.

I handed out Oreo cookies (yes, China does have Oreos!). The kids were excited because they rarely see chocolate. The first to receive his cookies was the biggest boy in the first row, after which I caught him in the usual ploy—sneaking around to the last seat—to try to get another cookie. When his second turn came, I told him he'd already had his share. I almost slipped him another because he was so darn cute, but I saw all the other children watching to see if he'd succeed, and I knew it would start a ruckus. I told him no and he laughed.

In the baby room, preparations were under way for the two cleft palate babies to go to the hospital for their surgeries. Chaos reigned. Without a translator, I struggled with my Chinglish (a combination of English and Mandarin) and eventually determined what was happening. I gave the babies a squeeze and tried to hold back tears. Feeling as if two of my own children were being taken away, I thought it should be me going along with them. And at least four babies had the flu; diarrhea and fever had taken over. The room smelled bad, and the babies weren't getting their weekly baths because the staff was shorthanded. That meant two weeks without baths, leaving us with some very stinky kids!

Once Macy had completed her paperwork, we showed her around and then got busy with our routine. She had all the usual first-timer's questions. Why do the babies share bottles when they are sick? Why are the toddlers using the same spoon? Why aren't there any toys? What kind of weird medicine is given from a bowl? Why do the *ayis* refuse to show compassion?

We had all struggled with these questions at first, but the bottom line is that we are there only to bring love, affection, and some brightness to the endless gray days of these children. Songs, smiles, hugs, kisses, and just plain old affection are what they need most. Changes can be incorporated, but only in a very subtle fashion.

One small step is that we have convinced the staff to use baby wipes and lotion. We've also supplied soft, new towels to replace the stiff, ugly ones they once used, making bath time a little more bearable for the kids. Little gestures such as these are all we can do. We are building relationships one visit at a time. I told Macy that when I first started coming, when my time was up they'd show me the door or point to their watch as if to say, "Okay, you're done . . . get out." Now, after months of continuing to reach out to them, they appreciate us and are disappointed when we don't show up. That's progress!

16

Yesterday I learned a valuable lesson. Right now, only two toddlers, Jin Ji and Yue Hua, are permitted to walk freely about the room. They are not allowed to play with toys or dolls; they just wander around aimlessly. Occasionally, I've watched as they try to feed the smaller babies a bottle, wiping at their mouths as though they are playing at being adult parents. That gave me the idea to bring them two little dolls to play with while I am there.

The next time I visited, I brought dolls that came with a bathtub, comb, and other accessories. The expressions on the girls' faces when I pulled the dolls out of my bag were unforgettable. It was sheer delight to show them how to play as though they were really taking care of the babies. Yet these little girls are so used to fighting over every scrap that they spent the next two hours sneakily trying to get each other's dolls or supplies. Several tugging battles went on for just a comb or powder! They clung to their toys with ferocity and never relaxed enough to play. Because of their possessive behavior, they found themselves in trouble with the staff. Yue Hua also kept throwing fits on the floor, which was very out of character for her.

When the rice came out, I retrieved the dolls and stored them in my bag. The girls needed to concentrate on eating. Afterward,

they sulked and both got spankings from the workers for misbehaving—all because I attempted to give them some semblance of
the normal childhood I so wish for them. While life is not exactly
fair for most of us, these kids get so few breaks that their daily lives
are downright wretched. But I must constantly remind myself I
cannot push American customs on people who have hundreds of
years of their own unique culture.

According to the directors, the children are not allowed to
play with donated toys because it makes them naughty. At the
time this sounded like a poor excuse, but yesterday I saw firsthand
that it is true. Still, it's depressing to think that a child cannot
enjoy the simple pleasures of being a child.

Adding to the drama yesterday, the staff had obviously had a
tiff. Xiao Jo, one of the more compassionate *ayis*, was in the next
room with tears on her face and the rest of the workers were sulking. It helped me once again view the *ayis* in a more humane fashion, realizing they also have lives outside of the orphanage walls.

They did not bring bottles until late. When the babies finally
got their milk, most were hysterical and had started sucking their
hands, sheets, or anything else available. Regina and I were disturbed but knew not to interfere. We tried comforting the children, but they would not be quieted. It was all so terribly loud.
Almost immediately after taking the bottles, they began having
diarrhea. Most of them had colds again and the room quickly took
on a foul odor.

Regina and I tried to help change diapers, but the staff waved
us away. It was easy to see their frustration with so many babies,
diapers, and feedings, and not many hands to get it all done. They
could have used our help, but their annoyance with our constant
optimistic attitudes won out over their need for assistance. It might
be silly, but sometimes I am embarrassed at my station in life compared with theirs. I can walk out and leave the drama, but they
must stay and face it day in and day out.

Everyone was overwhelmed—so much crying and such a tense environment! Before I left, one of the workers forced Yue Hua to apologize to me for misbehaving. Yue Hua had pinched and kicked me and tried to claw my face. I had sat her down on a chair and told her she was being a naughty girl. She is usually so sweet, but the toys got her agitated and she showed her frustration in the only way she knew.

The *ayi* was scolding her in Chinese and I was on my knees holding another baby. Yue Hua was staring up at me with her silent, serious face. The next thing I knew, she was flying into my arms for a hug, her pleading look telling me, "Please don't be angry." I hugged her tight and gave her a loud kiss to make her giggle. All was well when we left and I'd learned another good lesson.

* * *

MARCH 1, 2004

I can scarcely believe today makes ONE YEAR IN CHINA! I continue to be proud of us for the way we've adjusted, creating a life in this unfamiliar but interesting land. After the first six months, I was certain we would be more than willing to admit to failure and happily return home, but instead we have persevered and overcome so much. I no longer stand at the window and cry, and Ben is doing an outstanding job at work. Amanda has finally quit repeating the question, "When will we move back home?"

My outlook on China continues to change dramatically. When we first arrived here, I would have described Shengxi as an ugly city, filled with nothing but derelict buildings, having no sanitation, and with poor people and beggars everywhere—akin to a slum in the U.S.

I was so wrong! Of course, some places in Shengxi are run-down, but it's not that simple. As you get to know the city, complex layers are uncovered, and you discover the Chinese are doing more every day to make it a beautiful place to visit and live. Shengxi has been described as "a city with a mixture of the old and new everywhere." That couldn't be truer. Driving down the road, you may observe an ancient Chinese woman with a pole braced across her stooped shoulders, baskets filled with fruit hanging from either side. She is hunched and permanently deformed from the weight of this burden over so many years. Incongruously, beside her you might see a swaggering teenager, cell phone pressed to his ear and dressed in the latest trendy style. It will appear that an entire century has been skipped between the nineteenth and the twenty-first.

To feel real wonder, simply stand and watch men work at construction. You'll see them with no safety harnesses or any other kind of protective gear climbing all over tall scaffolding or buildings. Alternatively, take a trip down the highway, look to the sides, and watch farm people working their rice paddies the old-fashioned way—wearing the traditional flat, round Chinese hats with their babies strapped around their backs, reminiscent of scenes from an old movie.

Many country people live in tumbledown shanties with livestock tied to their front porches. In contrast, another thirty miles down the road you might see a skyscraper looming above you.

You can shop at the biggest grocery chain, yet the staff will still count your eggs out of crates, put them in a bag, and knot it. Next, you face the obstacle of getting the eggs paid for and then getting down the escalator to the parking garage while dealing with fifteen other bags of groceries. Last week I bought ten eggs and by the time I got home, all but three were broken.

I am further awestruck at Chinese housing. Those who are lucky enough to have a real home live in the midst of block upon block of enormous apartment buildings. At first glance, they appear slumlike, with colorful clothes hanging out of the windows to dry, yet they are considered middle class by Chinese standards. Many do not have hot water in the winter or the luxury of a refrigerator. Our driver is considered "middle income," yet he takes his daily hot showers at the factory where my husband works. He brings his suit to work and dresses in the locker room.

In many of these neighborhoods stand makeshift stalls, their proprietors selling all manner of produce and meats. Every morning small children play at the stalls with their grandparents while their parents are at work.

The buildings house hundreds of apartments, most of which contain only two small rooms and a bathroom. From what I have learned, usually a couple, their one child, and the paternal grandmother live crowded together in this tiny space. There are also square gray tents scattered throughout the city where people live until the officials force them to move to another location. If you peer inside, you'll see a cot for sleeping and occasionally a crate used as a table. All day long, you can find the locals squatting around a dishpan of water, washing their clothes. A familiar sight is the elderly gathered around makeshift tables on the sidewalks, playing cards or Chinese board games.

Wealthy people live here too, but they are in the great minority. Yet far too many cars choke the roads, suggesting many Chinese have enough money to own at least one.

In the spring, fireworks can be heard everywhere as young brides are shown to their new homes on their wedding day. In Chinese culture, a couple does not marry until the man has secured a home. Only after he has saved enough to buy his apartment will they proceed with the relationship. The couples share the privacy of their little nest until the birth of their first baby, at which time the paternal grandmother is usually invited to move in.

Ben is very interested in the architecture found in Shengxi and

the metropolitan areas of Beijing; he insists the Chinese are determined to keep up with the rest of the world in the construction of
tall, beautiful buildings on every available piece of land.

The Chinese people are amazingly artistic. Beauty abounds in
their paintings, carvings, buildings, and especially their gardens.
I have never seen such brilliantly landscaped gardens anywhere.
People here have an enormous capacity to empathize with nature.
They treat all wild creatures, trees, flowers, and water as sacred.

My views about the orphanage continue to evolve. I used to
be appalled by the treatment of the children and could see only
the negative aspects of how the institution is run. Now I understand why babies are strapped down, why they are only given half
a bottle of milk, and why the workers never pick them up or hug
them. There are reasons for all of it: the straps prevent them from
kicking off their blankets in the winter cold, and limiting their
feeding enables the sickest children to keep down a small bit of
nutrition. Now that I know how much work it takes to care for so
many children packed into one room, I can see why the *ayis* don't
have time to stop and give them individual attention; perhaps the
emotional barriers in place keep the *ayis* from experiencing more
grief than a heart can stand.

Certainly, there is room for improvement. However, while
I don't have to like their methods, I can empathize more than I
used to. I'm still homesick for America, some days more than others. While I've become used to Chinese food, I still miss eating
American food. Oh, how I miss the food. I would dearly love to
eat in an American restaurant where I could drink the water, eat
the meat with no foreboding, or just peruse a menu in English and
know what I am ordering is exactly what I'm going to get—instead
of the constant surprises I am presented in Chinese restaurants.

I miss American salad bars! I've never seen edible dressing on
a salad bar in China; in truth, I'm not brave enough to eat from
a salad bar here. I miss going for a drive in the car and listening

to the radio or my favorite CDs. I want to see a movie and have hot, buttery popcorn with an ice-cold drink. Most of all, I miss being with Heather and the rest of my dysfunctional family! I miss just hanging out with all of them, laughing and joking. I miss my phone ringing. No one talks by phone here; everyone uses email. If the phone rings, we look perplexedly at each other as if to say, "Who on earth could that be?"

I miss church. I long for that warm, goose-bumpy feeling when the hymns are sung, and I miss hanging around after the service to hear the local news. And yes, I miss the sermons. I have always been a strange one—I like sermons. I used to get them on tape from a friend of mine. Right now, I would love to be sitting on a hard pew, listening to a good sermon, all the while trying to control my growling stomach.

My Chinese speaking skills are improving steadily. In fact, when I run into new foreigners here and they hear me speak the language, they think I am fluent! Of course, that's far from true; nevertheless, I'm proud of how far I have come. I study in every spare moment and I've rounded the difficulty curve. The university course was beneficial in clearing up my initial confusion over the strange tones. It's all starting to make sense, and I've even had dreams where I'm involved in some drama and speaking Chinese. It's said that when you start dreaming in another language, it means you finally comprehend it. I'm so glad I didn't give up as I threatened to a million times. The payoff is enormous.

The question I'm most frequently asked is, "Do you like it here in China?"

Honestly, I don't know. That is impossible to answer. I do feel this is where I am supposed to be right now, and that satisfies me for the moment.

17

MARCH 3, 2004

Today we had a meeting of the orphanage volunteers, and I learned one of our cleft palate babies died over the weekend. I was there only yesterday and found her bed empty, but I thought she'd been taken to the hospital. We have already raised money for her surgery, but now it's too late. I was not surprised; last week while I fed her, she was having a terrible time. It was taking too long, and finally one of the staff took the bottle away.

Regina said she'd had the same experience. Sheila asked the worker what the baby had died from, and was told, "Because she wouldn't eat." She died simply because of her inability to take in nutrition. That happens far too often with babies born with a cleft lip or cleft palate. Unfortunately, as usual, the workers don't have the time necessary to feed a severely handicapped child; instead, they focus on those who are healthier and quick to eat. I cannot even describe how anguished I felt. She was so sweet and vulnerable. I never saw her cry; she would just gaze silently about with big, serious eyes that appeared to take in everything.

I am cheered a little to know that only a week ago I held her and sang to her. Several of us showed her what it felt like to be cradled, snuggled, and loved. That this innocent, intelligent child could have had a life if given half a chance makes me feel like crawling into bed and staying there, the covers over my head, for a week. All of us are despondent over losing her, but we must rally our strength and continue to help make the others' lives a little better.

The donations are extremely helpful. Every penny helps an innocent baby who never asked to be here, never asked to be a burden to anyone. There are so many more in this country who need help, and we still have babies in our room who need funds for surgeries. But we are making progress, however plodding.

The two babies who had cleft palate surgery this week are apparently doing fine. I haven't seen them yet, but I plan to go tomorrow. Tonight I will have problems sleeping—I always do for a while after one of the babies dies—but I'll try to imagine our lost girl is finally at peace.

* * *

MARCH 4, 2004

Eighteen-month-old Jia Jia is a beautiful little girl with severe spina bifida. She is paralyzed from the waist down but does a good job of supporting herself with her hands and arms. Often looking like a baby bird craning for its breakfast, Jia Jia provides an amusing picture as she tries to see everything that is happening from the confinement of her small crib.

Jia Jia has a lump of fluid the size of a large orange protruding from her spine. Lately the lump has begun to cause her great discomfort. When I first started at the orphanage last July, she always smiled and giggled. Now, more often than not, she is tear-streaked and clearly in pain.

The staff has discouraged any potential sponsors because her prognosis will probably never change. She will most likely never walk. However, we volunteers have taken a special interest in her and decided that we want to solicit an outside opinion. One of the volunteers talked to her husband, and together they agreed to pay for a specialist in Beijing to evaluate Jia Jia. That was done last week, with the specialist concluding that, with surgery, he could alleviate her pain and help her problem with bowel movements and incontinence. Those are big steps in improving her quality of life.

With the money donated thus far, we are going to pay for Jia Jia's surgery. She will also need a full-time nurse and follow-up therapy. Though we don't have the funds for the nurse or the therapy yet, we are simply determined to have faith that more donations will come. We also dream of someday getting a special chair that will allow her out of her crib.

Another example of God's goodness happened when, at the doctor assessment in Beijing, we asked about the cost of the surgery. The doctor's English was poor, so he handed us a piece of paper on which he had written 10,000 renminbi (US$1,300). We were stunned—10,000 renminbi is almost exactly as much as we have in our fund! The staff had expected this surgery to be very expensive. We don't know why the doctor would do it for so little, but we certainly won't question it!

We will keep working to help Jia Jia, who is at the top of our list of babies in need of medical assistance. We are continuing to brainstorm ideas to raise more funds. This project has turned into a mission.

* * *

MARCH 8, 2004

Today was National Women's Day in China, a celebration of women that is ironic in many ways, particularly where baby girls are concerned. We have far more abandoned girls than boys at the orphanage. Females are still largely second-class citizens here, making the celebration contradictory. Nevertheless, today Shengxi was alive with excitement and festivities. Shows, street performances, dinners, awards banquets, and all manner of other entertainment were scheduled around the city.

It was an unusual day at the orphanage. The absence of most of the administrative staff was disturbingly evident. Ordinarily when we arrive, the babies have already had their first changing of the morning. Clean diapers are put on at specific intervals throughout the day whether or not the babies need changing, and they are not changed again until the next scheduled time. This clearly isn't the most humane system, but it's reasonably efficient. Today, however, the entire room smelled of urine. As Regina and I made our rounds, we could see the babies hadn't been changed all night. They were not just wet, but soaked down to their bedding. We're not supposed to change their clothes, but after one and a half hours, it was clear no one else was worried about it, so we changed the messiest ones.

The few *ayis* on duty acted as though they were on vacation. They stood around aimlessly, chatting and laughing, leaving us alone in the room several times while they visited other rooms and halls. The orchestra of neglected, crying children escalated in volume as the usual diaper changing was ignored and then the feeding time delayed—these babies sure know their schedule! Bottles were eventually brought in, and then removed before the babies had had enough. Only one small bowl of rice was produced for five toddlers. The kids were still hungry and their crying was endless. When we asked about the remainder of the food, the frustrating reply from the *ayis* was, "*Mei you.*" Meaning, there was none.

On our way out, we passed an old man struggling to pedal his three-wheeled bicycle, weighed down by a huge pot of rice wobbling in the back. We were relieved to know the children were going to eat, just later than usual.

Le Men, the new baby boy who needs heart surgery, is becoming increasingly weak. I brought Regina over to see his little body underneath his coverlet. His legs look as if they belong to a ninety-year-old man, with shriveled skin hanging from twig-thin bones. His coughing is still horrible, and he is too weak to cry. The doctors told us Le Men's organs are on the wrong sides of his body, opposite of where they should be. He will need expensive surgery if he holds on long enough to get it. Nevertheless, he is adorable with his little mop of flat-topped hair. I took him from his crib and sat down with him, singing and then laughing because my singing frightened him. (It does scare a lot of people, but babies usually like it!) He raised his eyebrows at me as if to say, "What are you saying, and who are you, anyway, lady?" This child seems far older than his years.

Most of the babies are fighting colds. I'm in a very discouraged frame of mind today—the neglect of these helpless children has got me down. Nevertheless, tomorrow is a new day, and we must continue hoping things will improve.

18

MARCH 18, 2004

Today we brought along Kate, a new volunteer. She handled her tasks with professionalism and poise. Just like everyone else, she was surprised at some of the Chinese methods of child care, but took it all in without taking issue. She was concerned that none of the babies had toys. I told her they do have them, but every time we get them out, the workers remove them. It seems they prefer the babies to whine and be bored.

I want to say to them, "Don't you know your jobs would be easier if you gave the children something to entertain themselves with?"

Instead, they plunk the toddlers in walkers that are tied to the wall, where they stare at Chinese soap operas. The twenty-odd babies in cribs have only their fingers to play with; they are not allowed toys, rattles, or anything to stimulate their minds. Baffling as this is, it is just another of their many customs that we have no choice but to accept.

The majority of the babies were still sick with fever and colds. The one who just had cleft lip surgery was back in the baby room, her sutures looking raw from so much crying. In addition, with his defective heart, little Le Men was struggling to breathe. From the confines of his crib, he stared up at me with eyes that begged for release from his constant rasping and coughing. I'm doubtful that he will make it; his cold appears to have turned into pneumonia. Why won't they send him to the hospital? Upon leaving, my heart felt like a lead weight—I was emotionally exhausted.

* * *

I came home and crashed into a dead sleep. When I awoke, I was still in a funk and didn't feel up to tackling anything, particularly cooking. Instead, I decided to order from a pizza place that had just opened; if I wasn't in a good mood, at least I could make Amanda happy.

I called and got a Chinese person, of course. "Do you speak English?" I asked automatically.

"Okay, okay," was his reply.

Right there I should have known that problems were imminent. I told him I wanted two pizzas, but he had already passed the phone to another fellow. Same scenario, different voice.

"Do you speak English?"

"Okay, okay."

I repeated the two-pizza order and flipped into my limited Mandarin. "Wo yao liang ge pizza." Fine. He understood that much, but now I didn't know how to say "meat lover's and pepperoni." After a failed attempt at understanding me, he passed the phone to a girl. By this time, we were into fifteen minutes of nonsensical exchanges. Amanda was banging her head on the couch in hysterics.

With ridiculous cheerfulness, the girl said, "May I help you?"

Yes! English! "One pepperoni and one meat lover's, please," I said as politely as possible.

"Sorry, I not know." *Clink* went the phone in my ear. She'd hung up on me after twenty minutes of aggravation.

I think I'll quit trying to take a shortcut and throw together a pot of spaghetti. Fifteen minutes, no phone calls, and no communication blunders. But do I have all the ingredients?

* * *

APRIL 7, 2004

Yesterday was the spring festival called Heart to Heart, presented by students and staff of the international school. It was a charitable event for the orphanage, which is to receive one-third of the money raised. My duty was to give a speech on behalf of the orphanage and volunteer group. It went well despite me being terrified—I'm not a public speaker, and each time I stand in front of a crowd, my knees knock and my voice quivers. Oddly, my family insists I look poised and confident at the podium and they cannot detect a trace of nervousness.

I had to pause between sections of my speech while they were translated first into Japanese and then Mandarin. It seemed to take forever, but in reality, it only took fifteen minutes. I'm so glad it's over. Afterward, others said I looked calm and had done well. I'm glad they couldn't see my knees trembling or hear my heart pounding.

19

APRIL 16, 2004

My work at the orphanage today was a marathon of self-control and humility. Most of the babies are doing better than last week, but the four in the cribs against the wall are precariously ill. When the babies are placed in those cribs, we are not allowed to feed them. Left to languish there, these children shrivel up from malnutrition, with the skin hanging from their fragile bones. Their lips dry up and crack, and they take on an eerily vacant stare. It devastates us to witness this. We can only hope the staff feeds them at another time of the day.

One tiny nameless baby has jaundice worse than any child I've ever seen. The *ayi* told me that she was extremely ill and was not expected to live.

Xiao Su, whom I spent extra time with today, is only about six months old; according to the staff, she has some sort of brain problem. As I bent over her, I seriously thought I'd found another baby who had died. Her body was rigid and her eyes glazed and yellow, but they followed me as I tended to her. I pulled back the covers to examine her and was horrified at what I saw: her feet and legs had begun to turn black—by far one of the worst things I've ever seen on a baby's body.

I stroked her cheek and she began making a soft sound in her throat as if she were trying to communicate with me. I marveled at her tenacity to survive. Regina joined me, and even she, tough as she usually is, was visibly affected by this poor child's plight.

Sweet Le Men has at last overcome his cold. He was still coughing violently, but that is a complication from whatever is wrong with his heart. Overall, he is moving closer to being able to have his surgery.

Added to the room is the worst cleft palate case I have ever seen. Feeding her was nearly impossible because the part of her face that should be a mouth just disappears up into her nose. She can't suck at the bottle at all. The only way to get liquid into her is to squeeze a few drops at a time into her mouth, then pause to let her swallow. She is only four weeks old and I fear that she will be the next baby to become critically ill. I'm guessing her mother tried to feed her for a few weeks and then abandoned her. She has beautiful almond-shaped eyes that I fail to understand how anyone could abandon. However, it's easy to make that judgment standing in my position—but from her mother's perspective I am sure the choice was agonizing.

We certainly have many obstacles to overcome. Three of our volunteers were sick with the virus the babies had last week, but they're doing better now. We know we may lose some babies soon and we are all mentally preparing ourselves.

* * *

APRIL 28, 2004

I took an extra day at the orphanage this week to fill in for absent volunteers. One had become ill again and the other had a meeting. In any case, I needed to talk to the administrator, so it worked out well. I met with Director Yao to deliver the good news that the other international school is going to contribute some money to our volunteer group to be used for the surgeries needed. First, we have to earn it.

We've decided to hold another festival, with the proceeds to be divided between three charities, our orphanage getting the lion's share. I am part of the committee at the school that will organize this event. It's going to be huge, and I'm praying for a good turn-out so we can undertake some major projects with the donations.

At the meeting the orphanage's top director was also present. With a translator's help, he told me how impressed he was with my determination and that it was me who should be director. Of course, he was only joking, but it made me nervous. With the lack of expression on his face, I could not determine if he felt I'd been stepping on his toes or if he was genuinely complimenting me. One thing is certain: they emphatically do not want the public to think the children are in need, so we must tread carefully.

I think the directors are happy with my work thus far, but I could very easily overstep boundaries. I am always on guard not to cause them to "lose face."

While I was there, Sheila produced the file on the little girl she is sponsoring. The child's name is Xiao Li; her history shows that she was abandoned in a hospital emergency room when she was four. Six hundred renminbi (US$60) a year will pay for school and needed items for Xiao Li. Sheila will be allowed to host her on the weekends and spend holidays with her. In the girl's file was the note her mother had pinned to her when she was abandoned. Because I can't read Chinese characters, Sheila read me the note. In essence, it was a suicide letter stating that she was unable to care for Xiao Li because her husband had left her. More details in the file revealed that Li had been found crying and wandering around the hospital alone.

Later, we gathered Li from her bed and promised her that tomorrow she was going out for a visit. She was terribly excited, cowering behind her friend and peeking out at Sheila with a shy grin. Sheila is an angel—she's a Christian who spent many years living in Houston. She has the whole day planned for her new foster daughter. Sheila is an enormous blessing to us here, as a translator, friend, and volunteer.

In the baby room, I found Le Men propped in the corner of his bed. He had a strap tying him against the rungs to keep him sitting upright. This was an attempt to ease his breathing, but he was very upset over it: his solemn little face was scrunched and tears streamed down his cheeks. I immediately untied him and took him to the hallway, where the sun was shining through the windows and the air was warmer. I cuddled him and tried to calm him while he coughed incessantly. Ten minutes later, one of the *ayis* came for him, saying he was going to the hospital. She packed a bag, took him from my arms, and left. It is a relief that they are finally going to do something for him, especially since we have been asking about it for weeks.

Xiao Su, the baby who had looked so close to death on Monday—the one whose legs and feet had begun turning black and who would not move anything except her eyes—was gone today. When I asked about her, they refused to tell me where she was. Their reticence told me all I needed to know—she had probably died. Something inside me has definitely changed, because all I felt was relief that she is now free of her suffering.

* * *

Today was a beautiful day, the first one in a while. Spring is fighting its way in. The children were playing outside and some were lined up doing exercises to music—it amuses and cheers me to watch them. The kids were so excited at the release from their usually boring day that it was hard for them to rein in their energy. I saw a staff member kick a child for taking a potato chip away from another child. I turned away in disgust. That may sound cruel, but the only way for me to continue my work here is to try to look the other way when horrible things happen.

The victim of the *ayi*'s brutal kicking was a boy, perhaps five years old. When I passed him a few minutes later, I gave him a quick hug before we could be seen. So many children have cuts, bruises, and bandages—you have to wonder how they acquired these injuries. It's said the boys fight violently with each other at times, even the young ones. To the same degree that occurs in most institutions around the world, it is survival of the fittest here.

Though we have several staff members who should not be working with children at all, I can now see that some *ayis* genuinely care for the children. It isn't their custom to be affectionate and loving, but they at least treat them with care and humanity. In the baby room is an older woman named Lin who is very kind to the children. Xiao Jo is good to the babies as well. The longer I am here, the more I see the small gestures of compassion, where before I saw none.

* * *

MAY 11, 2004

Another day of heartache—Regina called me over to the crib of one of our babies. "Look at her," she said. "She is so thirsty." The lips of the tiny girl were parched from dehydration. Her eyes had the familiar foggy, glazed-over look I have seen just before a child slips away. The girl looked about three weeks old and weighed perhaps five pounds. Regina pulled back the covers and we gazed at her shriveled body.

"They look like this before they die," I said. The baby's skin hung in wrinkles, paper thin and dry.

"Do you think I'll hurt her if I hold her?" asked Regina. I shook my head and said I didn't know.

"Well, I just can't leave her there," Regina said as she gently swaddled the baby in a blanket and headed to a chair. I wrapped up Le Men, the baby with the heart condition, and sat down across from Regina.

We rocked the babies and talked for a few minutes, and suddenly Regina froze.

"Is she dead or sleeping?" she asked.

I knelt in front of Regina and touched the baby girl. She didn't move. Her eyes were fixed to the ceiling in an unblinking stare and her limbs were stiff, the arms outstretched rigidly. I felt a familiar chill run down my spine and touched her cheek again— no response.

"Regina, I think she's gone."

Regina snuggled the child against her breast and whispered, "Well, at least she didn't die alone."

As I rose to find a private corner to compose myself, I touched the tiny cheek one more time and saw an ever-so-slight movement in her face. She hadn't yet died, but she was only a few breaths from it. As I moved away, from the corner of my eye I saw Regina stroking the cheek of her little angel. I am so thankful for the women who have gathered to work together in this orphanage. We can't help all the children, but we can certainly be the ones to show them they are loved as they are passing through.

* * *

JULY 3, 2004

This has been a miserable day. I headed to the orphanage in good spirits, but after two near-miss accidents in the car, my back began giving me trouble. At the orphanage it was obvious Director Yao was on vacation, because most of the workers were nowhere to be seen. In the room with me was only one disgruntled *ayi*. I was busy, I'll say that much. Noses were running and we were out of tissues. Bottoms were dirty and no wet wipes were to be found. (I'm definitely going shopping before next Monday.) At bath time, the few workers who made an appearance remained in the wash-room, only to emerge long enough to dump the babies back in their beds. I counted and dressed eighteen babies in less than thirty minutes, causing me more back spasms.

The worst moment came when Hei Mei, the jolly, dark little girl with the heart problem, decided to be cute and kept standing in her bed when she was supposed to be napping. After Hei Mei had been laid down repeatedly and continued to pop up, Tilly yanked one of her shoes off and went at the girl with it.

I froze, thinking, How on earth am I going to take down that big woman with my skinny self after she hits that poor baby with her shoe? Fortunately, she thought better of her impulsive action and stopped just as she reached Hei Mei, then put the shoe back on her foot. She did slam Hei Mei roughly down on her back, but the child is accustomed to that sort of treatment and it didn't even upset her. In my mind, I chanted, Stay down, Hei Mei, stay down. I didn't want her to challenge Tilly's moment of mercy.

Jin Ji and Yue Hua, our two mascot toddlers, have left the orphanage for better lives. Yue Hua was finally adopted. It is puz-zling—we asked repeatedly when she would be leaving and they said they didn't know. Now I've returned and suddenly she's no longer here. I am saddened that I didn't get to meet her new par-ents or tell her goodbye. I have many memories of her solemn little eyes and the way she always gazed at me. However, even though I'll miss her, I know our prayers have been answered. She's now blessed to have a real family and will not know heartache from this place again.

Jin Ji is in a foster home here in Shengxi. Apparently, there are also plans for her adoption. I haven't any idea how that happened, but at least she's removed from the orphanage, even if only tempo-rarily. It's very quiet in the baby room without the two toddlers. I found myself continually looking up to search for them and then remembering they were gone. I know it won't be long before other babies discover how to use their legs and take their place, but I'll never forget Yue Hua or her partner in crime, Jin Ji.

After goodbye hugs and kisses, I went to wash up, but there was no soap to be found. Wonderful—the day just kept getting better. I briefly wondered what sorts of bacteria I was carrying out with me.

From the orphanage I headed to a grocery store called Auchan, where I must admit I lost my usual composure. People are always telling me I am "too nice." One of my best friends here is Australian and one day I asked her why in this expatriate circle, Americans get the most criticism. She replied that the thing that bothered her the most about Americans is that "they were just too darn nice and polite!"

She had me there. I am so courteous to shop workers and service people that even the Chinese look at me as though I'm crazy, but after the trials at the orphanage earlier, I'd had all I could take. The store was on the second floor, yet it did not have air-conditioning on. The temperature must have been over one hundred degrees inside. As usual, I was having a hard time finding the items I desperately needed. I was also having trouble pushing the rickety old cart with my back aching—the cart moved in every cockeyed direction. We're planning a cookout soon, but there were no beef patties, hamburger buns, mayonnaise, or mustard to be found. My next need was assorted drinks, which I know they have, and that's where the real problem began.

Since they didn't have soft drinks in cases this time, I decided to use an empty box I'd spied on the floor. As I began filling it, a worker stormed at me, yelling in Chinese that I must not take the box. She wanted me to set forty-eight single cans in the bottom of my cart, and then transfer them one by one into bags to tote them home! In the next moments, I discovered one thing: when highly agitated, I don't have to concentrate on my words—my Chinese is fast and surprisingly close to accurate.

I answered right back, telling the worker why I needed the box. With obvious surprise at my responding in her own language, she backed off to watch me from ten feet away. As usual, locals had gathered around me, staring into my cart and exclaiming in surprise at the money I was about to spend.

By the time I was able to extract myself from the growing crowd and reach the register, I was soaked with perspiration and seeing white spots. There, I had to deal with another common frustration—the clerk examined my foreign credit card and told me she couldn't accept it. After getting as far as the register and seeing freedom within reach, I was decidedly not happy to be deterred yet again.

Mustering as much patience as I could, I gave her my usual speech (reverting to my choppy Mandarin) explaining how I shop there all the time and how they always accept my card. I decided that even if I must camp out at her feet, I wasn't leaving until she processed my groceries. At that point, I was determined—even if I'd had cash available, I wouldn't have offered it. The cashier called over a manager, who called over another and then one more to complete the official credit-card approval committee. It was ridiculous. I gave them my obstinate "I'm not budging" look. Finally, they took the card and processed the bill.

Now that I'm back at home in my wonderfully air-conditioned house, let's think about it. Yes, it's hot. Yes, it's crowded. Yes, I'll have to make a trip to the import store and pay double or triple for casual food. Yes, life in China is always chaotic. Does realizing that make me feel any better right now? Well, maybe a little. It's just one of those days. Writing about it does put things in perspective and helps me laugh in retrospect at all the absurd situations. It's not as if any of this is new to me. Only a few more weeks and we will return to the States for our summer home leave. I am counting the days.

Now I'm going upstairs to take a long, hot bath in the middle of the afternoon. Hmmm, perhaps that should be a song if it isn't already! The too-friendly American woman that everyone knows will return soon.

* * *

JULY 25, 2004

As usual, our summer home leave was a blur of family gatherings, shopping, and getting reacquainted with our favorite restaurants. My body is probably in shock from all the clean, fresh salad and rolls I stuffed myself with at each dinner. Surprisingly, after two weeks of eating out, I missed cooking. I wish we had not sold our home when we moved to China, for I quickly get exasperated with hotel living.

Each summer at home we go on a shopping marathon to buy all the things we can't find in China, items such as deodorant, soap, medicine, snacks, and clothes. It's a revealing comment on our consumer-consumption society in the U.S. that the "necessities" we're accustomed to are either luxuries or nonexistent in China. I also stock up on salad dressings, seasonings, and soup mixes to get us through the cold winters, when we don't feel inclined to go out for a meal.

I always love the moment when I step up onto my mom's porch, throw open her door, and feel the welcoming atmosphere of her tiny, love-cluttered home. It's nice just to put my feet up, listen to her discourses on life, and catch up on all the family gossip.

It's also a time to spend as many moments as I can with Heather, who probably dreads the annual "life lessons" speeches I save up for her. At fourteen years old, she thinks there is nothing I can tell her that she doesn't already know. It astonishes and terrifies me how quickly she is becoming a woman.

Amanda's favorite part of home leave is visiting her aunt and

uncle—Ben's sister and her husband—at their farm in the country.
She rides the horses, swims in the pool, and plays with the many
kittens that run free. It's a great place for us to sit in the porch
swing, relax, and catch up with Ben's family. Before we know it,
it's time for us to jump on a plane and head to our second "home"
in China. The visit is far too brief but refuels us for another year
in the Land of Chaos.

20

AUGUST 28, 2004

Much has happened since we returned to China. Amanda is being treated for asthma; she's been on medication for a week and is doing much better. I have had serious breathing issues as well. The pollution and smog, combined with the suffocating heat, is the worst we've experienced in our time here. Not to mention that it took me a while to get my back and joint pain under control after twenty-five ruthless hours of travel.

Ben has a new manager and there have been changes at the factory. He is excited about how well his work is going and is obsessed with making this project successful. He often comes home late, when total exhaustion hits him. To make our lives even more hectic, I've hired a new Mandarin tutor to start this week for Amanda, Ben, and me. The poor woman will have her hands full with this bunch and our attempts at mastering a complex language.

While we were away, my team of volunteers at the orphanage also made some positive progress. Le Feng and Le Zi, the first two babies who had cleft lip surgery, are still in foster care. They have now been there longer than originally planned, which is a real blessing. I hope this means the families don't want to give them up. What a change in their lives—typically, to be born with a facial deformity in China means that the child will never have the love of a family or be accepted by society. These girls may now have a chance to fulfill some of their dreams.

Le Ci, one of our children with spina bifida, is currently in the hospital, awaiting spinal surgery. I'm not sure what the delay is, but my guess is that we were correct in our amateur assessment that she's suffering from a mean infection, which will need to be treated before any procedures are performed. I haven't been to the hospital this week because of some projects at home, but I plan on visiting Le Ci after my orphanage duty on Monday. We don't yet know whether her spina bifida has affected her future ability to walk. She is not yet one year old, and my research on the subject indicates that the longer surgery is postponed, the greater the chance there is of permanent paralysis. We just pray we've gotten to her in time. She is such a pretty child with lively eyes and little bow lips—a real beauty.

Getting each child into the hospital is a far more complicated affair than most people realize. Each case must go through tiers of directors at the orphanage, then to the board for approval. I plead with and aggravate them endlessly to get these children in for care. There are multiple levels of directors, and every one of them takes an inordinate amount of time to consider the request before it is moved to the next level. Each time we get a child into the hospital, a battle is won. This is a full-time job, and dealing with all the details and politics makes it that much more difficult. Why does it take so many approvals to get a sick child into surgery when we are paying for it?

Because of a steady stream of generous patrons, we have just enough to pay for the current child. I've decided to stop worrying about donations—that issue is under control. I'm spending most of my time dealing with getting the children into the hospital, and then making visits to bring in necessities such as diapers and formula. I also spend two days a week at the orphanage with the other children and countless hours on the Internet writing updates, scheduling volunteers, and coordinating donations and projects.

Next week we have a special person visiting the orphanage. John is a remarkably generous man who manages a shoe factory here. I've just received approval to bring him in to measure each walking child and teenager for a new pair of shoes. This will be a singular treat for children who have never owned anything new before. I will assist John with measuring. This should be interesting, considering we have more than one hundred sets of feet to measure.

I have stressed to the orphanage that we wish to include *every* child who walks, including those who are hidden away because of their mental or physical impairments. I'll fight if I must, even if it means pitching a fit this Friday, to ensure they are all included.

We have still more children for whom we are planning medical procedures. One girl who was badly burned will need additional skin grafts. The people who sponsored her first surgeries are gone now.

We volunteers concentrate on ensuring the cleft babies get one good meal while we are there; even so, we lost one while I was gone. There are still three children who require surgery, if only we can keep them healthy enough to reach the age requirement for the operation.

A nineteen-month-old boy named Le Bing lies in his bed every day, moaning in pain. His exact problem is unclear, but the source of the hurting is his mouth. His gums are swollen and bloody all the time. One of us spends at least twenty minutes each session with him, singing nursery rhymes and trying to console him. He resists being touched, and when he takes his bottle, he cries tears of pain. I have inquired about his needs and haven't received much information, but I'll keep trying. I know his days and nights are long—he never leaves that bed. He doesn't even attempt to sit up; he just looks as though he is in constant misery.

* * *

The atmosphere of the baby room has changed dramatically since only a year ago. No longer do continual crying and sadness pervade the room. In addition, the workers occasionally smile, and handle the babies in a much gentler manner.

The babies themselves have made great improvements in human interaction. A year ago, they would flinch in fear at the slightest touch, but that rarely happens now. These days, a touch often rewards us with a smile and an irresistible look, imploring, "Pick me up, please pick me up!"

There are still bad days and experiences. Sometimes I'm overwhelmed with the feeling that this is all too much for me. However, when I see the babies' pictures on my mantel and think about my local and overseas support teams and our successes, I can't bear to disappoint anyone. I know I've been handed a gift, a chance to do some good in life. I will continue until I just can't handle any more.

Reflecting on our accomplishments over this past year, I can definitely see the rewards. I am thankful for the others on my team—they are all angels. This entire mission has been a team effort of local and international volunteers.

21

Oh, the things I get myself into. Amanda's school is hosting International Day, and I volunteered to be on the planning committee. All the proceeds of this festival will go to charity. The committee chairperson appealed to me, and though I am far too busy, I felt compelled to say yes.

At the meeting, we began discussing local charities, and the school principal mentioned he'd heard about my involvement with the orphanage. He wanted me to elaborate, and when I was through, the room had become eerily quiet.

"Well, I'm convinced," the principal said. "We'll donate seventy-five percent of our proceeds to your orphanage."

I was in shock—happy shock.

Yesterday we held our second meeting. Halfway through, the principal asked if I would like to speak at two upcoming children's assemblies to explain the purpose of the event and describe the charity—our orphanage—that's been chosen as the main recipient of the proceeds.

Well, I am certainly not a public speaker. I grimaced and replied, "I can be there, but could you do the speaking?"

"Yes," he said, "I *can* do the speaking, but you relate it with such passion. You stir feelings in others that they might not have known they had before."

I was flattered that I'd moved him so much, so I agreed to speak. I know it was no accident that I was included in this committee, and I didn't just happen to find the words to move the principal to choose our orphanage as the school's top charity. Yet I hardly know what I said! He's right—my passion for these orphans surfaces without me even trying.

* * *

SEPTEMBER 7, 2004

In general, I dislike pessimism, but sometimes the things we see can't be glossed over. They simply are what they are. When we arrived at the orphanage yesterday, the preschool children were all sitting stoically in small wooden chairs in the hallway. They had no toys or books to entertain them, yet were expected to sit still for several hours.

When they saw me, they became agitated. As I handed out packs of cookies, some just couldn't wait until I reached them and rose out of their chairs. The supervising *ayi* immediately began kicking and smacking them down—it looked as though she were dealing with a pack of dogs. I became extremely upset. What should I have done? The children have come to expect a treat from me; they look forward to it. Sadly, I was the cause of their punishment and abuse. It's a difficult situation, and I don't know what the answer is.

* * *

SEPTEMBER 11, 2004

Today on our way to the nursery, we stopped at the watching room, a sick room where children are isolated after their arrival at the orphanage or after any illness or surgery. We were hoping to spend some time with Jia Jia to help shorten her long, boring day, but she was fast asleep and looking peaceful. The doctor said her surgery was a success; it put her bowels in functioning order and removed the lump on her back. Now we amateurs have to give her some physical therapy for her hip sockets. They are in terrible shape and always in an unnatural position.

After visiting Jia Jia, Regina and I crept along the forbidden territory of the corridor on the second floor. I showed her the room where the most severely disabled children are hidden away. Before announcing our arrival, we peered through the window and saw them sitting there, zombielike, in the cold, barren room, with absolutely nothing to stimulate their minds or bodies.

I had some cookies left but wasn't sure if there were enough for all of the children. The cookies come in packages of two, so we decided if we didn't have enough, we would split them. As we passed them around, the children were beside themselves with excitement over this special treat. When we ran out of cookies, only one child didn't have a pack. I looked into my backpack again and what did I find but one more package at the bottom—perhaps an angel stuck it there. Miraculously, we had exactly the right number of cookies for twenty-odd kids.

While we helped children open their cookie packs, some wanted to touch my hands. These children are hidden from everyone; they miss the human contact that is so critical for them. Some are dwarfs, others have severe deformities—there are all kinds of problems the average Chinese would rather not know about. Yet the majority of these kids are no different from children the world over. You can look into their eyes and see a little child in there who is aching for human touch.

Regina's first time seeing these children left her very moved. I hope we can sneak down again next week without getting into trouble. After my initial blunder of saying, "I'll be back *last* week," and then realizing the confused looks meant my tense was wrong, I corrected it and told the kids that we would be back *next* week. They will no doubt be expecting me and my bag of treats.

* * *

SEPTEMBER 18, 2004

I visited Le Ci again today. Surprisingly, she'd had her surgery last Thursday—I didn't expect it to happen so quickly. I wasn't able to speak to a doctor, but I managed to extract some information from the attending *ayi*. The spinal surgery took three hours and it was the doctors' opinion that Le Ci would eventually be able to walk. That was marvelous news! With all the prayers and support, we reached this child in time to change her life.

Le Ci was bandaged, so it was impossible to confirm, but I'm assuming her lump was removed. She was in a great deal of pain and cried incessantly during my visit; the *ayi* said she was not sleeping at all. Recently she learned how to flip over, but she's not allowed to do this because of the wound on her spine. I'll return to see her on Wednesday or Thursday and deliver some more milk formula.

More good news: Jia Jia is in foster care! When a couple came to the orphanage to consider fostering a child, they were shown the baby room. Upon seeing Jia Jia sitting in her stroller, they were both struck by how closely she resembled their recently deceased son. Apparently, they felt it was a sign that they were meant to bring Jia Jia into their home.

The administrative staff explained her disability, which would ordinarily deter any prospective families from further interest, but not this couple. They adamantly stated that they wanted her. We are all excited for Jia Jia—we hope she will become transplanted deep into the hearts of this couple and is never returned to this place.

* * *

SEPTEMBER 20, 2004

I learned on Monday that the health of Le Bing, the boy with the gum and mouth problems, has declined considerably. Before my visit home to the States, Le Bing had been healthy-looking, chubby, and always smiling. Upon my return, I was shocked to see how he had deteriorated.

Le Bing had been moved to a toddler bed, where he had become increasingly ill. His mouth and gums were still bleeding and he was obviously in pain; he'd also lost a lot of weight.

I wanted to insist he see a dentist—my amateur assessment was that he was suffering from some sort of mouth or gum disease. If I'd had any inclination of the seriousness of the illness, I would never have waited. I feel awful about it. It is *so* hard to intervene in these children's lives. We try to be careful to select the most serious cases first, such as the heart babies. In doing this, we sometimes overlook the cases that appear less urgent but are actually grim.

When I arrived at the orphanage on Monday, Le Bing wasn't in his bed. When I inquired, the staff said he had been moved to the watching room for further observation. Our new volunteer, Lucy, and I went looking and found him in very bad shape. He was even smaller than he had been last week, and extremely dehydrated and weak. At the office, using our two drivers/translators, we communicated that we wished to take Le Bing to a dentist immediately.

The office workers called Director Yao, who said Ji An, the orphanage social worker, had just taken Le Bing to the hospital earlier that morning. We'd been there all morning, so we knew that could not be true. When we tried to stress the baby's dire condition, Yao refused to consider a dentist, but said they would take Le Bing back to the hospital that afternoon and then call us.

I received a call later that afternoon reporting that Ji An and Director Fu had taken Le Bing to see the doctor, who determined he had a non-treatable genetic disease. Ji An informed me that Le Bing could not be helped and would soon die. I was appalled—even if they can't cure him, how can they simply leave him to suffer? I asked our translator to intercede on our behalf, insisting that we get Le Bing to Beijing immediately for a second opinion. No one knew the English word for his condition, and I wanted answers.

It is now Tuesday evening. This morning the translator phoned, informing us that Beijing was out of the question, but that the orphanage doctor had entered Le Bing into the Shengxi hospital. I'm certain the hospital visits they'd claimed took place yesterday were bogus, because he's now in the intensive care unit, where the care is expensive and usually saved for only the sickest children. Two other volunteers and I went there to learn what was happening. The doctor showed us a book of medical terms with the letters *PKU*[3] written next to a description in Mandarin. He also showed us a CT scan that suggested Le Bing has bleeding in his brain. In addition, he has a mouth infection and a severe urinary tract infection. The doctor confirmed that Le Bing was in a lot of pain. He told us Le Bing is mentally challenged, which agrees

---

3 Phenylketonuria (PKU) is a rare condition in which the body does not properly break down (metabolize) an amino acid called *phenylalanine*. PKU occurs when a person is missing an *enzyme* called phenylalanine hydroxylase, which is needed to break down phenylalanine. Phenylalanine is one of the eight essential *amino acids* found in foods that contain protein. Without the enzyme, high levels of phenylalanine and two closely related substances build up in the body. These substances are harmful to the *central nervous system* and cause brain damage. If the proteins containing phenylalanine are not avoided, PKU can lead to *mental retardation* by the end of the first year of life. Older children may develop movement disorders (such as *athetosis*) and hyperactivity.

Source: http://www.nlm.nih.gov/medlineplus/ency/article/001166.htm.

with research I found later today, that if PKU is not addressed at birth, irreversible brain damage can occur. The medical team is going to treat the infections, pump him up with antibiotics and fluids, and send him back to the orphanage.

According to Kate, our group registered nurse, most likely Le Bing will become increasingly sick from PKU unless they change his diet. Kate found a website with helpful information that she passed on to me; armed with this information, there is a possibility we can obtain special dietary needs for him. I will try to research it and see what we can do. Unfortunately, we won't be successful in paying for a surgery that will cure his PKU or reverse the damage done to his brain, but thanks to our stubbornness, he'll be treated for the infections that have caused him so much misery. I was relieved to see that he looked better already after just one morning of pain medication and antibiotics.

I don't know what his immediate future holds—he may not have long to live. I do know that if Le Bing's destiny is to die now, he will do it with one of us holding his hand and singing to him softly. We'll be watching out for him when he returns to the orphanage, and we'll see what we can do about the special milk he needs. If he is to die, we will show him that he did matter to someone. No one deserves to die alone.

Right now it looks as if we have enough to cover the costs of this child's medical visits. We told them to go ahead with whatever it takes to clear up the infections and lessen his pain. If we don't have enough in our fund, we'll find a way to come up with it. No child should have to suffer.

* * *

SEPTEMBER 28, 2004

Two steps forward and one back. Tilly—the abusive *ayi*—has softened lately. A little at a time, she is changing her reputation; she is still unemotional and treats the babies like insects, but she rarely hits them or screams at them.

Now, however, we have another *ayi* with issues. The woman in charge of the bigger children—I'll call her Xiong—is completely out of control. On Monday and Tuesday, I watched helplessly as she beat and kicked the kids, while screaming at them like a drill sergeant. These children are ages four to ten and very active, yet they're supposed to sit in cramped wooden chairs in the hallway all morning without moving. They are allowed no toys, no singing, and no touching one another. Can you imagine trying to force kids to behave like that hour after hour, day after day? Expectations like this are simply not realistic; the children get so antsy they can't help but stand up every so often.

It sickens me to see how violent the new *ayi* is with them, and she goes so far as to lash out right in front of us. Regina calls her an evil woman. It is obvious that she hates her job, and yet we're helpless to do anything but give her disapproving looks. Perhaps her life is hard and pushes her to act out at work. Whatever it is, it's hard to imagine what put such cruelty in her heart.

Li Li, one of the heart babies, is deteriorating rapidly. Her symptoms bewildered me until I investigated online and discovered they were very common for patients with heart issues. Li Li is weak and thin; five minutes after she takes her bottle, her face and body break out in a tremendous sweat, her fever goes up, and she begins shaking. Today I wiped her down and held her upright until her body temperature lowered a fraction. This is one very sick little girl. We have raised enough funds for only one heart surgery, but we don't know who is in worse condition, Li Li or Le Men.

We must wait for Director Yao to return from Beijing to decide whom to send to the hospital. I only hope both of these desperate children will make it until their surgeries are approved. Losing either of them is hard to fathom, especially knowing that if intervention is allowed quickly, their prognosis could become favorable.

We took a new volunteer to the orphanage yesterday. I was excited to learn she is a registered nurse, which could be a marvelous addition to our team. Unfortunately, during her tour she could not stop crying, which started to get under my skin because it was infuriating the *ayis*. On the ride home, she confessed she didn't think she could handle going back. She is going to inquire about working with the older people instead of the children.

This really got me down, but I tried to remain positive, telling her it gets easier with experience. I still have days when I feel it's all hopeless, but I remind myself that we have made many improvements. It is not all in vain. The encouragement received from our friends and families have been instrumental in pushing us along. It helps to know there are people out there who care for these babies and that we are not working alone.

* * *

OCTOBER 6, 2004

A food poisoning episode at home made me quite ill, thus I didn't go to the orphanage at all last week. It appears I was missed; yesterday when I arrived, the *ayis* were happy to see me. They greeted me with, *"Ni hao!"* (hello) and called me by name. I was even able to tell them in my much-improved Mandarin why I had been absent.

* * *

OCTOBER 11, 2004

This week we had some drama at the orphanage with Jia Jia. I spotted her in the hallway sitting in her stroller with her foster father standing behind her. Oh, I thought, a visit—how nice of him to bring her to see all of us. As I moved closer, the man pushed the stroller up beside one of the baby-room doors and then silently slipped in, leaving Jia Jia sitting in the hall. He then exited the other baby-room door and crept down the stairs.

What was he doing? I could only imagine. When Sheila, our translator, arrived, she asked the staff what was going on. They informed us that Jia Jia was being returned because her foster mother was too sick to care for her. I didn't believe this for one moment; we have had many children returned and this is always the story given.

By this time, Jia Jia had begun to realize something was wrong. She twisted around in her seat, looking for her foster father. Her eyes welled with tears and her mouth started to tremble. I went to her, digging around in the bags hanging from the stroller's handles. Snacks! I calmed her with one of the goodies her foster parents had sent with her as a consolation.

I could scarcely believe her foster parents had kept her all this time and now decided to return her. She would be devastated to be back in the baby room full-time. Compared with when she was last here, Jia Jia now looked like a completely different child. She was much plumper and her hair had grown, so she looked like a girl. (The orphanage always keeps the children's hair so short that you can't tell the girls from the boys.) Jia Jia looked so much healthier, and I dreaded the moment when she would realize her second family had abandoned her just like her first.

The room *ayis* instructed us not to give her special attention—it would only make her more upset. We had to watch her become increasingly agitated and bewildered as she watched the hallway to see if her father would reappear. As I left the room that day, I said a prayer that her foster father would reconsider and return for Jia Jia. Judging by past situations, many of our approved foster parents are terribly fickle. Often a child is "tested out" by a family for a few days, only to be returned for some insignificant reason. This game of I-want-you-no-I-don't is cruel to the children; on the other hand, the alternative would be for them to go through their childhood never experiencing a semblance of family life.

* * *

OCTOBER 12, 2004

The administrative staff wasn't on site this week because of the annual National Day holiday, the day the People's Republic of China was founded. All was quiet and calm. Lucy and I enjoyed a session of playing with the kids, feeding them, and administering some minor physical therapy. There were no new illnesses or serious fevers as is usually the case. We were allowed to bring out as many babies as we wanted, so we lined them all up on the mats for a change of scenery and a brief break from their cribs.

Sheila informed Director Yao that we have raised enough funds to send one of the heart babies to the hospital for surgery. Yao will decide which one and let us know next week; deciding who is in the most critical condition must be left up to her and the medical staff.

Anna, our Singaporean volunteer, has begun teaching English to the older kids. She is even sharing the teachings of Jesus with them. Initially we were uncertain whether this would be allowed, but so far we've met with no disapproval. Anna is doing a good job of balancing the English lessons with messages that can bring them hope. I would love to be doing this, but I must get better at speaking the local dialect. The older kids—ranging in age from four to ten—are lots of fun. I can't leave the baby room, though, because that is where my heart lies.

22

OCTOBER 16, 2004

My information books liken China to an onion; the analogy describes the different layers of this country and how peeling each away reveals increasingly more of China's true nature. The longer we are here, the more I understand it. When we first arrived, we were completely amazed by the outer layer. We focused on the masses of people, the unkempt look of the city, the inadequate housing. After a year and a half, however, we are starting to see more layers. We see the grace of the people dutifully tending the gardens, the beauty of the land, the intricately designed pagodas, and the long-lasting and diligently maintained paddy fields.

Yes, this can be a difficult place for a foreigner to become established, but it is also a great experience in learning to respect another way of life.

We've discovered that a smile goes a long way when you can't communicate with words. Our eyes have been opened to a part of the world harboring some very needy people; they are real and not just pictures on television or in the mail. And when our spirits are down and we're frustrated with the *foreignness* of it all, once we get behind our front door, we can still be happy. A family is a family no matter what continent you live on; all you need to survive is love and a lot of patience. To live for a time in China as a foreigner is a guarantee that your outlook on life will change forever. For most, it is a positive change, but for those unfortunate few who cannot adapt and evolve, it is invariably difficult.

* * *

OCTOBER 18, 2004

On Monday morning the orphanage was bustling with energy. We arrived to find the babies getting the most thorough baths I have yet seen. Ordinarily, they are either briefly dunked or just their bottoms are sprayed off. This time they were getting real baths: immersed in the sink and soaped up all over. We soon learned that the *ayis* thought the babies' cribs had bedbugs. This is one disadvantage to the babies sleeping on bedding instead of only on bamboo mats, as in the summer.

After they had all been bathed and dressed, we were instructed to change the bed liners and pillowcases. Regina and I shook out the thin mattresses as best we could and settled the babies into clean bedding. Several of them were swollen badly with bug bites—one was suffering so severely that a nurse was summoned to look at her. The majority had the worst bites on their faces, with a few on the feet and arms. The staff moved in fast-forward all morning, and Regina and I were exhausted by the time we left.

I had a discussion with Director Yao today concerning the details of our volunteer group paying for a heart surgery. Because of the great health risk, we will not provide transportation or take responsibility for the baby following the surgery. We will pay only for the hospital charges. The surgery will be done in Shengxi, and Yao indicated that Le Men would probably be the one to go. She will let us know next week. This operation will take all of our collected funds, so we will be praying that the needs of the other sick children will somehow also be met. As of now, we have three babies needing heart surgery, one who needs spina bifida surgery, and two who require cleft palate surgery.

A new baby was admitted yesterday while I was working. I don't know yet what her disability is—if any—but she is unbelievably tiny. When she cried, she sounded like a baby kitten mewling for its mother. I still haven't seen her open her eyes. It will undoubtedly be difficult for her to adjust to this harsh environment.

We learned that the orphanage's top director has requested a meeting with us to express his gratitude for our work and contributions. This is a first, that we know of, in this institution. We've developed a wonderful team of women, and I'm very proud to be leading them. I never dreamed this project would grow to the extent it has. In the beginning, I thought simply visiting to hold the babies and demonstrate some affection would be enough. But when you see the multitude of constant needs, you cannot help but step forward and become more involved. Sometimes I feel I'm the wrong person for this work, as I have no previous experience in raising donations or organizing such a large group of volunteers. When I feel overwhelmed and want to walk away, a higher power gives me a gentle nudge and tells me I can do it—and my newly discovered stubborn streak kicks in to keep me going.

* * *

OCTOBER 28, 2004

Yesterday morning at home, I cut open all the snack packages and put them in a baggie for easy access. The children are not used to eating anything that isn't put in a bowl in front of them, and individual packages are troublesome to open in their frenzy to get the food into their mouths. I stuffed the baggie into my backpack, along with fifteen new pairs of underwear, and headed out the door.

After a long and chaotic drive in heavy traffic, Regina and I arrived at the orphanage. Regina headed up to the baby room, while I made my weekly stop on the second floor to hand out goodies—cheese sticks today.

By now when the children see me they know there are treats coming, and some become quite stirred up. One of the first to receive a treat was a boy of about ten or so. He never looks up or has any kind of expression—just stares blankly ahead. I put the snack in his hand, as usual, and he dropped it to the floor. I picked it up and tried once more. He dropped it again. I picked it up and set it on his lap. I knew he wanted it, but I couldn't take any more time with him.

I continued to hand out snacks, much to the delight of the other children. They rushed to cram them into their mouths. A few minutes and many smiles later, I headed for the door. On my way out, I passed the first little boy again, and noticed the snack was no longer in his lap. Sitting beside him was another small boy, who had broken the cheese stick into bite-size pieces and was feeding it to his "brother," one tiny tidbit at a time. The gentleness of his actions as he placed the bites into his brother's mouth made me want to capture that moment in my heart and hold it forever.

* * *

NOVEMBER 1, 2004

Jia Jia is doing much better after her spina bifida operation. She no longer appears to be in pain and hardly cries anymore. The removal of the grapefruit-size lump on her back has given her a much improved life, without pain dictating her every moment. Because she is in better spirits, the staff has begun to treat her more humanely. She is now allowed out of bed and can crawl on the floor by using her arms and a special wiggle. The current prognosis is that she will always be paralyzed. In November, Jia Jia will be two years old. We're discussing the possibility of sending her to a different doctor for another opinion on her physical-therapy needs. We also know that one day she will need a special chair and that will mean more fund-raising.

On Tuesday, the staff decided it was time to take Jia Jia off the bottle. While their decision may have been right, the way they went about it brought tears to our eyes. We had taken her out of bed and put her in a stroller, and when the bottles were wheeled in, we hurried to get all the babies back into their cribs for feeding. When I started to pick up Jia Jia, they waved me away and gestured for me to leave her in the stroller. I was confused but kept quiet as I began feeding a cleft baby. Jia Jia's face scrunched up with a confused expression as if to say, "Help! Get me back to bed for my bottle!"

A while later, Tilly, the *ayi* with whom we've had problems in the past, pulled up a chair in front of Jia Jia. She loudly declared it was time to change Jia Jia's diet from milk to rice—no more bottles. Without any kind of coaxing, she proceeded to force some rice into Jia Jia's mouth. The child has never had anything other than bottled milk, so naturally she was upset—there was no way she wanted that strange stuff in her mouth. She immediately spit it out, angering Tilly.

Lately I'd begun to think Tilly's disposition was softening, but today there was no evidence of that. Her face contorted with rage, she screamed at Jia Jia and continued shoving in spoon after spoonful. Jia Jia tried blocking her mouth with her hands, prompting Tilly and another *ayi* to tie her arms to the stroller. At this point Jia Jia was hysterical, and it was all Lucy and I could do not to interfere. "Just look at what they're doing to her!" Lucy said helplessly.

I knew that if we intervened, Tilly would take it out on Jia Jia, but it was excruciating to simply stand there and watch.

Mercifully, they gave up, and Tilly shoved Jia Jia and the

stroller away from her. I immediately put down the baby I was holding and found another half-full bottle. I asked if I could give it to Jia Jia, but Tilly angrily waved me away.

"But she is so hungry . . . ," I began. My heart was aching to give her comfort and fill her empty little tummy.

The other worker, who has some respect for me, said, "Xiao Ti Ti . . . *bushi*"(don't).[4] She was warning me in a gentle voice not to interfere.

I picked up Jia Jia despite the warning and tried my best to console her, though I know she was hoping I would give her a bottle. I felt as though I'd let her down when she was certain I would be the one to help her. The *ayi* put her back to bed hungry and it weighed on me all day—I'm sure dinnertime was a repeat performance. I know I'm not supposed to question Chinese practices, but it was very hard for Lucy and me to stand by and watch such a scene without becoming involved.

I suppose we'll find out on Monday if they were successful in their feeding attempts. Will they have put her back on the bottle, or did she give up and eat the rice? I know she needs the nourishment, but it would have been much better to start her gradually and with a gentler person feeding her. It would take so little to make life easier for these children.

* * *

There is no doubt that my work at the orphanage is affecting my home life. Last night I was exhausted from the emotional drain of the past few weeks, so we splurged to go out for dinner at the

---

4 In my first few weeks of volunteering the director asked me what I would like to be called at the orphanage. I chose the nickname that my nieces and nephews had given me years ago, Ti Ti.

local hotel. As Ben talked about issues at work, my mind wandered back to the orphanage children and which of their needs required the most urgent attention.

Finally, Ben asked, "Have you heard a single word I've said?"

"Of course!" I lied.

I wasn't fooling him, and as Amanda took a turn regaling us with her adventures at school, Ben observed me with a concerned expression. I know he is worried about the toll this work is taking on me, but it's something that has taken on a life of its own—and a meaningful life at that—and to step away now would mean that the quality of lives of many children would be affected.

I have to find a way to balance the two worlds I'm living in.

23

NOVEMBER 4, 2004

In rural areas or smaller cities it is common for people to abandon their sick children at hospitals. The child is admitted under a false name, and the parents frequently vanish during the treatment or operation. Sometimes this happens because the parents cannot afford to pay for the care and treatment; but more often the parents, because they are allowed only one child, simply choose to start over and try to have a healthy baby. Others abandon their daughters because of the age-old cultural preference for a boy.

Another popular abandonment site is the train station or large markets. Most of these places have security guards posted about, but the crowds are so thick that it is impossible to notice parents wandering away from their crying child. I always ask the *ayis* where a newly abandoned child was found, and if they are privy to the information via the grapevine, the most frequent answer is, "Wandering around the train station." This sad reality brings me to the story of Xiao Gou.

* * *

One afternoon several months ago, another volunteer and I were at the hospital visiting one of our orphanage babies who was being prepared for heart surgery. While we were in the ICU area, a little girl named Xiao Gou (a nickname meaning little puppy—pronounced "shall go") drew our attention. She had an engaging smile and personality; we could tell immediately that she was highly intelligent. We spent time coloring with her and looked forward to seeing her each time we visited the other baby. We learned that she was not an orphan; she was one of the lucky ones to have parents who were supportive and waiting for her to recover. The nurses had become attached to Xiao Gou and she was able to stay in the ICU much longer than she actually needed. Through my translator, the head nurse told us Xiao Gou's tragic story.

A happy four-year-old with parents, she spent her days entertaining herself while her parents worked outside. In the countryside, it is common for small children to stay alone while their parents work the fields. One afternoon, while Xiao Gou was playing near her home, a car struck her.

The exact details following the accident are unclear, but we learned that her parents took her to Shengxi and admitted her to the children's hospital. Xiao Gou's injuries were traumatic and doctors were forced to amputate her right leg at the hip socket, leaving no remaining bone structure. Xiao Gou was not expected to live and spent many months recuperating in the ICU.

Months later, on a return visit to the ICU, we asked for Xiao Gou and were told she was no longer there. Apparently, her parents had initially paid their daughter many visits, but after a few months the visits became increasingly infrequent, until one day they just never returned. After that, Xiao Gou was taken to one of the local orphanages. Imagine our surprise when we requested to know which one and were told it was the very institution where my volunteer group works! I asked the nurse to write down Xiao Gou's name in Chinese and told her I would be going to find her.

The next day, with the slip of paper in hand, I approached Director Yao. She informed me Xiao Gou indeed was there, but her name had been changed to Sheng Rui. The two parts of her name, given by the directors, sounded similar to "Sun Ray," so we nicknamed her Sunshine. (Later, she told us that her mama had called her Xiao Gou and that's what she preferred.)

At the orphanage, we found her on the second floor—the most avoided and desolate area of the institution—with the group of severely mentally and physically challenged children. One look into Xiao Gou's eyes told me how devastated she was at the turn her life had taken. She hardly resembled the child we'd known in ICU; if it weren't for her amputated leg, I would not have recognized her. The orphanage barber had sheared her beautiful hair into a chopped-up bob and she looked completely beaten down by her circumstances.

I knelt in front of her and tried to make her smile, but no matter what I said, I could not bring her out of her shell. I felt unspeakably sad at her situation and the difficulties she'd been forced to experience. First to be in such a painful accident, then to lose her leg, and most terrible of all, to be abandoned by her parents and brought to this gloomy place. I vowed to do everything possible to help her.

I left Xiao Gou and went to speak with the director again. I told her that my group wanted to sponsor Xiao Gou and try to have her fitted with a prosthetic leg. To our disappointment, the staff was not open to our suggestions; instead, they said our available money must be spent on a child who would "have a future."

"Xiao Gou will have a wonderful future," I insisted, "and it would be wonderful if she can walk again like other children." They relented somewhat, saying they would discuss it with their board of directors.

Weeks later, I had still not received approval to take Xiao Gou to a doctor. I continued insisting until the staff and board finally yielded. Soon after, we made a day trip to Beijing. Xiao Gou was still silent and withdrawn.

Unknown to us, Xiao Gou's injuries were much deeper than just the amputation of her leg. When the doctor pulled back her diaper, we all gasped in shock. She had at least four inches of colon extending from her body and she no longer had a rectum. Her genitals were maimed and unrecognizable. The scars from her accident were deep and many. As we stood gaping at her mutilated form, Xiao Gou wept silent tears of humiliation and fear. I wiped her tears and reassured her that no one would hurt her anymore.

The doctor called in a colleague and they decided Xiao Gou should be admitted for a series of tests to see what else might be going on internally. To my dismay, the orphanage staff declined, saying they would have to consider it, and Xiao Gou might be brought back to the hospital later.

The doctors were not happy with this decision. They said it was imperative that Xiao Gou return to the hospital as soon as possible. Her risk of serious infection because of the extended colon was extremely high.

Back at the orphanage, the staff said they would inform us when they'd made a decision. We were left with the feeling that they considered this single exam the only step they needed to take. However, we continued to badger them for weeks until they finally agreed to the testing.

One morning soon after, I took Xiao Gou back to Beijing and she was admitted. Two weeks later, the test results showed she had internal problems that needed immediate surgery. One of the lines that transported her waste was broken and particles were backing up into her kidneys, causing a life-threatening infection, which was evidenced by her continual fevers.

The doctors did not want her to leave the hospital, but the orphanage staff would not approve the surgery, so they ordered her discharge to be processed. The doctor recommended that

Xiao Gou's body be kept dry and warm at all times to cut down on outside infection to the traumatized areas. I knew this was not happening at the orphanage so I volunteered—demanded, actually—to foster Xiao Gou until we could get her into surgery. Much to my surprise, this was approved, and she came directly from the hospital to our home.

At first I was nervous about this, seeing how withdrawn she had become and how easily she cried. I should not have worried—within two days she had returned to the joyful and spunky child I had met at the Shengxi hospital. Not only that, but she was extraordinarily affectionate and easy to care for. She got around fine on one leg by crawling or using furniture to support her. In fact, she was very fast. We had already known Xiao Gou was intelligent, and she picked up English words very quickly.

Like most girls her age, this little one just loved a bath. I gave her baths frequently because her scarring and extended colon made bowel movements quite messy. I knew it was important to keep the area clean, and a bath was the best way to do it without hurting her. Each day at about noon, she would start begging for her bath. If I said she needed to wait a while, her spirits would sink. As soon as I relented, she would throw her arms around me and smile all the way upstairs to the bathtub.

If we had not instinctively already known it, we would have soon discovered that Xiao Gou was a very special child. Ben, Amanda, and I all fell for her easily and dreaded the time when she would leave our home. Finally, the orphanage gave permission for the surgery to take place. We took her back to the hospital, where the plan was to repair the internal damage and attach a colostomy bag.

Leaving Xiao Gou at the hospital was traumatic for both her and me—she cried and screamed each time I left her side to attend to any small detail. When they finally pulled her away, we were both sobbing. The many curious Chinese who had gathered appeared astonished at how an American woman and a Chinese child had formed such a close bond. As I was leaving, I promised her I'd return soon. I imagine she was thinking she'd be there for another stay of many months, as she had been after her parents abandoned her. This time I was doing the walking away, and I felt as if I were betraying her.

The scheduled surgery was canceled many times because of Xiao Gou's continual fever. When her fever finally abated and the surgery took place, it lasted more than eight hours. The doctor repaired the fistulas and removed over eighteen inches of damaged colon. He determined that the colostomy was not needed right away, and Xiao Gou was returned to her room. The following weeks of recovery passed quickly and the day soon arrived for her discharge.

Throughout this ordeal, the orphanage administrators had assured me they would have a foster family prepared to receive Xiao Gou after her release. However, this proved not to be the case. I was angry—I felt as though they hadn't even tried. Xiao Gou was going back to the orphanage and there wasn't a thing I could do about it.

I saw her three days after her return. She had regressed to being withdrawn and silent. However, I can now happily report that she has made some progress in healing and has returned to her former exuberant self. Most important, the staff did not return her to the second floor of special-needs children but instead installed her in the watching room, where she'd be held for an observation period with other kids who have undiagnosed or contagious illnesses.

Because of her bowel problems and the poor care she receives, Xiao Gou frequently has severe diaper rashes and bleeding around her still-exposed colon. The only way to clear this up and give her relief is to remove her from the orphanage, so we've brought her back to our home a few times for short visits. Each time, she proves to be a delightful addition to our family and brings a new level of life to our home. Small things make her happy: a warm bubble bath or a trip to McDonald's, a bowl of potato chips and a cup of milk. She is entirely lovable and has an exquisite sense of humor and a dauntless spirit. She is playful with Amanda and loves to play hide-and-seek with Ben. She has learned to move about quickly using a physical therapy walker; we can hardly keep up with her. I see a child thriving who would otherwise be languishing in the unemotional environment of an institution.

The doctor has said Xiao Gou will not need any further surgeries; furthermore, they say she will never be able to wear a prosthetic leg because of the lack of bone structure on her side. However, I firmly believe that another doctor in another country could figure out some way to make this happen. She wasn't given the colostomy either, which I think was a mistake.

The orphanage staff claims they are still trying to find a Chinese foster family for Xiao Gou. Meanwhile, I continue to show her lots of love and affection. She knows I am not her mama, and I have had translated to her that we're trying hard to find her a new mama and daddy. She told her *ayi* that her parents left her "because they didn't like her." What a burden on this child's heart. Xiao Gou remembers them clearly, and when other Chinese discuss how her parents abandoned her, she becomes withdrawn and quiet again.

Ben and I will not give up on our goal to improve her quality of life. I feel as if the Lord has a plan for her. We want to help her find it.

* * *

Sometimes I am frustrated with the fates that brought me into such close contact with so many children when I know that we likely won't be adopting any of them. On many occasions I've left the orphanage with the intention of discussing the possibility with Ben. I think we could afford it, but what always stops me is the thought that bringing a baby into my family will make me too busy to continue my work with the rest of the children. I feel as if this desire to adopt one of the orphanage children is selfish, and it's unfair to the many kids who have come to depend on me. How can I do the most good? The answer is obvious, so I'll keep this constant thought to myself and try not to become too discouraged by it.

* * *

NOVEMBER 5, 2004

Le Bing, the PKU baby, is back at the orphanage. Part of his disease requires that he receive special milk. His urinary tract and oral infection have healed, and he appears to be pain-free. This baby has been the cause of several sleepless nights for me, as well as for a new volunteer named Maggie, who has bonded with him. The dilemma is that he is severely mentally challenged and will always need special milk. Some very special people in the States have donated the milk we currently have on hand. We can't find it in China, so the question is, should we continue to keep him going when we know he'll eventually end up in the ward of mentally challenged adults? Do we go on hoping his quality of life remains merely adequate? Or should we stop supplying the special milk and let nature take its course, which it may do in any case? What is best for him? I don't have the answer, and several volunteers have asked me the same question. No one wants to make that decision. Personally, I would rather die than be banished to that building behind the orphanage. I see those poor, neglected adults through the bars on the windows and it is not a pretty life. But we may not have to decide Le Bing's fate: if we cannot get any more milk, it will be in God's hands. For now, Maggie and I are smothering him with love and hoping for some sign that we are doing the right thing.

Xiao Li is an eight-year-old girl who was just released from the hospital and is now in foster care. She has a bone disease that has her in a full body cast, and soon she'll need rods inserted into her leg. She is an extremely precocious child. While she was in the hospital, I brought her a doll with five dresses, and we played at changing the clothes for a while. That was followed by more playtime with the electronic game Lucy had brought. Next, Xiao Li showed me all the goodies Sheila had brought, and she was anxious to know when we'd be back. This child knows how much we all love her. She is a real trooper. When I asked her if she was in pain, she looked up at me with big eyes and solemnly nodded. Once I informed the doctor that we'd pay for any pain medication, and he confirmed that she was indeed receiving it, I could only offer her a heartfelt *"Dui bu qi"* (I am sorry).

There are more surgical needs to be met, including four cleft lip babies who will soon need operations. One baby with a tumor in his stomach is in the hospital, but we can't find out what kind of costs are involved or determine who will pay. Before we commit to anything else, we must pay for all the current babies' medical care. We'll make decisions on additional children once we have a better grasp of our present expenses.

It is painful to look at a child who you know desperately needs medical care, and not be able to give immediate approval for his or her surgery. We want to help every single one of them! We've become so attached to these children, it's as though they're our own.

* * *

NOVEMBER 9, 2004

This morning at the orphanage, Regina and I first visited with the older children before heading up to the baby room. When we got there, we found the babies had not yet been changed—the staff had decided to have a lazy day. The babies were in misery, their diapers soaked through, but the worst was yet to come.

Tilly was in a stormy mood, blatantly demonstrating her evil side to all of us. (I must have been dreaming when I thought she was improving in September.) When Jin Ji, the two-year-old, whined because she wanted the lap of another *ayi*, Tilly began spanking her severely. We were sitting in the hallway, with some of the babies in walkers and others on our laps, playing with and singing to them. At the sound of Jin Ji's screams, we stopped our activities and silently observed the scene, unable to intervene.

After the spanking, Tilly grabbed Jin Ji roughly, carried her to the window, and dangled her halfway out, three stories above the ground, all the while threatening that she was going to drop the poor child. Jin Ji was terrified, screaming and grasping at air. Just as I leaped up and raced to the window, unsure of what I was going to do, Tilly pulled her in and brought her back into the room. She sat Jin Ji in a chair while the girl sobbed pitifully. Next Tilly produced a piece of rope and strapped Jin Ji to the chair, which started the fear all over again. Clearly, Tilly was making a show to see how much terror she could cause, and after a few minutes she removed the rope. Then, unbelievably, she carried Jin Ji around while her sobs subsided. Strangely, as soon as Tilly started show-ing Jin Ji sympathy, the child warmed to her affection, as if she'd immediately forgiven the trauma she had just endured.

Jia Jia was next on the list for trouble. She still craves a bottle, which she is no longer permitted, and when she saw the rice bowl coming, she began to cry softly. Tilly and another *ayi* immediately pinned her to her bed, pulled her arms out straight, and tied her wrists to the side rungs. They proceeded to shovel rice into Jia Jia's mouth, while plugging her nose until she was forced to swallow. She cried and choked, trying uselessly to keep her face averted from the relentless onslaught.

Jia Jia evidently had not had much nutrition in a few days and was listless and weak, but they will continue this inhumane feeding routine until she surrenders and eats out of sheer starvation. As soon as they gave up and left her alone, Regina and I took turns hugging and consoling her. She kept pulling our hands to her face—she wanted the comfort our touch would bring.

In my opinion, Tilly is the single biggest problem in this orphanage; I can't help but speculate on what kind of life she must have had as a child to put such cruelty in her heart.

Among all these horrors, our volunteer group had some good news: Le Men will go to the hospital this week for his surgery. It was going to take all the money in our fund to cover this, but a kind of miracle happened. On Friday I learned that an expatriate Scottish woman had a conversation with her husband about the many surgeries needed.

The following day they set up a new project called the Happy Fund. Together with their friends and colleagues, they have raised enough to pay for Le Men's surgery. That means we can use our own funds to pay for Li Li, the other baby needing heart surgery. Our gratitude on behalf of these children is boundless.

With many more children requiring medical procedures, I refuse to doubt that we'll succeed in making them happen. How could I when I've seen firsthand the wonderful things happening here? I have been blessed to meet such generous people in Shengxi and around the world.

* * *

Yesterday a friend and I attended an expat association lunch at a Japanese restaurant. In China, many restaurants do not have public washroom facilities. Unless you're in a hotel or very expensive restaurant, you'll usually find only Chinese "squatters," which are simple porcelain pots placed flush against the floor that you must squat over to relieve yourself.

When I warned my good friend about the squatters, she said she just couldn't wait, and followed a waitress upstairs. About ten minutes later, she returned.

With a twinkle in her eye, she said, "They do have a bathroom, and you have to see it to believe it."

I was also getting desperate after chugging down four glasses of cola to abate my hunger. (The food options had been slim and I declined the only offers of sushi and cooked fish.) I followed the same little Chinese girl up several flights of stairs, around a winding hallway, and to a door marked with a high-heeled shoe indicating the women's room.

Inside was a paradise far removed from the primitive facilities I was expecting. The counter was inset with a beautiful glass sink, completely transparent under an exquisite mirror. In the stall was the most futuristic contraption you could imagine. This "toilet" stood majestically placed, with a small sink built into its top and an array of digital buttons surrounding the sink.

When I sat down to take care of business, much to my astonishment and delight, the seat began warming up under me—a wonderful treat, considering the rest of the restaurant was icy cold. To my further surprise, birds began chirping. As I gazed in wonder around my tropical oasis, the sound became increasingly louder, but I could not see any birds . . . I laughed aloud when I realized the sound was coming from below and behind me! As I stood, the toilet automatically flushed and the sound of birds gently faded away until, at the precise moment the water disappeared, the room became quiet.

I laughed again at what extremes China presents. Usually I can't even find a public washroom, but yesterday I happened upon a paradise of bottom-warming and birdsong accompanying my bodily functions.

24

NOVEMBER 10, 2004

The feeling was buoyant in the baby room today—what a difference from yesterday! The babies were given baths and a good shake of baby powder, and then we dressed them in clean clothes. Two of our babies had been moved to the other room with the bigger kids, which confused me. I went in to investigate and discovered that one of them had a large, dark bruise on her face. The other was a small mentally disabled girl with whom I was only vaguely familiar.

I later discovered what all the fuss was about and why the two babies had been temporarily moved. A Chinese television crew was coming to film us, and all the healthiest babies had been primped and polished for their benefit. There could be no signs that orphanage conditions were less than perfect—in China, appearance is everything.

The crew filmed their piece and promptly left the room. Soon after, however, he returned with the director, who said he wanted to interview me. I agreed, and held Le Men while Sheila translated his questions to me about our volunteer group.

He also interviewed Sheila, but they spoke entirely in Mandarin, so I'm not sure what questions he asked. I hope this initiative will spur the public's interest in helping the local children. There are many generous Chinese, but they need to be made aware of what the needs are. On the other hand, I was frustrated that the cameras did not capture the reality of daily life in the orphanage; appearances had been "airbrushed" for the media.

I learned more about Tilly today. She has been with the orphanage less than a year. Prior to taking this job, she'd worked in a paper factory for years but was let go. Her husband is unemployed and they have a daughter starting college this year, so she is likely under a good deal of financial stress. I feel bad for her circumstances but they still give her no excuse to treat the babies so cruelly.

* * *

Tonight, after Amanda had her bath, she sat on my bed as I braided her hair into many tiny plaits, the same way I had done her sister's when she was younger. Amanda loves this tradition because the next morning, when we take her braids out, her hair falls in beautiful waves.

As I methodically worked through Amanda's sweet-smelling hair, I thought about how fortunate we are to have such an affectionate child. She is growing up far too quickly. I recalled when, at three years of age, she'd been hospitalized with a mysterious bacteria racing through her veins. Terrified for her life, Ben and I spent two weeks sleeping on a cot in her sterile room, refusing to leave and praying for her recovery. How would we have survived if she had been taken from us, or if she had been diagnosed with a fatal disease?

What anguish the mothers of these children must have experienced to have to abandon their babies. Perhaps they hoped their children would receive the medical care they themselves could not afford to provide. Or did they leave them for selfish reasons?

Cultural pressures? I struggle with these thoughts, which jump from empathy for the mothers to outrage at government officials' lack of interest in helping their people avoid such desperate acts.

* * *

NOVEMBER 20, 2004

I visited Le Men in the hospital yesterday. He was supposed to have his heart surgery but was too weak. The attending *ayi* told me the milk sent from the orphanage was not good enough, so we left, returning with formula that was more nutritious. The plan is to try to strengthen him and possibly have him ready for surgery in a few days. The doctor also found something else in his lung area that doesn't look good, and now he says Le Men's surgery will be riskier than first thought. He needs to be as strong as possible before they proceed.

Le Men was happy to see us, but it was obvious he was bored. He had no toys or entertainment, which is such a difference from American pediatric patients. In the States, children would be able to watch cartoons or be entertained by toys and colorful mobiles hanging from every pole or bed rail. Observing the sparse hospital room with its filthy walls and bedding reminds me how lucky I was to be born in a country that strives to place its people in adequate medical environments.

The *ayi* was happy for our presence—she could now have her first break in three days. She's been hired to give Le Men twenty-four-hour care, but she's an older woman from the fields and gets a little skittish in the cramped room. She's paid thirty renminbi for each day, which is about four American dollars. She's usually very good—we've used her for the last three babies.

When I laid Le Men down and told him goodbye, he started to whine and that got the curious local women laughing. As was the case with Xiao Gou, they find it amazing that a Chinese baby could become attached to a foreigner. After our visit, I went shopping for toys for Le Men's crib. At the same time, I bought a few more towels for the *ayi* to use when bathing him.

* * *

NOVEMBER 30, 2004

Ben and Amanda came with me to the hospital today to meet Le Men. I thought meeting him would help them understand why so much of my energy is directed toward these children. The *ayi*'s face lit up when she saw us. We'd brought her a fast-food lunch—always guaranteed to win favor. After she'd left the room, clutching her bucket of chicken in satisfaction, I stripped Le Men, rubbed him down with baby lotion, and dressed him in his new shirt. He smelled lovely and basked in the attention.

When she returned, the *ayi* reported that the milk we'd brought Le Men on Friday was "too good." Is that as compared with the milk from the orphanage that is "too bad"? She had quit feeding it to him because it caused him to have diarrhea. He is marginally better than he was on Friday, but it's difficult to tell. And there's no new information on a surgery date—only that it will happen when they think he is strong enough.

It's interesting to see how babies are so attracted to other kids. Le Men was mesmerized by Amanda and was pleased with the toys. According to the *ayi*, he wasn't sleeping well at night and she's had to stand and hold him for hours. She looks exhausted— she's been with him almost nonstop since Wednesday, but he couldn't get better care from anyone else—she is struggling to do her best.

* * *

DECEMBER 1, 2004

We went to the hospital to drop off more items for Le Men and were told that he is still too weak for surgery this week. They are giving him IV fluids and weighing him every day to evaluate his progress. A few days of vomiting and diarrhea set him back, but he's now taking in milk again. If he starts gaining weight quickly, there is still a possibility they will do the surgery early next week.

Le Men is clearly bored, but he's in good spirits when he has visitors. Although she claims not to be, it's evident the *ayi* is very exhausted; we're concerned she is too tired for adequate care. We may need to hire an additional *ayi* to help her out in shifts since Le Men is not sleeping well at night. We'll talk to the orphanage administrator about it. In the Shengxi hospital, the child's parent or caregiver does most of the work. They bathe and feed the child, take temperatures, and must be attentive to the child's needs. This requires the caregiver to be alert and well rested, which our present *ayi* is not.

We've learned that as soon as Le Men has had his operation, his story will be featured on the news because of the involvement of foreigners paying surgery costs. That should make for an interesting piece; we hope it will generate more awareness of the desperate circumstances of some of these children and perhaps prompt some prospective foster parents to come forward.

More worries today. At the orphanage this morning, Li Li was looking weak and listless. She still has a small smile for us, but she's not moving about much. We will talk to Director Yao about preparing her for heart surgery soon. She is in the same weak health as Le Men, and without the necessary surgery will only become worse. No one has a clear answer. The hospital nurse has said that the orphanage food is not nutritional enough for the babies, yet they need to be fattened up before going into a risky heart surgery. It's a vicious circle: without a substantial weight gain they cannot have surgery, but without the surgery they will die. It's very complicated and keeps me awake at night trying to figure out a solution.

* * *

DECEMBER 5, 2004

Two days of diaper changes, sleepless nights, red-rimmed eyes, and a critically ill baby in the house has been quite an experience. Sheila requested permission for me to take Li Li home to strengthen her for her upcoming surgery. She was not getting adequate care or feedings at the orphanage. That the request was approved was surprising—all the hours I've put in appear to be paying off. It's been a long while since I've had to take care of an infant around the clock. It turns out that Li Li is much sicker than we thought. She sometimes takes up to two hours to suck down one bottle, her stomach and other organs struggling to pump in and out. She perspires through her clothes just from the effort of trying to drink from her bottle. She is ten months old and weighs a mere ten pounds.

One volunteer immediately jumped in and offered a porta-crib, a bumper seat, and loads of used baby clothes. Another volunteer, Darlene, who lives next door, offered to keep Li Li one evening so I could have a break. She's offered several times since then, but the fact is the little sweetheart is very little trouble, other than not sleeping at night. I've grown quite attached to her in this brief time.

At first I rushed around trying to ready everything; sorting through and hanging her clothes, getting her room ready, and setting up all the baby items. At night, Li Li sleeps only about twenty to thirty minutes at a time, due to her problems breathing. She can't hold her head up, turn over, or do most things a healthy child can at that age.

Once we knew Li Li would be joining our household for a time, Ben and Amanda had to learn the important rules of not spoiling an orphan who eventually has to go back to living in an institution. I gave the strict instructions that we would only hold her when necessary, and under no circumstances were we allowed to rock her to sleep. I felt it would be distressing for her to get used to something so comforting and then feel the heartache when that comfort was removed.

Well, that plan lasted no longer than a few hours. What did Ben say when he entered to find me and Li Li snuggled in the rocking chair together with a look of rapture on both our faces? Not one word—he just shook his head. He knew I was all talk.

Both Ben and Amanda have completely lost their hearts to her. Ben stayed up with her last night for three hours to let me sleep, and I took the rest of the night. We're all exhausted but it's mitigated by the reward of seeing this lovely child so content.

* * *

DECEMBER 8, 2004

It's the fifth day of the little orphan Li Li adventure and I'm happy to say that she has gained two pounds! We have eleven more days to plump her up, after which we hope she'll be able to go directly to the hospital. Sheila will talk to the orphanage today to let them know how important this is. If Li Li goes back to the orphanage even briefly, I have no doubt that she will lose the weight we've worked so hard to help her gain.

I have been seeking permission to have her checked out by the foreign hospital. Her cough is violent at night and she likely needs to start a round of antibiotics before surgery, just as Le Men did.

After almost a week, I really miss him and his serious face. I'd like to visit him, but I cannot leave Li Li.

These two children have been nothing less than enchanting. Li Li has become more animated and smiles easily after only a few days of family life. She is no longer the extremely weak and listless child we had become so accustomed to seeing. She is now preparing herself for a fight for her life.

* * *

Amanda has a new best friend and the positive change in her is remarkable. Our volunteer Darlene has a daughter named Madi, and the girls have become inseparable. What a wonderful coincidence that another American family would move into the house next to ours and have two daughters that are the same age as our own daughters. Madi and Amanda both love animals and playing with Bratz dolls, and they are even in the same classes at school. Their bedroom windows face each other's, and each night Amanda has to be told to close the window and stop shouting to Madi across the way. We're just thrilled that Amanda finally has someone nearby with whom she can bond; there's nothing like seeing your child happy.

* * *

DECEMBER 12, 2004

Darlene and I took Li Li to the local doctor this morning. He was horrified at her poor condition, informing us that she has pneumonia with the possibility of heart failure! I was not very surprised at his comments; though Li Li appeared to be improving in our care, it was obvious that her little heart struggled too hard to do the simplest things. We were instructed to take her directly to the local hospital. We met the administrator and Sheila at the children's hospital, and then sat and awaited the doctor. Soon we had a cluster of curious onlookers standing in the hall and trying to determine why I was holding a Chinese baby as if she were mine. I was very worried for our baby girl, and not happy to be the center of attention among a dozen nosy people.

The doctor eventually arrived and asked what the problem was. Sheila translated to her that Li Li might possibly have pneumonia. When this was understood, the doctor and the gathering outside the doorway began to giggle as if it were the most ridiculous thing they had ever heard. The doctor procured her stethoscope and began listening to Li Li's chest. Her expression turned serious, and she gestured to another technician to fetch her colleague. After the professionals were satisfied that Li Li was truly in serious condition, they ordered X-rays and had her transferred to the ICU in the other building. Relieved that Li Li was finally getting some professional care, I watched closely as the orphanage staff signed all the pertinent admitting papers.

As we left, they ordered no further visitors. Being the rule-breaker I have evolved into, I made it clear to the doctor that we would be back to see her despite his orders. Someone needs to be responsible and step up as this child's advocate, and it appeared that Darlene and I were going to have to team up to ensure Li Li receives the care she deserves.

As we lingered to tell her goodbye, Li Li fought against the tube being inserted through her nose to drain her lungs. With the sound of her irregular breathing still fresh in my memory, I knew she had no alternative but to endure this treatment.

It was agonizing to walk away and leave her, when I somehow felt entirely responsible. I know Darlene and Sheila were as sick about it as I was. We've done all we can, and now it's time to let the medical team do their job. I am thankful that Li Li was allowed to come stay with us—we'd thought she had pneumonia, but no one would listen to our amateur diagnosis. At least the temporary stay in our home put a few pounds on her and gave her the opportunity for nine days of unconditional love.

Meanwhile, Le Men hadn't left our thoughts. When we stopped by to see him later, we found he was doing much better. He's putting on weight, and he may be ready for surgery in another week. The orphanage administrator fussed at the *ayi* for leaving trash in the cupboards and for taking all of Le Men's toys away. After this verbal spanking, the *ayi* pulled out the hanging mobile that Elaine, one of the founders of the Happy Fund, had bought. Rather angrily, I hung it back up.

Over and over, I'm infuriated that Chinese customs prevent any type of entertainment for sick children. Day after day, Le Men has nothing to stare at but four grungy walls. His boredom must be mind-numbing.

* * *

JANUARY 7, 2005

I have a newfound awareness of life that makes me feel joyful every moment that my family is alive and healthy. We've just returned from an excursion to Thailand—Ben's company allows for two excursions a year to get us out of the high stress of living in China. Heather had flown over to spend Christmas with us and she was able to join us. Up until the last minute, we were debating whether to stay on Koh Samui or Phuket. Spontaneously, I made a quick decision and chose Koh Samui. We had been in Phuket the year before and thought it a gorgeous place, but the atmosphere was not family friendly. That decision may well have saved our lives, as Amanda is now fond of telling everyone.

We arrived in Koh Samui in the morning, unaware there had been a natural disaster. As we entered our room after a day on the beach, the neighbor next door burst in, telling us to turn on the news. An earthquake in the Indian Ocean had caused a tsunami to hit the city of Phuket as well as several other areas. Already the deaths were numbering in the thousands, with many still missing.

In disbelief, Ben and I watched the newscasters as they attempted to describe the various areas of impact and the rapidly increasing death toll. We spent a few hours trying to get an open telephone line to call our families in the U.S. Finally, almost ten hours after the tsunami, I was able to get through to my father.

He answered the phone immediately. "Hey, Dad," I said, attempting to be casual. I didn't yet know how much the rest of the world had heard of the catastrophe. Even here in Koh Samui, the extent of the destruction wasn't fully known. When Dad recognized my voice, the line became silent. Libby, my stepmother, picked up the phone.

"What's wrong with Dad?" I asked anxiously. "Why isn't he talking to me?"

"Honey, he can't talk; he's crying with relief."

As it turned out, our families did not know which city we were visiting, only that we were in Thailand. Many people were afraid that we would not be coming home at all. They'd been calling the embassies and waiting for hours for some word of us. Koh Samui was indeed a part of Thailand, but it was a remote island on the other side of the mainland and not affected by the tsunami.

Still not convinced, my father wanted us out right away, but that was impossible. All flights were solidly booked, and the airports were in chaos. My family had idealistic notions of hiring a magical helicopter to drop in and whisk us away to safety. Forced to stay on, the rest of our trip was bittersweet. Many of the people working at our resort had family members who were dead or missing. In the restaurants and massage huts where the staff was made up of local families, the grief was palpable. It was embarrassing to be lounging around while hotel employees were dealing with personal tragedies. As a small gesture of respect, we took up a collection from the guests and gave it to the local women at the massage hut to help their stricken family members.

Getting back to China was a relief. Once there, I had only a few more days with Heather, after which we had to put her on a plane back to her father. Our short visit together only left me wishing she would agree to live with me full-time. I left the airport crying for my big girl, who was turning into a beautiful young woman right before my eyes, and yet with whom we could no longer share the most memorable moments of her young life. Having her with me for a short time and then sending her back to her father was difficult. I wanted to find a way to persuade her to stay with me but knew that it would be futile; her teenaged life was in the States and those years are so important socially to a fourteen-year-old.

* * *

JANUARY 25, 2005

Amanda's international school held another fund-raising event this weekend. Our orphanage was one of the charities to receive part of the proceeds. It was beyond disappointing that only twelve of the more than one hundred and fifty children at the orphanage were allowed to come.

However, those twelve children proved to be exceptional. They tugged at many heartstrings in the audience as they sang a series of songs onstage. We gave them tickets for games, but it was overwhelming for the usually isolated children to be surrounded by so many people. To calm them before the performances, we took them to the basketball court to release their energy. I kept some of them busy playing Duck Duck Goose and Ring Around the Rosie and giving piggyback rides. When it was time to perform, we headed upstairs and had fun watching all the different nationalities do something to represent their countries. Amanda and her friends performed wonderfully in a cheerleading routine.

Because of my involvement, many of Ben's colleagues attended. The school did a remarkable job with the entire event; it was deemed a great success. But the bottom line is what share of the proceeds our orphanage will receive. We don't yet know, but we're optimistic that it will be generous and we're very excited.

Monday we arrived at the orphanage to total chaos. We should have known there was a superficial reason—government officials were arriving for a "promotional" walkabout. We had to hurry and change beds, line the babies up after haircuts, and assist with quick baths. We were instructed to make everything look neat and tidy for this facade. The *ayis* even put real diapers and Western-style sleepers on the children instead of their normal shabby clothes. The beds were cleaned, plumped, and toys placed in pleasing arrangements. Regina and I were introduced to the top officials—and the next day we were mentioned in the local newspaper. Our biggest hope is that our babies will benefit from the media attention.

On Tuesday the orphanage was back to normal. Calmer, if that's a word to be thrown lightly around this place. The children remained in the same clothes they'd worn the day before, and they hadn't been attended to, other than to be fed. I noticed that one of babies with spina bifida is looking listless. Another infant, this one with a cleft lip, cannot get anything without having the bottle squeezed into his mouth. I know he gets only one good meal a day, and that's when we volunteers are there to work with him.

Leaving the orphanage, I quickly made my way across town to a charity committee meeting; it was a great success, with an inspired group of women interested in our new fund-raising ideas of visiting the children's wards in the hospitals, raising awareness in the media, and doing donation drives. Our goal is to get more expatriates involved in hands-on charity work in several differ-ent areas of Shengxi. I was asked to be the chairperson for this charity; once again, I felt intimidated yet compelled to accept the challenge. This work will be separate from the orphanage volunteer group and is going to take a large chunk of my already limited time.

After the meeting, I stopped by the hospital for a visit with Le Men. The doctor was there and informed us that he is still too weak for surgery. They'll continue feeding and weighing him, and perhaps he'll be ready next week. He was clearly glad to see Lucy, Darlene, and me. We all took turns cuddling and spoiling him. He is such a handsome little boy with a surprisingly stoic personality. We're confident that after his heart is repaired, a loving family will want to adopt him.

25

It was inevitable that a wave of depression should hit me after such a long time of steady work at the orphanage. I hesitate to use the terms "negative" or "miserable," because they're relative. Nevertheless, a dramatic change has gradually come over my normally buoyant psyche. To work in those surroundings for months on end tears at one's heart, and for a short time, I lost perspective. A black cloud of depression finally put me down for almost a week. Ben and Amanda thought I was sick with a virus, which is what I told them, but in truth, I just couldn't function anymore. When I felt it coming, I thought I'd be able to stay ahead of it, but this time it was stronger than my will to keep it at bay.

I paid my dues in my dark, silent bedroom; I had no interest in watching television, reading, or seeing anyone. I gave up on feeling anything, and mercifully, my mind allowed me to sleep for hours on end. Every time I awoke, I pushed myself to force down a little food, going right back to sleep to escape from reality.

I remember the last time depression hit me to this extreme. It was thirteen years ago, just before I'd met Ben, when Heather spent her first night away from me. She was just a toddler and her father was scheduled to start his visitation weekends. As I watched him take her away, the worry and fear pushed me past logical thinking and I spent almost two days in my bed before my sister became worried and visited to check on me. She eventually had to beat on my bedroom window to wake me, after which she forced me out of bed. By the time Heather was delivered back to me, I was functioning normally and relieved to see my baby girl.

I try to hide this part of myself from those around me, and because I'm ordinarily optimistic and positive, most people in my life would be shocked to know of the secret I harbor. Those who haven't dealt with or don't understand depression think that the afflicted person can simply choose to be better and their mood will improve. Some think slipping into an episode is an act of cowardice. I know it is much more than that. I do not like gloom, misery, or feeling hopeless. I have spent my life trying to outrun those feelings. I don't *want* to be depressed. I want to be healthy and happy, a functioning part of my family.

On the last day of my "illness," as I lay listlessly in bed, I could hear talking and giggling wafting up the stairs. My heart latched on with a yearning to be a part of my family again. The heaviness began to lift from my body and I stumbled to the bathroom for a much needed bath and a clean set of clothes.

An hour later, when I slowly made my way downstairs, the relief on the faces of my family was clear. They were thankful Mom had made it through her bout with the mysterious "sleeping flu." As for me, I am hoping that it will be at least another decade before that ominous cloud catches up with me again.

* * *

FEBRUARY 18, 2005

Thailer, a new little boy, has not yet reached seventeen pounds and is waiting to have heart surgery. He does not look fully Chinese; judging by his eyes, he may be of Thai descent. For weeks we referred to him as the Thai baby until one of our volunteers cleverly nicknamed him Thailer (pronounced "Tyler"). His health appears to be stable compared with some of the other heart babies I've dealt with. Thailer is a serious fellow with a somber little face. When I lean over his crib, he holds my finger with a strong grip for a tiny nine-month-old. We hope that he'll quickly gain the weight he needs for his surgery to be scheduled.

The second-floor room and hallway of the disabled and mentally challenged children will be painted before we return from our annual summer break. I had begun to doubt my decision to approve this cost from our donation funds, but I soon received a direct answer that it was the right thing to do. One of Ben's colleagues gave a cash donation this week in exactly the amount needed to paint the room! Oddly, he had not even known I was worried about the cost for this project.

After the summer, a group of Shengxi artists will donate their talents and paint a mural on the walls of the room. These children are hidden away and live their entire lives in this small area—it will be such a blessing for them to have fun and bright surroundings. The new environment should bring much delight to these deprived children.

* * *

FEBRUARY 20, 2005

Amanda and I had a mother-daughter day yesterday. The previous night, Ben and I had scolded her about not sleeping in her own bed. Ben took her to her room and immediately I felt bad for her. I realized it wouldn't be long before she is a teenager and decides she doesn't want to be around us at all. The next morning I decided it was time we spent some quality time together. I have been utterly buried in the orphanage, the children's hospital, and fund-raisers. I know that she has likely been thinking that I love everyone else more than her!

I didn't get her up at the usual 7 a.m. A few hours later, I crawled into bed with her and asked her if she'd like to skip school and hang out with me for the day. She was overjoyed. Our first destination was the Copy Street to find seven matching T-shirts for Ben and his rowing crew. This weekend the famous dragon boat races are taking place and Ben is on the men's team. After a few hours of walking and shopping, we were hungry. Amanda chose McDonald's for lunch, of course—what else would a nine-year-old want?

After thirstily sucking down my drink, I had a problem: I desperately needed a washroom and just knew all they had was a squatter. Amanda thought it was quite funny, but I told her I was going to have to use it and hope my knees held out. I went in and was pleasantly surprised to find a Western toilet—and miracle of miracles, there was even precious toilet paper!

As I pushed out of the stall to wash my hands, I couldn't wait to tell Amanda. Much to my amusement, a young mother was holding her son over the sink while he urinated all over the faucets, the mirror, and the wall. The mother clearly did not know the difference between a sink and a urinal, and I knew it would be useless to explain. I washed well and used my elbows to get out the door, much to the amusement of people entering.

As we left, I was anxious to fulfill my last promise to Amanda. I had agreed to ride in a *sanlunche*, the pedicab that many pedestrians use to get around. I detest them because they are always dirty, but Amanda takes great pleasure in the ride, and this was her day. We found just the right *sanlunche*, gave directions, and offered the driver six renminbi, which is what I had available without breaking a big bill.

He agreed, but as soon as we climbed into the cab, he demanded, "*Shi kuai*." (Ten renminbi.)

"*Bu yao*." I grabbed Amanda, and proceeded to climb out of the cab.

"Okay, okay—*liu kuai!*" (Six renminbi.)

For a local, the price would have been no more than three renminbi, so he was actually getting double the normal fare. Finally, we headed home in a real taxi, and none too soon for me. To go out for the day here is an exhausting exercise—I'll never get used to the masses of people that crowd every corner of China.

Despite my fatigue, we'd had a wonderful day. I'm sure Amanda now knows that she is still loved, even though so many other children get a large piece of my life.

26

MARCH 12, 2005

Last weekend we took a mini holiday to see the Great Wall. Along with another family, we rode the train to Beijing and, once there, made our way through the hordes of people at the train station, grabbed a taxi, and headed for the hotel and a much needed shower.

After we'd freshened up, we spent the day visiting Tiananmen Square and the Forbidden City. I learned why it was called forbidden. Emperor Pu Yi was believed to be the Son of Heaven. He and his family required a special home away from ordinary eyes. The palace was built and the local people were forbidden to see behind the grand walls. The many buildings and rooms set up for the emperor's family and concubines seemed as though the palace would have been a cold, sterile place to live.

Walking around the city, I was mesmerized when we happened upon a group of elderly Chinese performing ballroom dancing in a small park. They were dressed in bland clothing and flat shoes, but the dreamy looks on their faces suggested that in their imaginations, they were transported to another place and time. As the young people looked on, the seniors glided gracefully around and around the square, the sound of a soft tune the only noise.

The next morning we headed up to Chang Cheng (Great

Wall). We decided to go to the Badaling section so we wouldn't have to do so much climbing. It was truly an amazing sight. Throngs of people milled about everywhere, and Amanda made it clear that she was captivated to witness one of the Seven Wonders of the World. I don't think she'll grasp the scope of what she has seen until she is older, but I hope she'll remember more than the exhaustion we all felt at the end of the day.

* * *

APRIL 20, 2005

We lost Bo, the cleft lip baby boy. The *ayis* reported that he refused to eat, but he'd never given me a problem. He tried his hardest, but it took time and patience to get a full meal into him. Maggie, another volunteer, had a special bond with Bo and she has taken his passing particularly hard.

I don't like to think about him, but I try to remember that he is now in a better place and being comforted by a loving God. Maggie's son is an athletic director in the States, and his students had raised money for Bo's upcoming surgery. They had all become enamored of him from photos and email updates, but now their donations will be used for a different project.

Le Men is out of the hospital, doing well, and in foster care. So far, his heart surgery is a success. We only hope he will continue to recover and that his foster family will fall in love and adopt him.

Li Li is still in critical care. She went through an eight-hour surgery and was in recovery when her heart stopped. They rushed her back to surgery and implanted a pacemaker. She is still unconscious and on a morphine drip. This is very worrisome; how common is it for such a small baby to live with a pacemaker? The thought of her being in so much pain that she'd need morphine is very upsetting.

I won't lie—going back into the orphanage today was difficult.

After a three-week break it was like entering the institution for the first time. My time away was a much needed respite that ended too soon. This time we were lucky enough to tour the Great Barrier Reef in Australia, where the reality of my life in China was far removed. A week of intense family time was just what we needed, and we were able to add many more memories to our growing list. I missed the babies terribly, but did not miss the orphanage's depressing atmosphere. Arriving in the Chinese airport, the disparity between the beauty of Australia and the squalor of China hit me hard. However, I jumped back in with both feet.

When I entered the orphanage, Bella was sitting in her walker, her head down on her hands. When she saw me, she immediately began crying streams of silent tears. It was as though she was saying, "Finally . . . you came back."

I produced cookies, which she usually loves, but she wouldn't eat them. I held her and rocked her, asking the staff if she was sick. They claimed not, but later her temperature was taken and they found she had a high fever. I sat on the floor with her head in my lap until feeding time, trying to console her. It makes me shudder to think of her lying in bed all night with no one to comfort her while she was so ill. When my daughters are feeling bad, they want to be pampered and taken care of. It's unimaginable to think how alone these children must feel in their most needy moments.

In my early days at the orphanage, Bella was one of the first toddlers I fell for. After her bath, I'd dress her and then hug her close. She would wrap her arms around me and hug back, which is unusual for the orphanage children. The workers frightened her—with them, she preferred to hide under her blanket. One night when I came to the orphanage for a party, I tiptoed up to the baby room to see her. She was lying in her bed with the blanket completely covering her head. I had thought that was just her naptime habit, and it saddened me to think she was that scared all the time. I slowly lowered the blanket and her face filled with fear.

"It's just me, Bella!" I whispered. She was surprised to see me there at that time of night.

On another occasion, I came to the orphanage with a bus to pick up twenty or so of the bigger kids for a field trip to the park. I insisted that I wanted to take Bella and ignored the protests of the *ayis*. They gave up trying to explain why Bella wasn't allowed to go and reluctantly dressed her. I grabbed a few diapers and, with Bella on my hip, headed for the door.

As Bella realized what I was doing, she began to shriek in fright. I'd never heard her cry aloud and it stopped me in my tracks. The *ayis* looked at me as if to say, "We tried to tell you." Perhaps if I got Bella out of the building, I thought, she would calm down.

I continued but she only became increasingly afraid. By the time we reached the waiting bus, Bella was hysterical. She emphatically did not want to be carried out that orphanage gate. I'd never seen one of the children react this way, and I knew to force her any farther would have traumatized her even more. In defeat, I turned and headed back up the stairs; the closer we got to the room, the more Bella's sobbing subsided. I took her into the room and laid her in her bed, where she immediately covered her head to hide.

Six or so months later, one of our younger volunteers, Claire, took a special liking to Bella. She also saw the panic that overtook Bella if any attempt was made to remove her from the room. Claire decided she wanted to help Bella overcome this fear of the unknown so that one day Bella could come and go as some of the other children do or be considered a candidate for foster care.

Claire signed a sponsorship agreement that gave her the privilege of taking Bella out on the weekends. The first time was traumatic for them both; Bella screamed and sobbed all the way out of the orphanage and down the alley leading to the main road. At one point, Claire sat down with Bella on the curb and prayed for guidance. She so wished to help the child but didn't know if she was doing the right thing. She decided to go a little farther and if Bella wouldn't calm down, she'd turn around and come back. A few minutes later, Bella fell asleep in her arms, exhausted from crying. Claire felt this was a positive sign and carried her to a taxi and then to her new part-time home on the local nursing school campus. Maggie also teaches and lives there, and together they taught Bella what it was like to feel special and to be loved.

In the subsequent weekends, Bella began to open up and get braver with each visit to Claire's home. Now a new Bella has emerged, one who giggles and jabbers and holds our hearts like play putty in her hands. Claire, with Maggie's grandmotherly guidance, has successfully helped Bella overcome her phobia of the outside world, and now she finds delight in new experiences and well-meaning people.

27

MAY 8, 2005

Kate and I went to visit You Ming in the ICU yesterday, one day
after his heart surgery. We had just learned this little boy was taken
there directly from his abandonment site. He had not yet been to
the orphanage. We were notified that he needed immediate surgery and we quickly approved the funds.

The doctor said he was doing well. Kate, a registered nurse,
did her own examination and found that his heart rate was high
and he had a fever. He appeared achingly pitiful lying in that huge
bed and hooked up to a ventilator with his little chest heaving—
how I wished he had a mother to comfort him. At least now he
has a chance at life, thanks to the donations from the Happy Fund
that are paying for his medical care.

Lately the issues at the orphanage have been taking their toll
on several of us. I know our accomplishments are substantial, but
they pale in comparison with the many things we are powerless
to change. Each project takes an inordinate amount of time to
get through the red tape for approval, making every new idea for
improvement a challenge. There continue to be many children in
need of medical help, but it takes months to get approval for each
one. It is sometimes frustrating beyond my capacity for patience.

I know that I need to simply relax and take one project at

a time, but that is just not in my nature. I like to roll through and make things happen quickly. Despite the delays, in two years we have been able to improve the lives of many Shengxi children. I only wish it hadn't torn up so much of my heart to see it through.

* * *

MAY 16, 2005

While visiting You Ming last week, my attention was drawn to another boy whom I'd seen there for more than a year. He was lying in exactly the same bed and position as the last time I'd seen him. I checked with the doctor to find out if he was the same child, because he was so much bigger. I'm glad I asked.

He is a seven-year-old named Fen He who was treated for leukemia. His body was enormously swollen due to past aggressive chemotherapy treatments. The doctor said he was in a coma.

"Does he understand what is going on?" I asked.

The doctor said no. I approached the child and saw his eyes shifting rapidly back and forth. When Kate checked him, she said that was clearly not normal for coma patients, especially the way he was looking. I spoke soothingly to him, stroking his head while telling him he was a big, brave boy. After a few seconds, I was shocked to see tears begin pouring out of his eyes.

I turned to the doctor and said, "He *does* understand!" The response from this child was so heartbreaking that I began to cry too, all the while continuing to stroke his head, face, and eyebrows. Kate moved closer and began to speak to him because I was simply too emotional to say any more. This poor boy has been lying there, on a ventilator for an entire year! When I asked if anyone ever moved his limbs, they said someone does it every three hours. Apparently, his father comes to see him often. With his crying, it was almost as if this boy was pleading for help. He could not move and looked trapped in his body. His crying was not just tears; it started deep in his throat and was like the sound of a wounded, suffering animal.

The doctor said Fen He's blood no longer tests positive for leukemia but they do not know if he will ever get better. Yet the hospital is paying his bills, which is completely perplexing. Why would they keep a child on life support for a year?

This boy is hovering between living a hopeless life and moving on to a merciful death. If I were to hazard a guess, I would say his family will eventually abandon Fen He, if they haven't already. I also suspect the doctors tell us what they think we want to hear; in reality, his father may not come to see him at all. Who knows?

I will be back to see Fen He, to talk to him, and to try to break up the monotony of his desolate world. Next time I refuse to cry. I will force some laughter and lightheartedness, and do my best to bring a little light to his dark world.

* * *

MAY 30, 2005

The new baby room—the additional one—is finished and the "bed" babies have been moved there. There are twenty small babies in the new room and eighteen "floor" babies in the old one, including Bella.

Babies I have never seen before (I wonder where they came from so suddenly?) help fill the new room and several are very frail and sick. One tiny girl is obviously a preemie and already has the hanging skin of a malnourished child.

Some of the babies have contracted a strange rash. At first glance, it appeared to be small bumps on their hands, feet, and knees. Upon closer viewing, we saw the spots were blisters. Lucy said it looked like hand, foot, and mouth disease. We discussed this with the room supervisor and the doctor came to examine them.

He concluded they were symptoms from being exposed to high temperatures, but my own daughters struggled with heat rash and I know this is something different. We could learn much more if we just isolated these children instead of exposing them to the whole room, but that is not my call to make.

I looked forward to seeing Xiao Gou today. I brought her promised milk and potato chips. When I arrived at her room, the children were being bathed. The *ayis* were obstinate today and wouldn't let Xiao Gou leave with me. I bent down and whispered in her ear to take her bath and then I'd come back for her—with some treats.

I went on to the baby room, but returned soon after to see if Xiao Gou was ready. There I witnessed a touching scene. Xiao Feng, the eight-year-old girl with a stump for a hand, was dressing Xiao Gou and had laid her on the floor while she spread diaper cream on her scarlet rash. I'm sure it was the cream I had secretly provided for her that she keeps hidden under her bed and away from the scrutiny of the *ayis*. When Xiao Gou stayed at our house, I always rubbed her with it, and she loved the instant relief it gave. Even when she forgot the other English words she'd learned, she always remembered to ask for "cweam" when I changed her.

Xiao Feng helped Xiao Gou up, and she reached out her arms for me to pick her up. I snuggled her tenderly all the way back to the baby room.

Once there, she received her promised snacks and happily sat in the corner eating and observing the commotion. After bathing and feeding were over, we sat around holding babies; Xiao Gou was at my feet. Suddenly, one of the *ayis* told me they had let Xiao Gou see her mama on television! Apparently, before Xiao Gou had been abandoned in the hospital, her mother had done a television interview. In the piece, she lamented how sick she felt at having to give up her daughter, but they had no money. The mother was crying and pleading for financial help during the session, with an image of Xiao Gou pictured directly behind her.

Xiao Gou was listening intently as the *ayi* related this story. I didn't want to discuss it any further in front of her, so I said nothing, trying to discourage the subject.

The *ayi* kept on and on—until I finally interrupted and asked incredulously, "You actually let her watch it?"

"Yes," she replied nonchalantly.

I quietly asked if Xiao Gou had cried when she saw her mother.

"Yes," the *ayi* said, "she cried a lot."

I looked down at Xiao Gou, who had withdrawn into her shell of silence. Her mother loved her very much, I told her gently, but didn't have the money for her operation. It was clear her little heart was breaking from listening to this. They must have let her watch it just to see her reaction. The *ayis* can be so cruel without even intending to.

For the remainder of my visit, Xiao Gou would not look at me or anyone else. Finally, we had to take her back to her room. There, a small, scrawny girl, about three years old, was sitting in a stroller. Her face was drawn and the skin hung loosely from her arms and legs. I'm still not confident with the local dialect, so I had Sheila ask what was wrong. She was informed that the doctors do not know. They say she is well fed, yet she keeps losing weight. I handed out my remaining cookies to all the kids and the little girl took one too. Even without a medical background, I could tell that she needs a hospital bed.

I tore my eyes from the child and returned to Xiao Gou. Bending down, I told her I would be gone for four weeks, but when I returned I would come to see her right away. I promised her a new dress and shoe. Her eyes filled with tears and she slowly took the cookies we had hidden in her dress pockets and threw them to the floor. Xiao Gou loves food, so I know this was her way of telling me she was angry. I kissed her, swallowed the lump in my throat, and walked away. At the doorway, I said goodbye, but she wouldn't look at me. I headed downstairs and out of the building, reflecting on how this singular child had worked her way into my heart over the past months.

I had known helping these children would make me feel good in so many ways, but I'd never counted on the profound sadness I would deal with daily. I had attempted from the beginning to make Xiao Gou understand that I am not her new mama; my words had even been translated for her—but how can a child help but gravitate toward the person who shows her love and comfort during her most painful moments? Her home visits with me had begun as a way to keep her clean and dry in order to ward off infection. I continued bringing her out of the orphanage to give her a break and prepare her for a possible upcoming adoption. I knew that it would be difficult for her to be shuffled between two such different worlds, but it felt like the right thing to do. Now I am far from sure.

28

After a month of vacation, I am finally back in Shengxi and oddly glad to be here. Our annual home visit that we had so anticipated was wonderful for the first few weeks, but suddenly we were ready to return to China. In the States, we are constantly on the move, and there are too many distractions. Here in China, I feel I can focus on the more important things in my life. I would never have imagined it, but getting back to the chaos of my Shengxi life was a relief.

Heather is here! Over the summer, we decided together that she would try China, and she committed to staying for one school year. I am so happy to have both my girls under one roof again. I thought she would be a little frightened of the new experience, but in her usual Heather style, she wasn't a bit apprehensive. Before leaving the States, we shopped for new bedding and room accents to decorate her space and sent the items, her clothing, and her stereo via air shipment to Shengxi.

Heather was an instant hit among her culturally diverse group of peers, and now our house is always filled with teenagers, music, and laughter. She has made five close friends very quickly; they're from Germany, Italy, England, the States, and Mexico. Knowing Heather to be a natural leader, I was amused to find her in her room one afternoon, teaching the other fifteen- and sixteen-year-old girls how to dance "American style."

* * *

I've received some good news: Le Men is healthy and well! He is living with the same foster family and has become somewhat of a celebrity on Shengxi television. The local station reported on how foreigners had jumped in to take care of the cost of his heart surgery. I really believe that due to the amount of media exposure, his foster family may not give him up—they have a TV star in the house! Le Men's doctors declared that his surgery was a complete success, and that without it he would have surely gone into heart failure.

Recently I had a chance to see him and his new foster mother. She had him all spiffed up wearing one of the special little necklaces that the Chinese put on their small children. Seeing her treat Le Men like a true son warmed my heart. He was completely content and his mother looked satisfied. His foster father is a driver and they have a child in the university, which means that little Le Men has a foster sister or a brother. I am thankful that the one-child policy doesn't affect families wishing to take on foster children.

Little Bella is still wearing her cast but is improving after the surgery to straighten her leg. All the volunteers have taken turns writing and drawing on her cast, much to Bella's delight. Regretfully, Claire, the volunteer who sponsors her on weekends, will be leaving for the States in a few weeks and will not return. Bella will have a hard time dealing with the loss of Claire—they have bonded like mother and daughter.

Many volunteers have come forward to host Bella for weekend visits just to keep her secure in leaving the orphanage. Because of her schedule, Maggie cannot pick up the sponsorship, so we will have to wait and see what the directors have planned for Bella. This little girl is such a character; we love seeing her wobble around but are hoping this latest sponsored operation will make her limp less noticeable. She has also had surgery to repair a place in her spine that was responsible for her lack of growth. She may be short, but she is oh so adorable.

Li Li, my other special little angel, was adopted by the daughter of the elderly woman who was her *ayi* in the hospital. She has had a happy ending, but it was a complicated journey getting there.

To begin with, Li Li was taken back to the orphanage after her surgery. She cried incessantly for the *ayi* to whom she had grown so attached during her six-week hospital stay. It became so bad that Director Yao called a reporter to ask if she could run a special piece about Li Li needing a foster family. The *ayi* heard about this before the story ran, and called Yao, suggesting she would foster Li Li. It was determined that the best solution was for her own daughter to adopt Li Li, making her the official grandmother! I am thrilled with the outcome, especially since on Li Li's last day in the hospital, the doctor told us she had been in such bad shape with her pneumonia and failing heart that she would not have lasted through the summer without intervention.

Our volunteer group has been asked not to return to the orphanage for at least a few weeks until further notice, due to a virus. This was quite an alarming request—it's the first time we have been asked not to visit due to illness. Three of my volunteers have emailed me with the same concerns, but perhaps the children are just too ill for us to visit.

I desperately hope we'll be allowed back soon. My heart is heavy with worry about all the children, especially Xiao Gou and the babies.

* * *

JULY 16, 2005

I traveled to the orphanage today to pay for some new tables and chairs we had ordered from Beijing. Thanks to donations from our fund, the new furniture will go into the second-floor redecoration project. We've learned that the mysterious illness that had us banned from visiting is measles. Director Fu said many of the children are ill, which made me wonder if the babies have been immunized against anything at all. To assuage my fears, I did some research and discovered that a baby must be at least one year old to receive the mumps/measles/rubella vaccine. We made a deal with Director Fu that we could come back if we were immunized with the MMR vaccine (and most of us already are).

As we stepped through the gates, I spotted Xiao Gou in the classroom. Her serious face broke into a great smile as she saw me—clearly she had recovered from her hurt feelings. I knelt down and hugged her close, telling her about the new shoe and dress I'd bought. We were able to spend some time together, but too soon it was time for me to go.

As I left, Xiao Gou's face drooped, causing me great anguish. On the way home, I decided to bring her to our house for the weekend, no matter the consequences. My Mandarin skills are terrible on the telephone, so I had my translator call to obtain permission. I'll pick her up around noon tomorrow, which means I need to dash to the store for diapers, wipes, and snacks. I called my *ayi* at home with instructions to prepare a batch of congee. I try to keep Xiao Gou on her regular diet so her stomach doesn't rebel, though she will get her favorite chips and milk.

Sometimes when I leave the orphanage now, I feel as though I'm not doing enough. Some days I'm proud of how far we've come and all that has changed; other days I think that with more commitment and intervention, we could do so much more. It's embarrassing to return to my air-conditioned house knowing the children are sweating and being swarmed by mosquitoes all night. Each time I see them, they have bites upon bites on their arms and legs. They eat the meager cookies I bring as if they haven't had a meal in days. The world is not a fair place for these innocent angels.

* * *

JULY 19, 2005

On Saturday, Ben and I drove to the orphanage to pick up Xiao Gou. As we arrived and passed through the gates, many older children—from ages six to about eleven—were outside playing on the sidewalk in front of the classroom. They had one bicycle to share and were taking turns helping the smaller deaf children ride it. They looked happy, though seeing the adjacent empty playground with a padlocked chain-link fence enclosing it infuriated me. It seems the playground is only for appearances—I rarely see any children allowed to play there. Instead, most of their outside time is spent wandering around on the concrete courtyard.

We went upstairs to find Xiao Gou, but first I wanted to show Ben the nursery area where most of my time is spent. We remained in the hall and looked through the windows to see the babies. Among them were Gracie, Jia Jia, and many other of my favorites. Bella, along with a tot we call Buddha Baby, is living with a Chinese foster family now. This is marvelous news—the family should feel grateful, because Bella has a brilliant, lively personality hiding in that tiny body. Let's hope they'll keep her long enough for her to come out of her shell and show them what a delight she can be.

We found Xiao Gou on the third floor in her living quarters. When we walked in, she was there all alone; the *ayi* had set her on a chamber pot because of her diarrhea. Xiao Gou is very fussy about being clean, but she had been sitting there so long that she'd given up holding herself out of the pot. Her little bottom was wedged deep in the bowl and she looked utterly ashamed.

An *ayi* approached, ranting about what trouble Xiao Gou was, and said she'd give her a bath.

"No. She can have a bath at our house," I insisted.

The *ayi* ignored me, jerked Xiao Gou up, and roughly put her in the industrial-size sink. I know they don't have hot water up there; I've seen it brought up in buckets on bath day. So there sat little Xiao Gou, shivering, with her leg pulled up to her chest and her forehead rested on her knee in a submissive pose. The *ayi* scrubbed her angrily and then put on a dress that was far too small. Xiao Gou evidently thought it was nice, so we made a fuss over it. Not surprisingly, the many clothes I have bought her have disappeared.

While this was going on, Ben and I played with the children who sat at the tables waiting for their food. Several were so skinny they looked sickly, but when they saw us, they became animated and crowded around us. When Xiao Gou's bath was finished, she was somewhat shy with me, which was puzzling. Still, she nodded when asked if she wanted to come home with us, so I'm not sure what the problem was.

We got her in the car and I immediately gave her a bottle of water and a bag of chips. She quickly ate the chips and promptly fell asleep leaning on my arm. Ben and I both commented on how sweet and blissful she looked, happy to get out of there even if only for a short reprieve.

Once at our home, her behavior was still strangely quiet. She wanted me in her sight at all times. Heather met her for the first time and, like everyone else, she fell for Xiao Gou completely. Later we went to a friend's house for a cookout, where Xiao Gou played with my daughters a little, but kept saying she wanted Ti Ti. Finally, they brought her back and I put her in a chair in the kitchen to watch me prepare food—that satisfied her need to keep me in sight.

Saturday night I gave her a bath, which turned out to be the highlight of her visit. Afterward, I coated her with Olay Body Quench while she smiled from ear to ear; she certainly loves to get girly. I dressed her in Amanda's shirt and fixed her hair (what is left of it after the orphanage barber hacked it all off). I told her she could play for thirty minutes and then we'd go to bed.

At bedtime, she was feeling poorly. She had a low fever, diarrhea, and a slight cough. I tucked her into our bed, and turned the air conditioner off, instead using a fan to keep the air circulated. Xiao Gou lay there and played with her fingers until she drifted off to sleep. Every few minutes she'd touch me to make sure I was still there—that satisfied her and then she slept well. I remained restless because my thoughts were whirling. I dreaded taking her back the next day.

We had a good day on Sunday, even though Xiao Gou was still feeling bad from her cold. Ben and I took her to lunch at a Western restaurant and disobeyed orphanage rules by ordering her a hot dog and fries. The server was incredulous that such a little girl could eat so much, but we didn't elaborate on Xiao Gou's circumstances or how she was unaccustomed to eating anything but rice. Once settled back in the car, she slept contentedly until we carried her into the house.

When it was time for her to go back to the orphanage, Xiao Gou became stone quiet and shook her head stubbornly. I told her that her friends missed her, but that had no effect. I pulled out my cell phone and pretended I was talking to Xiao Feng, her favorite sister there. I pretended Xiao Feng was telling me to bring Xiao Gou back. It didn't help that Heather didn't want her to leave— she had taken Xiao Gou to her room and set her up with another bag of chips. The girls were having a good time spoiling her, but I had to pull her away.

Xiao Gou stayed silent and pouted all the way to the orphanage; she spoke to me only once when I asked her if she wanted a lollipop. She ate it so slowly that I told her she had better hurry up before her *ayi* took it away. When she saw the gates, she hurriedly crunched it up and swallowed.

When we took her inside, children were playing in the classroom. They all shouted her name and were happy to see her. I set her in a chair, where she wouldn't look my way or talk to me. I said I'd be back in two days to see her. That opened her up a little, and I asked for a kiss, whereupon she leaned over and shyly gave me the sweetest butterfly kiss. I told her goodbye and left.

Even Ben agrees that someone has successfully broken Xiao Gou's spirit a little. With much love and patience, I think she will bounce back eventually, but it makes me unspeakably angry to see her in a state of such submission.

I believe I have been led to this child to attempt to help her, but I struggle with knowing what to do and wonder if I am hurting her even more by the attention I lavish on her.

When I have these doubts, I think to myself, How can loving her hurt? I pray she will be adopted by a good family. She is such a wonderful, smart, and beautiful child. She deserves a family, and someone deserves her and the joy she can bring.

* * *

I began a new tradition tonight. Because of the girls' busy social lives, it is becoming increasingly difficult to bring all of us together for meals, so I've implemented a new policy of one family dinner per week. The girls grumbled that this plan prevented them from eating in front of the television or in their rooms, but I am standing firm on this.

Tonight was our first attempt. To set the tone I arranged the dining room table with an exotic cloth from Thailand, candles, and fancy dinnerware. We drank our water out of delicate wineglasses and listened to soft background music.

Heather said it was silly, but I think she secretly enjoyed it. Amanda thought it was the coolest thing. We didn't go to the trouble of dressing up, but we didn't need to. The atmosphere along with the comfort food of pork chops, salad, potatoes, and corn on the cob was enough to make it special. Listening to the girls taking turns to tell about their day, I reveled in the knowledge that I am a good wife and mother; I am finally proud of the woman I've become. Why did it take being uprooted from my home and moving to a third world country to achieve and recognize that?

29

JULY 29, 2005

I arrived at the orphanage a little after nine today. I collected all of our recent donations: many toothbrushes, bars of soap, shampoos, and another new air conditioner that a departing volunteer had donated.

My driver, Mr. Li, asked if he could accompany me to observe the children. He and his wife are considering fostering a girl. I doubted we'd get permission, but I was happy to try. Since he is Chinese and they see him with me regularly, they hardly raised an eyebrow when he came through the security gate.

We stopped at the little classroom to look for Xiao Gou and found her poring over the notebook I'd given her—I can't believe they let her keep it. Her new shoe had been replaced by a tattered old one, but at least she had her little writing book. Xiao Gou would rather "write" (doodle) than anything else—and she will do it for hours.

I gave her the usual "There's my girl!" and she looked up and smiled that gorgeous smile. I hugged her and told the new *ayi* I was taking her upstairs with me, which, judging by the disdain on her face, did not go over well.

We stopped by the second-floor room to find that the donated tables and chairs still had not been installed, even though I'd been told otherwise. I was certain this delay would happen; nothing is simple in dealing with this institution.

In the baby room, even more babies were missing. Last week I asked the *ayi* who speaks some English if many babies had died during the measles outbreak, and she confirmed they had lost a couple of infants. Xiao Gina, the room supervisor, quickly reprimanded her and informed me no babies had died. What, then, could account for the great number of missing children?

Many of the remaining children were wearing old, soiled bandages where IVs had been in place. One little boy had bandages on both wrists and on his head. He was crying pitifully, so I went to console him. I peeked under one loose bandage on his wrist and found a hole the size of a nickel eaten through the skin. It looked so painful! I rubbed his small back and whispered gently until he was quiet and gazing at me in wonder.

It was now bath time, and my driver was standing in front of the bathing room, captivated by the scene he beheld. There were four *ayis* involved in the routine: one to retrieve the babies from the room, one to undress them, one to wash them, and one to diaper them and drop them back in bed for us to dress and put down for their naps.

I motioned to Mr. Li to move away from the washroom door; the workers didn't like to be observed in their tasks. As I went about my work, Mr. Li inspected the babies. He especially took a shine to Jia Jia and Xiao Gou. Jia Jia held her hands out to him and with beseeching eyes said, "*Baba* . . ." (daddy). Recently, her foster family brought her back to the orphanage for the third time, and she is having a tough time dealing with it.

Mr. Li picked her up and began talking to her.

"She is paralyzed from the waist down," I said tentatively. It startled him a bit, but when she got on the floor and began pulling herself around rapidly using her arms, he was astonished at her speed.

I pulled out my snacks for Xiao Gou—chips and milk—which made her giddy with happiness. I set Jia Jia next to her and asked Xiao Gou to share her treats. In the orphanage, sharing is a foreign concept; the children so seldom receive snacks that when they do, instinctive greed takes over. I was proud to see Xiao Gou passing Jia Jia one chip at a time, and praised her manners, making sure Mr. Li noticed.

When I announced we had to leave, Xiao Gou's attitude instantly became icy. Her expression could have been carved in stone and she refused to talk or look at me. I carried her down to the classroom and put her at her desk, where the *ayi* scolded her for pouting.

I heard the *ayi* tell her in Mandarin, "If you cry, she will never come back!"

I understood exactly what she said and it fueled my temper. I reassured Xiao Gou not to worry, I would be back. I gave her many kisses but she was still downcast. As Mr. Li and I reluctantly turned to go, I looked back to see her watching me with tear-filled eyes. I blew her more kisses and left.

In the car, Mr. Li said he was shocked at how roughly the *ayis* handled the children. Chinese parents usually treat their babies with care, he said. I explained that the *ayis* don't have time for attention or gentleness; there are too many babies and not enough hands.

I find it harder and harder for me to leave Xiao Gou there. Last night I talked to Dawn, a psychotherapist from Germany who also volunteers at the orphanage, about what she thinks is the right thing to do. She believes the love and hope I bring to Xiao Gou keeps her going. I just don't want to damage that little girl's spirit any more than it is already, so I second-guess all that I do.

Most of the other volunteers should be coming back from home visits this week. The usual routine will return and it will be a relief to have a full staff of volunteers on hand.

* * *

AUGUST 1, 2005

On Tuesday, my friend from Beijing, Cassie, and her driver met me at my home. Cassie and her husband are contributors to our surgery fund and have worked closely with a group called the Sunshine Dream Team to find Xiao Gou a family in the States. Cassie had met Xiao Gou once before but wanted to see her and the rest of the children again.

We drove to the orphanage and dropped off the many donated diapers Cassie had brought with her. Then we walked over to the children's side of the campus so she could get a good look at the entire area.

On the second floor, the kids became excited to see us when they saw we'd brought cookies. We moved on to the third floor and found Xiao Gou, then snatched her up to bring her to the baby room with us. We were there only a short time when the staff brought in a terrified two-year-old girl; she had just arrived at the orphanage after being found abandoned in the city. I'm not sure why they brought her immediately to the baby room instead of the isolation room as they usually do new arrivals, but I am glad we were there to welcome her.

The *ayi* dumped her on the floor and abruptly walked away to continue her duties. The girl sat petrified, her eyes glistening with fear as she frantically looked around. I picked her up and settled her rigid body in my lap, softly crooning and rocking her. She was an adorable little thing with an elfin face and beautiful eyes. She calmed down a little and clung to me. After a time I felt she might be ready to be on her own, but when I tried to put her down, she became hysterical. I continued to hold her close as she sobbed, her little body heaving with exhaustion.

After an hour of rocking, she closed her eyes, hiccuping and moaning softly. I tried to lower her to a bed, but she clung to me.

I thought this odd considering she'd probably never been close to a foreigner before. It must be true that affection knows no nationality. Even though she smelled strongly of burnt sulfur, I kept hugging her and tried to will strength into her. Her long night ahead was on my mind, and I ached knowing how frightened she was going to be without her mother at her side.

During this time, Cassie made herself at home and familiarized herself with many of the infants. She did a marvelous job for her first time in a Chinese orphanage—some women quickly become overwrought with emotion and break into tears. Cassie was very moved by some of the babies, but didn't let that get in the way of adopting a professional demeanor while demonstrating as much love and tenderness as possible.

Finally, the new girl allowed me to lower her into a crib and I slowly backed away. I needed to save time to feed the cleft baby. He had become entirely too skinny and looked close to dehydration—his little legs were like toothpicks. It took a long while but eventually, with me doing the squeeze method, he drank the whole bottle.

Judging by her sulking and refusal to give me a smile, Xiao Gou was becoming increasingly jealous. I tried to make her understand the girl was distraught because she was new, but Xiao Gou continued to pout. Near the end of our time, I began to feel so bad for Xiao Gou that I decided to take her home for the night. I sent my driver to ask the director, and my request was approved. Cassie and I took Xiao Gou out to lunch.

After a fun hour together, Cassie left for Beijing and we headed home. When the girls got off the school bus, they were excited to see Xiao Gou. Heather immediately carried her to her bedroom, but soon brought her back because of the many diaper changes needed. This visit has reinforced my opinion that Xiao Gou really needs that colostomy; she had constant diarrhea and I changed diapers many times over the next twenty-four hours.

From almost two hours of holding the little two-year-old and two more hours of toting Xiao Gou around, I must have strained the muscles in both my arms as well as my back. Xiao Gou is five years old and can be very awkward to handle because she has only one leg. We have quite a number of stairs and I am continually going up, then down, then back up again. Usually it does not bother me, but combined with the earlier strain of holding the new little girl, it was all too much.

I had a rough night trying to get Xiao Gou to sleep. In the morning, my muscles were on fire, making climbing the stairs difficult. Lifting Xiao Gou was so painful that I had no choice but to take her back. I treated her to McDonald's and then returned her to the orphanage.

When we arrived, she was very upset with me. She was sobbing with real tears this time and my heart broke yet again. The *ayis* immediately stripped off her pants and placed her on her chamber pot in anticipation of the next bout of diarrhea. They force her to sit there, naked, in front of all the other children, and it is highly embarrassing for her. She is hyper aware and ashamed of the diaper situation and becomes upset when she has to be changed.

To know she is forced into this humiliation makes me ache for her. However, I try to put it out of my mind at home so I can function properly with my own family. This isn't easy, and that's why I say *I try*. It has been several days and Xiao Gou and the new little girl have been on my mind constantly. The newbie will get no consolation from the room *ayis*, which is what they deem best to help the new children adjust. It appalls me to think of the mental anguish these kids are put through while they are still reeling from the trauma of losing their mothers.

I received the news that our two cleft lip babies left today for Luoyang to receive their surgeries. A group of Stateside doctors are performing the operations and many babies from surrounding cities are coming to the hospital for the free surgeries. It was complicated getting through the red tape but will be worth it. I am thankful for all the people who refuse to look the other way but instead use their gifts to make a difference in these children's lives.

* * *

AUGUST 10, 2005

It is 11 p.m. and well past my usual bedtime. I can't get the image of a new tiny baby off my mind. How can parents abandon a one-week-old infant outside in the sweltering heat? Her tiny face was covered in what I first thought was some sort of disease but soon discovered was a vicious mosquito attack. The skin was extremely red and raw, and the baby was clearly in severe pain. I cannot imagine what this defenseless child went through as the insects tortured her with repeated bites.

The baby girl has one deformed hand turned completely backward—obviously the reason for her abandonment. The hand looked like such a minor handicap—something easily repaired.

Why do people in China still believe they are living in a time where disabilities mean lifelong hardship? They need to join the rest of the world and agree that a hand is just a hand—it doesn't affect the child's brain or change her right to be treated like a human. I'm praying tonight that the baby will not feel any more pain. Sometimes the things I see are beyond my ability to comprehend, and I will never respect customs that cause harm to innocent children.

30

Most people think I am a very easygoing person. I have endured a good deal of nonsense here in China, but I'm proud to say I usually take it all with a little humor, or at least an attempt at patience. Even when I am frustrated, I usually try to contain it until I get home. However, today my wide boundaries for patience and humor were crossed. For the first time in almost two years, the orphanage staff witnessed a rare glimpse of my temper. Elizabeth, a volunteer from Canada, later said she was shocked to see my ears turn red—a sure sign of my frustration.

Elizabeth, Mr. Li, and I went upstairs to fetch Xiao Gou and bring her with us to the baby room. When we entered the sleeping quarters, I didn't see her right away, but all the children were jumping around wildly at the sight of my bag of cookies. I quickly scanned the room as the kids started chanting, "Xiao Gou, Xiao Gou," and pointing to the corner.

I looked to the corner and there, sitting on the metal chamber pot, was Xiao Gou with her clothes stripped off and a completely beaten-down expression on her face. Slouching down into the bowl, actually sitting on top of the waste, she appeared to be thoroughly exhausted. I felt the red heat creep up my neck and knew I could not keep a neutral tone of voice.

Fortunately, I had Mr. Li there. I looked at him evenly and said, "You ask that *ayi* how long Xiao Gou has been sitting on this pot." My finger was already poised in the accusatory gesture.

He asked her and she replied, "All day, because she's had so many bowel movements."

The heat rose higher and I became so furious I began stuttering. "No way—absolutely no way—is this going to go on day after day! *No way!*"

She saw how upset I was, tried to change her story, and spewed out some nonsense that Xiao Gou had *not* been sitting there all day and that they were potty training her.

My response was an angry and abrupt, "*Bullcrap.* Translate *that*, Mr. Li."

I then began a blazingly heated discussion with the *ayi*—most of it translated by Mr. Li from my choppy Mandarin to the local dialect—about how they were unjustly punishing Xiao Gou for her lack of bowel control and humiliating her in front of all the other children. I said I was going to bring this atrocity to the attention of the top director. I demanded a diaper and told the *ayi* in an adamant, indignant voice that Xiao Gou was coming with me. The *ayi* said they wanted to bathe her and I retorted that they had ten minutes before I came back for her. I stalked out of the room and stopped in front of the baby room entrance to compose myself before entering.

Before ten minutes were up, they had sent Xiao Gou to me clean and dressed. They've never sent her out of the room alone before, so they clearly didn't want me coming back. I'm not in the least sorry for intimidating them. I am still furious, hours later. When will these people realize that these children have feelings?

In the baby room, Director Fu appeared and with the help of Sheila, we had one of our most heated conversations yet. If they had allowed the colostomy in the first place, I argued angrily, Xiao Gou wouldn't have to be *punished* for having so many bowel movements. Fu tried to tell me they were trying to train her to *tell* them when she needed to go.

In total exasperation, I replied, "She doesn't know *when* she has to go because *she doesn't have a normal colon!*"

Making an effort to calm myself and show the proper respect, I said, "I insist on another doctor's opinion about the colostomy." Sheila translated.

Director Fu's first answer was no, but then she finally agreed. *Yes!* A local doctor will do the exam and if they cannot give us good news, we will take her to Beijing.

"I want to be there for the consultation," I said, "so don't give me a load of crap about 'the doctor says it isn't needed.' I'll bring my own translator and I'll be involved." Sheila did not translate the "load of crap" statement but got my point across, for Fu agreed that I could accompany them on the visit.

A colostomy might sound drastic, but the humiliation of sitting naked on a pot for hours is far worse. The original doctor had shown me another five-year-old girl on the same hospital floor as Xiao Gou who had recently received a colostomy. She could empty the bag herself and was fine with it! This is by far the better option. I pray this plan will not collapse, as so many others do in this place. I will nag until we get the exam—and nag even louder until we get the colostomy.

Something amusing arose in all this drama. Xiao Gou recognizes my irritated voice from hearing me deal with my own girls, so when I was using it with the *ayi*, she had a little grin on her face as if to say, "Uh-oh, Ti Ti's mad." When the conversation ended with my ten-minute ultimatum, I blew her a kiss and she gave me the sweetest thank-you smile. She is a smart child and knows she has someone who cares about her. I wish she knew how many people outside the institution love her and want to help. One day, she'll be astonished to learn how the ongoing telling of her story by email resulted in a landslide of support for her and other children.

As I was taking her back to her room, I gently explained she couldn't go home with me today, but the October holiday was approaching and she'd be permitted to spend five days with us. That made her eyes light up with anticipation. Perhaps bringing her home again is not a good idea, but the alternative is for me to leave her where she'd surely be sitting on a pot for a full five days.

* * *

The new two-year-old girl has regressed and now lies in a crib curled up in a fetal position, a vacant look on her face. Because of her failing condition and sudden weight loss, she was unrecognizable to me; the *ayi* had to point her out. We have named this precious little girl Tuesday.

Seeing her so ill was shocking. The *ayi* says she won't cry, talk, or walk now. It is troubling to see how defeated she is after just two weeks. I'm sure she will come out of it eventually, but the treatment these children receive when they arrive invariably damages their spirits permanently to some degree. What must they feel when they are left to cry alone and no one touches or comforts them?

* * *

AUGUST 20, 2005

Last Monday at the orphanage we encountered endless frustrations trying to budge the adoption process for Xiao Gou and a little girl named Dai An. I should not have been surprised, as this is always the case when we want a child to be considered for adoption that the Chinese deem inappropriate.

After speaking with the director, I headed for the classroom from which the children's voices emanated. Some of them saw me and started shouting at Xiao Gou that I was there.

They ran out and told me in Mandarin, "Don't go near her—she really stinks!"

Xiao Gou was sitting at the desk, her cheeks scarlet with shame. The other children would only get so close, then cover their noses and point at her, chanting, *"Hen chou, hen chou"* (very stinky, very stinky).

"That's just fine. She's *my girl!*" I said, pulling her into my arms and smothering her with kisses. Ordinarily, I waited to do this until we were alone, in order to prevent jealousy, but this time Xiao Gou needed to revel in my attention. In my arms, she was beaming. I thought, Whoa! Must get diaper changed now, but I got her out of the room without letting any of them know the smell bothered me.

Upstairs, I went to Xiao Gou's room for a diaper and laid her down to change her. Her diaper rash was so bad that she jerked back in pain even as I gently tried to clean her. I suppose last week, after I complained about her sitting on the pot, they decided instead to let her sit in soiled diapers all day. I felt guilty—perhaps they are punishing her because of my outburst. I don't know if she'd rather sit on the pot for hours or sit in a soiled diaper for hours—she is ashamed of both. She is such a feminine little thing.

Bringing her to the baby room with me, I sat her on the counter and produced her secret treat of potato chips. She was content just to sit and watch us crazy foreigners do our thing: playing with the children, cooing to them, and tickling them. Elizabeth and I played with her the entire morning and she was full of joy, crawling around, giggling and laughing.

The little girl whom we've nicknamed Tuesday is now doing a little better. They'd shaved her head and it took me a minute to identify her, but she was smiling faintly and much more at peace.

Tuesday can't stand up, even though she's just over two years old. It's not clear what is wrong—she may be next up to rally and fund-raise for. I want to learn if she has a disease and if so, what it is, and then explore the possibility of getting her some sort of physical therapy.

When it was feeding time, Tilly approached her with a bowl of rice and started roughly shoving it into her mouth. Tuesday was lying on her back, unable to swallow one spoonful before the next was crammed in. I interrupted Tilly and asked if I could finish the feeding. It was a painstaking effort, but Tuesday got fed and I had a lovely (one-sided) conversation during the feeding session. I also took time to massage her scrawny little body between bites. After three weeks of lying in that crib, I'm sure she is stiff and sore, especially coming from a real home where she must have been more mobile.

Tuesday afternoon, Sheila and I met the administrators in the office for a discussion about Xiao Gou. I asked Director Fu if her file had gone to Beijing, because we volunteers knew of an adoption agency that had taken an interest in trying to place her as a special-needs child.

Fu immediately erected a barrier by insisting it was not possible for Xiao Gou's adoption dossier to be filed. The orphanage does not have legal guardianship of her; she came from the hospital and her parents could not pay their financial obligations, so her case was different from those of other abandoned children. Apparently, another child had been in the same circumstances, and just before she was adopted, her parents suddenly came forward and demanded their daughter.

Conveying my frustration to Sheila, I suggested this was a skewed argument; we might wait forever for uncertain parents to claim their child. We'll just have to be patient—now almost impossible for me—and keep attempting to cut through all this red tape.

* * *

I arrived at the orphanage today to a great commotion. They were expecting another visit from local officials and everyone was scurrying around, preparing the children and the rooms. Fifteen of the bigger children donned band uniforms and carried cymbals or drums as they stood at attention inside the gates. All the other babies and children were dressed in clean clothes and kept indoors to ensure they stayed clean.

The old gray wall in the courtyard has had a makeover. This wall has jagged glass glued to the top to keep out unwanted visitors, but it's been transformed into a delightful wall of 3-D cartoons. Zoo animals and dinosaurs bring much needed color to the formerly drab area where the children like to play. Many of the archways were painted an offbeat shade of light green, adding character and charm to the area. Around the other side of the wall someone has hand-painted many other animals. The children were obviously enthralled with the new look and I was impressed with the Chinese government for loosening its purse strings to pay for the improvements. Now if they would just concentrate on something other than cosmetic changes, I would be happy.

I went searching for Xiao Gou and found her in the almost empty classroom. The *ayi* would not let me take her upstairs; they wanted her available to see the officials. Next, I headed up to the baby room and spent some time feeding a few babies before the magnetic pull of wanting to spend time with my girl brought me back down to the schoolroom.

Since the officials had arrived by then, most of the children were released to go outside to play. Some children were held back: Xiao Gou for some inexplicable reason, Le Bai because the sun hurts his eyes, Xiao Feng because she has hepatitis and is only allowed limited interaction with others, and a little boy who is mildly mentally challenged. I decided to remain inside to play with them and help them practice their English. Le Bai told me he was five years old, which I had not known. He was in a happy mood and kept sneaking behind me to wrap his arms around me and squeeze tightly.

Xiao Gou soon became envious, so I decided to take her outdoors despite orders to the contrary. She hit the drums and tried on one of the boys' band hats. Local police officers arrived to join the growing crowd of visitors, so I took Xiao Gou back to the room. Giving her and the others a hug goodbye, I stepped outside again. I was quickly surrounded by half a dozen TV cameras—they love to film foreigners, but I was not in the mood to cater to the charade. As I was leaving, the band children began pounding and clanging on their drums and cymbals.

* * *

Director Fu recently introduced the orphanage's new social worker, Ji An, and instructed me that we can utilize her for requests and information. Ji An will be in charge of helping with adoption dossiers, accompanying children to the hospital for medical checks, and closely monitoring children in foster care. This week, Ji An said Director Fu has not had time either to take Xiao Gou for her exam or to petition the court for guardianship. She promised to talk to Fu about this for me. As with everything we undertake, it will take much pushing and many requests. I know they wish I'd stop asking and pushing, but I never will. Several of our babies have been placed in foster care recently—wonderful news if the families will keep them! It's so traumatizing for them to feel the warmth and comfort of a family, only to be rejected and returned to the cold and unemotional orphanage environment.

Lucy took Jia Jia to a physical therapist in Beijing, where we learned that to straighten her legs she would need to be placed on an electrode machine every day for several minutes. With optimism, Lucy bought the machine, but we've yet to find someone to do this each day. The doctors predict that Jia Jia will never walk because she is paralyzed from the knees down. However, we're still encouraged that if we find the right doctor, her prognosis will improve.

31

Many infants in the baby room have colds now. When I arrived today, the staff immediately instructed us to remove clothes and prepare for baths. We stripped the babies down and then quickly redressed them as they were returned from their baths. There was much wailing and confusion—the babies decidedly do not like to feel the chill of the room on their bare bottoms.

When we'd finished giving bottles, we were instructed to feed several toddlers who are bed-bound and cannot sit up. I fed a special-needs boy who, at just over three years old, was unable to sit up or move his limbs. Feeding him was difficult because he continually bit the spoon and tried to spit out the rice. Each time he swallowed a bite I stroked his cheek and talked softly to him for encouragement. I eventually succeeded in getting the whole bowl of rice in him, but it took some time.

I left the room early to find Xiao Gou, and as I entered the hallway, I spotted a little boy of about five dragging another child up the three flights of stairs. I looked closer and realized the smaller child was Xiao Gou! My guess is she convinced him to help her make her way to where I was. Fearing he would drop her, I rushed over and grabbed her from him.

I took her into the hallway to give her the potato chips I'd brought. She sat on my knee to eat, giving me many kisses between bites. When it was time for me to leave, she ran off so quickly that I didn't see the tears on her cheek.

The *ayi's* sharp voice rang from the room: "Stop crying! You'll see her next week!"

On our way out, Sheila voiced her opinion that Xiao Gou had imagined she was coming home with me. I felt so bad that I couldn't help but return and scoop her up, promising McDonald's on her next outing. Still, I felt guilty. Is it doing her any good at all to come home with me, only to be returned? On the other hand, because of the circumstances of her abandonment, she is well aware of what life is outside the orphanage. Unlike the majority of children there who don't have anything to compare it with, Xiao Gou needs the respite away from the bleak surroundings . . . I think.

In a long talk with Director Fu today, I learned the adoption for Xiao Gou has taken a very complicated turn. Every time we seem to be close to making progress, another obstacle is placed in our way.

She had some good news, however. The orphanage has taken the painting project even further, adding more imaginative and colorful paintings all over the building's exterior. The government has paid for the project, she said, which very much impressed me.

* * *

OCTOBER 2, 2005

Such dramatics at the orphanage by Xiao Gou today! I found her in her room, miserably sitting on her pot, and asked the *ayis* to dress her and send her down to me. Soon she appeared in the baby room smiling widely.

As usual, we worked diligently peeling layer upon layer of soiled clothes off the babies to prepare them for baths, and then dressing them in clean clothes after baths. Director Yao came in later to answer some of my questions about our planning of the Christmas party for the kids.

While we talked, Xiao Gou was playing quietly, when suddenly Jia Jia screamed and began to cry. Yao turned to Xiao Gou angrily and snapped, "What did you do?"

Xiao Gou solemnly shook her head, indicating she'd done nothing. I know she hadn't; they were in my sight the entire time.

"You bad girl! You tell Jia Jia you're sorry," demanded Yao after further confirmation from Jia Jia's accusing pointed finger. Xiao Gou looked beseechingly at me, but I cowardly cast my eyes down. I couldn't make the director lose face by interfering.

Xiao Gou, my usually stoic little soldier, scrunched up her sweet face and began to sob desperately.

At that point I thought, to heck with losing face. I rushed to her and pulled her into my arms. Yao swatted me as I passed but said nothing.

"I know you didn't do anything!" I whispered to Xiao Gou. *Ayis* gathered around, trying to get her to stop crying, only because it made the director look bad for making a child so upset.

"Do you want to go outside with me?"

She sniffled and looked up at me with a small smile. I took her out to the playground for a few minutes of special attention.

Her feelings were hurt, but I also know she had played it up— just as any five-year-old would.

On another note, the little girl we nicknamed Tuesday is once again in poor condition. Removing her shirt for her bath, I found legs like little sticks with flesh hanging from them. Her cry is weak and she no longer tries to sit up, just lies in her crib, moaning and staring at nothing.

It appears no one is taking the time to feed her when we're not around. She whimpered in pain, probably from dehydration. I spent some time rubbing her legs, but it didn't seem to calm her.

However, after her bath she quieted down a little—I think the hot water felt good for her.

Not so long ago, all of our cribs were full, now six stand empty. What happened to those babies? They haven't graduated up to another room; that doesn't happen until they can walk. It's best that we don't ask. I don't think we could handle the truth.

* * *

OCTOBER II, 2005

I am very upset about a situation at the orphanage and hardly know how to write about it. Yet I know this is the best way for me to deal with difficult situations, so once again, I'll let my flying fingers cry my tears.

Jia Jia, the three-year-old girl whose foster family kept returning her, now alternates between two foster homes, a Chinese foster family and the home of Lucy, one of our American volunteers. After a brief time, Lucy's family has fallen in love with Jia Jia and now wants to adopt her. This is slowly coming together, but in the meantime, she circulates between Lucy's home, the Chinese foster family, and the orphanage.

Jia Jia is more attached to Lucy and her family than she is to the Chinese foster family. Each time Lucy brings her back to the orphanage, she cries incessantly. The *ayis* get very aggravated, particularly Tilly.

Last week, when Lucy arrived at the orphanage, she was shocked to see what appeared to be a footprint-shaped bruise on the side of Jia Jia's head as well as a bloodied ear. She was informed that the child had tried to climb out of bed and fell. This is impossible— she is paralyzed from the knees down! We believe Jia Jia was crying for Lucy and was severely punished for it.

Now, whenever Tilly is around, Jia Jia becomes quiet and withdrawn. There's not a thing we can do about it because we don't even know for certain what happened. We can be thankful that last week Director Wai, the big boss, called and got special permission for Lucy to adopt Jia Jia. The situation is complicated because the regulations for Chinese adoption state that children aren't supposed to be chosen by prospective parents; they are matched by agencies unless there are extreme extenuating circumstances. Lucy is now deep in the first stages of paperwork. She hopes to have the administrative work completed and Jia Jia safe in her arms by the time she leaves in July.

Today I spoke with the *ayis* about Xiao Gou and her bowel issues. She is not faring any better, they say; in fact, she was perched on the chamber pot when I arrived. As I was readying myself for another battle about that situation, a boy in more serious condition caught my eye. He was about five years old, seated on a wooden chair and looking forlorn. His lips were chapped beyond dehydration stage and completely bloody. Sheila asked the *ayi* for some Vaseline, but she said it wouldn't help because he "doesn't want to eat." What sense does that make? I lifted the boy's shirt to find wrinkles and folds of skin hanging from his rib cage. It was dreadful. He looked like a shrunken, desolate old man who was resigned to his hopeless circumstances.

This boy needed to be on an IV immediately, and something done for his bloody lips. He needed a soft bed and some love and compassion. Sometimes I feel as though I can't possibly witness one more instance of the neglectful treatment these children receive.

Winter is coming fast and the orphanage is freezing, dark, and depressing. Today I wore long johns, jeans, an undershirt, a long-sleeved shirt, and a coat all morning, but I was still cold to the bone. The rooms now have electric heaters but we are only permitted to use them at bath time.

I left there feeling overwhelmingly sad. Tomorrow I've scheduled a meeting with the volunteers, primarily to plan our Christmas party for the children. In the winter, people often drop out because of how depressing and cold it is within the gray walls, but hopefully this year we can be stronger and stay united.

* * *

OCTOBER 28, 2005

What a stench we walked into when Elizabeth and I arrived upstairs yesterday; the two baby rooms were unbearably suffocating with the smell from the stain the workers were using on a new floor that had been installed down the hall. The babies weren't uttering a sound; I'm sure it was because their little heads were spinning from fumes. Their room was absolutely frigid, causing all four of us volunteers to agree that, even though we're dressed in multiple layers, we find it almost impossible to tolerate the cold in that room.

The toddler side was warmer but reeked of excrement, worse than I've ever experienced. My gag reflex kicked in and I tried to breathe only through my mouth. Where was the problem coming from? I didn't have time to ponder; I was late after stopping off to use donations to buy eighteen coats for the bigger kids. The baths were already done, so I put the stench out of my mind and went directly in to playtime with the toddlers.

Elizabeth has been away awhile, so I took her to see our new preemie. In the middle of describing last week's episode when the little one had projectile vomited all her milk, it began happening again! I held her head up out of the mess while Elizabeth ran for an *ayi*. If the vomit rolled off the blanket and into the bed, I knew the baby would have to smell it until the next bedding change, which could possibly be a week away.

By the time the *ayi* came, I had vomit up to my wrists. She took over and I tried to wash up, but I couldn't get enough water out of the spigot to get clean. Finally, I wiped my hands on the only rag I saw, soiled and flimsy as it was. I tried not to show my disgust. I checked to ensure the baby was adequately cleaned up and exclaimed over how tiny she was, with a head no bigger than a softball. She should still have been in an incubator and she really needed to be fed by small droplets in frequent doses. When the regular feeding comes, she gobbles up too much and then loses it every time.

When the rice came out of the kitchen, I spent thirty minutes trying to feed Tuesday. I had thought that this toddler was a girl, but I was wrong. The day he came to the orphanage, he was wearing a dress—I remember vividly. I suppose his family must have been too poor to buy him proper clothing, or had they tried purposely to pass him off as an abandoned little girl? I am learning more each day that long-held beliefs can make people behave in strange ways.

Tuesday is now beyond doing anything other than lie on his back and cry. I discovered he is actually about four years old, but oh so small. When I feed him, I have to use a quick technique with the spoon because he tries to bite down and grip it each time, which leaves me trying to pry it out of his surprisingly strong teeth. The rest of the time, the *ayis* give up and let him go hungry. Yesterday, I bluntly asked the *ayi* to move and allow me to feed him, to ensure he will have at least one satisfying meal for the day.

As I finished feeding Tuesday and put the bowl up, a screaming toddler the *ayis* had strapped down grabbed my attention. His bottle days were proclaimed over and it was time to transition him to solid rice.

Though hard to witness, this is standard practice here for this rite of passage. The *ayis* are not purposely trying to be cruel (with the exception of Tilly), but they simply don't have time to wean the children gradually from the bottle as we do in America. It's discouraging, but in these overcrowded institutions, the *ayis* have no time for coddling.

The temperature was somewhat milder today and many of the

kids were playing outdoors. I spotted Xiao Gou. When she saw me, she instantly turned her head away as if she was angry. Lately she's been acting aloof, and I don't understand why. Perhaps her *ayi* has told her, "Ti Ti doesn't love you anymore." As I approached to give her some attention, she tried to move away with her walker. Hugging her close, I said, "I missed you so much, Xiao Gou." However, as soon as I let go, she continued on her way with her lip stuck out.

"Can't I give you a kiss?" I called. She stopped in her tracks and tolerated a kiss without turning to face me.

It hurts me deeply to see her so sad all the time. I know she's angry because she wants to come home with me, but we've decided to suspend home visits unless we can get her closer to adoption. Those visits are like dangling happiness just out of her reach. The parents who were going to try to adopt her have reconsidered— there's been an unexpected change in their lives. Now I must pray that another family will come along and fall in love with this child enough to add her to their family.

As I was leaving, I noticed Le Bai—our little boy with albinism—crying in pain. The sun was hurting his eyes. He was so blinded by the light that he didn't know who was standing in front of him. Over a month ago, I brought him a pair of sunglasses that had been sent by his future family in a care package, but the glasses were nowhere to be seen. Sheila asked the *ayi* why he wasn't wearing them, and this started quite an exchange. A group of *ayis* and two cooks were sitting around playing cards, and this was when we discovered that Le Bai's foster mother is the orphanage cook.

She took offense at our interference, saying she only gives him his sunglasses and hat at night, away from the orphanage. He needs them during the day while it is sunny, I argued, because being outdoors is making his eyesight worse; moreover, it is painful for him. I put my own sunglasses on him and he started smiling, as if to say, "Hey! I can see!"

I'm sure the cook imagined we were criticizing her mothering skills, but I only wanted Le Bai to be able to enjoy being outside like the rest of the children. They are cooped up in that dark, dungeonlike room most of the time, and when they are finally allowed outside, their happiness is obvious.

On another note, Yu Jun, one of the babies who had cleft lip surgery, is still in the hospital three weeks later. He must be doing very poorly, because usually they leave the hospital only a few days after that procedure.

Overall, it was not a good day. Lately I've been especially homesick for the U.S. and my family, so perhaps I saw only the negatives all morning. I've been trying to think of something good to write about the day or even about the last visit, but cannot come up with a thing.

Ben came home and after sitting through his weekly conference call, he casually asked, "How was the orphanage today?"

"Fine," I said dully. There is no way he can imagine what it's like to witness such constant misery and to know there is little one can do to change it.

Then my husband did one of the small things that make me love him so much. When he saw the forlorn look on my face, he shut down his laptop, crossed the room, and held me in his arms. With that small show of devotion, I know that even if Ben can't walk through the dark clouds with me, he'll always be waiting on the other side to comfort me when I make it through.

32

Song Li, a teacher at the orphanage, is an absolute angel. Song Li is from Shengxi and, remarkably, she grew up in the orphanage. She is disabled and needs a wheelchair, and she teaches and cares for the ten or so deaf children. When she was old enough, someone sponsored the education of this young woman, and among other things, she learned sign language. She now lives in a building close to the orphanage with her new husband, who also grew up as a Shengxi orphan.

Song Li has the marvelous gift of easily bonding with the children. All her deaf children live together in one room with their own small dining and bathroom areas. She allows them to have personal belongings such as books and toys, which are not permitted elsewhere in the orphanage. The room is the only one in the institution even close to being warm and inviting.

One late afternoon when I went to find Xiao Gou, I was amazed to discover Song Li, who had somehow managed to get upstairs, sitting on one of the beds with the deaf children surrounding her and singing along to a DVD. They looked so happy—a rare sight in this desolate place. With Song Li, the children feel maternal love; she always makes sure her kids are dressed in clean clothes and even does up the girls' hair in pigtails.

This small group of kids is so lucky to have Song Li. These children will never have to worry about a lack of love while they're with her. Now, if only more angels would come along for the other children—but that seems like a faraway dream.

* * *

NOVEMBER 18, 2005

I thought I'd finally reached the end of my tolerance for the orphanage staff, the hospital administration, and all of China. I actually told Ben I wanted to go home. The corruption, inefficiency, and continual stress had taken its toll on me, and I felt that if I had to face one more baby who needed medicine or surgery and was being denied, I would fall apart entirely.

It feels as if I have been fighting these battles for such a long time, and I'm mentally exhausted. While our team has had many success stories, we have also lost many innocent children. My two closest friends and fellow volunteers here are also feeling the strain from the burden of responsibility we're carrying.

Even though I scarcely had the energy to do it, yesterday I asked permission to take Xiao Gou home for the weekend. Now that she's here, I am relieved I was able to break out of the chains of my self-pity. My heart never fails to be lifted over what a joyful child she is so much of the time; right now she's singing a nursery song at the top of her lungs—and what a set of lungs this little girl has!

When Ben and I picked her up, she was a little overwhelmed. She demolished the potato chips I had ready for her in the car and at once fell asleep on me. After a long ride home, as soon as we got inside she insisted, "Ti Ti, *da bian*." I have learned a number of new words recently, but that one has been etched into my brain permanently. It means, "I've pooped."

In twenty-four hours, we went through half a bag of diapers.

Each time I'd get her cleaned up, apply the cream, and wash my hands, about twenty to thirty minutes later I'd hear, "Ti Ti, *da bian.*" Last night in my sleep I heard, "*Da bian da bian da bian . . .*"

On Friday night, Ben's coworkers came over for a visit. Xiao Gou has a way of capturing everyone's attention and she didn't hesitate to show off to this new audience by exhibiting her perfect balancing skills, her rapid moving-around-furniture technique, and her infectious giggle. Not surprisingly, they all fell for her charms. She doesn't like to use her walker much at home; she prefers to pull herself alongside the furniture. She is quite fast, moving in that way.

Ben, the girls, and I took Xiao Gou to McDonald's on Saturday. Seating her on the counter, I told her to choose what she wanted. Excitedly she pointed at french fries, a cheeseburger, chicken nuggets, ice cream, and just about everything else on the menu. We laughed and ordered a chicken nugget Happy Meal. "*Xie xie,* Ti Ti" ("thank you"), she said to me repeatedly. I was pleased at the improvement in her manners. The last time she spent three weeks with us, I had a hard time getting her to say please and thank you.

Now every time I change her diaper, she whispers, "*Xie xie,* Ti Ti."

As I carry her upstairs for a bath, she giggles, "*Xie xie,* Ti Ti."

Setting her meal in front of her, I hear, "*Xie xie,* Ti Ti."

Amanda said she sounds as if I programmed her. It is amusing, and I must always remember to return the polite response, "*Bu yong xie*" (no thanks needed).

* * *

Ultimately, this weekend Xiao Gou's presence added joy back into my heart and opened my eyes to my purpose once again. It was like a nudge from above, saying, "Get it together and don't give up!" It's a bittersweet visit though, because I will have to take her back today.

I desperately want to find a foster family for her. She has so much to offer, so much love and affection. What a saucy personality! She is also very sensitive; she hates me to show disappointment in her. If I scold her at all, she gets very quiet and cries silent tears.

Just now, she called Ben downstairs (*Baba, guo lai!*) and they're playing hide-and-seek. He pretends as if he doesn't see her, and she scoots from room to room on her bottom as fast as she can to get away from him. If he gets too close, she shrieks loud enough to wake the neighbors. If I'm not in the room, she wants him to play, but if I'm around, she doesn't want anything to do with him.

* * *

NOVEMBER 27, 2005

I was not able to go to the orphanage today. Both my girls woke up with fever and sore throats, and thus had to stay home from school. I called Sheila early this morning to prep her for the talk regarding Xiao Gou that we had planned today with Director Fu. Sheila called me afterward; apparently, the discussion did not go well at all. Fu said there was nothing anyone could do to change Xiao Gou's circumstances.

According to Fu, the orphanage takes in two types of children. The first are the children over whom the orphanage has guardianship and who can be adopted if the medical staff believes they are fit. These are the children who have been abandoned with or without a note; the parents are deceased or completely absent.

The second type are the children who are removed from homes due to neglect or abuse, and also the sick or injured children who have been abandoned at the hospitals due to lack of funds, facilities, or other such impediments. These children's cases are all under ongoing investigation and the orphanage does not have guardianship. It is paid a monthly stipend by the government to care for them and allow them to live at the orphanage.

Xiao Gou falls into type two; in addition, she has other complications. Prior to her abandonment, her parents were on TV pleading for donations, and after they abandoned her, the local TV station did another three-day piece on her. She has had much public attention, though she likely understood little of it. Fu says the authorities are actively searching for her parents and for the people who caused the accident that began Xiao Gou's tragic story. This case is too highly publicized for the government to allow her be adopted. This is beyond my comprehension.

I asked Sheila, "Well, then, why did Fu tell us that the orphanage could petition the courts for guardianship?"

She couldn't tell me. Apparently, Fu now says they cannot petition the courts and no one will have guardianship until the investigation is closed.

"How long will they investigate?" I asked. She does not know.

Meanwhile, my frustration level is building steadily because of the inconsistent information we constantly receive about adoption dossiers, regulations, and other bureaucratic matters. I could manage better with the truth than with all the misleading promises we are forced to sort through. Just when I think we've made progress, I am brought back to the reality of China's appallingly unfair welfare system.

* * *

DECEMBER 1, 2005

These past few weeks have been some of the most difficult I've yet experienced in dealing with the orphanage staff and hospital officials—if that's possible. I'm exhausted and discouraged. To make things worse, just this week China blocked access to our volunteer group's website. Now it can be viewed only from the U.S., which is no help to my team, because all of us are here. Our best communication tool has vanished and we don't know when we'll be able to use it again.

The next blow fell when last week one of the newest infants was in danger and looked as if she might die. She was a cleft lip baby; one of the many that I have seen here in the past few years. Several have died because of malnutrition; it's a frustrating reality that their inability to eat is taking their lives. That brings to mind a related story—one that proves there are blessings among the deepest tragedies.

Several weeks ago, a stranger from the other side of the world heard about our volunteer group and wanted to help. I get many promises from faraway people, but more often than not, they don't follow through. I replied to this woman with some of our needs, including those of cleft lip bottles and nipples, though I thought it unlikely that I would hear from her again.

This morning at home, a knock at our door startled me; a postal worker stood with a parcel in front of him. Receiving a package in China is usually a frustrating process. First, a man on a motorcycle will arrive at our door and wave around a piece of paper to prompt me to bring him my passport. He will then write down the passport number and leave the paper with me. Next, I take the piece of paper to one of the many postal outlets and try to wait patiently in a throng of people that refuse to form a line—all just to show my paper. Sometimes I'm directed with charades out the door, meaning I have the wrong post office. On rare occasions, I am mercifully given my package after a lengthy wait.

Today the package itself came to my door. No charades and no aggravating wait or crowds. Inside the box were the promised items of Vaseline and cleft baby bottles and nipples from the faraway stranger of two weeks ago. This woman doesn't know me or know to trust that I actually need these items. She knows only to listen to her heart and to the whisper that she has the resources to help, even if she is a world away. Perhaps her package was a message to me that there is still much work to be done here, that God is beside me and knows of my heartache and will provide for our greatest needs.

* * *

Last night Ben, Amanda, and I went for foot massages at the local spa. After a half-hour wait, we were led down dark stairs and into a basement. If not for the strategically placed candles, we would have tripped in the dark and fallen into the shallow water surrounding the stone walkways. These led to several luxurious armchairs, where the accompanying gurgle of fountains was a tranquil backdrop for the rich surroundings.

Speaking in whispers, one tiny Chinese girl offered us steaming cups of jasmine tea. Normally, I don't drink the flowery-tasting tea, but with the recent stressful events wreaking havoc on my stomach, Asian tea was exactly what I needed to help me ease into the moment.

We each chose a comfortable reclining chair and waited with anticipation for what would come next. Soon, a group of people filed in, all dressed in identical blue pajama-type clothing and carrying steaming buckets of water, which were placed in front of us. As I eased my aching feet into the mixture of black, cloudy tea water (an Asian custom to soak sore feet), a small, older woman placed a warm rice bag on my abdomen.

The young fellow who knelt in front of my chair used his gentle, callused hands to wash the street dust and grime from my feet. As he cleaned between my toes, I wondered idly which region of China he had come from, because his dark skin wasn't common around here. Rising quietly, he took the rice bag from my stomach, lifted my hair, and placed the bag around my neck.

He reclined my chair and began methodically kneading the knots from my tension-filled shoulders. As he administered to me, my mind jumped from thought to thought:

It is late; I wonder how many people he has massaged? He looks so young to work and not be in school. His haircut is different from the other two fellows. I need to call Heather in the morning to remind her to make a doctor's appointment. My water is getting cold; when is he going to massage my feet? Is that my husband making that low buzzing noise? I like the way my masseur has one lock of hair falling over his eyes—he looks so mysterious.

Finally satisfied that he had done all he could for my pitiful upper body, Mystery Boy silently moved back to his stool in front of the chair. He placed a towel in his lap, and then, as though he was handling priceless glass, he lifted and dried each of my feet and placed them on another stool between us.

I'll bet he's glad I don't weigh much, considering how many times he's already lifted my legs, I thought with amusement.

Wrapping one foot in a towel, he began massaging my other foot with a mint-scented ointment. The friction coming from his hands was unexpectedly hot but extremely comforting. I was also surprised by the thick muscles on his small frame; I suppose massaging people hour after hour is an effective way to tone one's biceps. In his hands, my feet began to feel weightless.

Listening to my husband in an all-out snore, I wished I had his capacity to simply shut off thoughts, but the distraction of a stranger working on my feet cut into my usual mental rambling and wouldn't allow me to ponder one subject at a time—instead they came flying at me all at once.

I wonder if he thinks my feet are big. I think I forgot to let the cat in. I have to get to the grocery store! I wish he wouldn't grind that knuckle into the sole of my foot! Oops, I forgot that my toenail polish needs retouching. Did Amanda finish her homework before we left? Wow, he has some strong hands. I am really, really going to finish my latest short story by the weekend! I wonder how much is a good tip for this fellow?"

In the chair next to me, my daughter had her head leaned to one side and appeared to be sleeping while her designated young man rubbed her tiny feet. I marveled at how she could be so relaxed and carefree. I peeked at my watch and saw that we only had ten minutes remaining to be pampered. Knowing that one day our time in China will be over and impulsive trips to the spa will cease, I laid my head back and forced myself to concentrate on what should have been a mesmerizing sound of gurgling water.

Five minutes later, I peered through my eyelashes to see what kind of expression Mystery Boy was wearing. He was concentrating on my foot extremely hard, deep furrows across his brow. Perhaps he had spotted an imperfection—perhaps he thought my scarlet toenails needed a trim or my heels were too rough. Oh! I wished he'd just finish up and let me out of this chair! Why is relaxing so hard for me?

He caught me looking at him, so I figured, What the heck, I might as well talk to him now.

"Ni ji sui le?" (How old are you?)

Flashing a shy smile, he whispered, *"Er shi er sui."* (Twenty-two! Wow, he looked only about sixteen!)

"Jintian ni gei duo shao ren anmo?" (How many people have you given massages today?)

"Liu ge." (Six.)

I wondered what kind of money he made and whether he had a family. He rose from his stool and left to bring out a bucket of clean water. After rubbing my feet and calves with an exfoliating cream *(I wished I had shaved my legs before coming!),* Mystery Boy eased my feet down one more time and softly wiped away the lotions he had used.

He patted my feet dry and stood up. Bowing to me with

his hands clasped in a prayer gesture, he murmured, *"Hao le."*
(Finished.)

"Xie xie ni!" I said as I popped out of the chair and went to
retrieve my shoes. With all of us now awake and ready to go, we
walked up the stairs and out into the light, paid the bill, and exited
the spa.

In the taxi on the way home, Ben murmured, "That was *so*
relaxing."

"Yeah, I wish we could do it every night!" Amanda agreed.

"Yeah, yeah, it was nice." While marveling at how good my
feet felt, I began to remind myself of the many things urgently
waiting to be done at home.

33

I'm in a reflective mood. As I sit here and stare out my window, I wonder what it feels like to be tied to a chair for hours without any diversions. How could people knowingly inflict such unconscionable suffering upon defenseless, innocent children?

This single thought swirled relentlessly in my head today after I discovered such a child tied up for the third or fourth time in a matter of weeks. I crouched in front of him and rubbed his little legs; they were icy cold from lack of circulation. Loosening the old, heavy rope around his abdomen, I saw it had made deep red welts in his skin. I offered him cookies and talked to him soothingly. Somehow, my sympathy invoked tears that began to trickle down his cheeks. The room *ayi* told Sheila that this child needed to be tied up to prevent him from running in the halls. How ridiculous—if we tied up every child who ever ran down the halls where I come from, we'd need a lot of rope. The boy was about seven years old and undoubtedly full of the energy that makes a boy a boy.

As I left the room I couldn't help but give the *ayi* a glare that unequivocally told her how ashamed she should be.

* * *

DECEMBER 14, 2005

Our orphanage Christmas party was fabulous. Considering our planning and teamwork, it could hardly have turned out differently. However, there was one thing that was out of our control. The orphanage allowed only a small number of children to attend, approximately twenty of one hundred eighty. Even though the party started at 5:30, they told us the others were sleeping. We know that was an outright lie, but could do nothing. Forty-five elderly people from the nursing home attended and were thrilled about the gifts of scarves, gloves, and hot-water bottles we'd prepared.

The volunteers' children—including Heather and Amanda—sang a series of Christmas songs, after which we honored the elders by presenting them with plates of goodies. We couldn't understand why they weren't helping themselves, until someone explained that, as elders, they must be served. We were happy to comply.

Santa was a big hit. (I'd warned my girls not to let the smaller children know that their daddy was pretending to be Santa.) The kids were awestruck and had a great time interacting with him and receiving M&M's as a special treat. Chocolate is banned at the orphanage—understandably, because the orphanage cannot afford dental care—but this is Christmas! I played the part of Rudolph, joining in with the rest of the volunteers, who were dressed as the other reindeer, to perform a dance routine to "Rudolph the Red-nosed Reindeer." The elders and children were enchanted with our "Southern country" rendition of the classic.

The children sang a song, using hand signs to enhance it. The theme of the second song they performed was "Mother . . . why didn't you love me?" It brought tears to the eyes of all the volunteers and made me wonder with sadness why they would teach orphans such a song. The children's faces became so serious that it was evident they understood what they were singing.

I was proud of Ben and our girls; they sang, helped children open candy, and served the elders. It's lovely to see they enjoy helping me in a world they don't ordinarily share.

Xiao Gou was unusually sedate—I'm concerned about her. She sang her heart out with the rest of the children but didn't smile much. She balanced on that one foot of hers for the longest time so she could use her hands for the motions and not hold on to her walker. I felt like scooping her up and running off with her, taking her to a better life somewhere.

* * *

DECEMBER 16, 2005

My emotions are in turmoil once again. I have been feeling melancholy all day. Yesterday when I left the orphanage, I found myself in the path of a teenage boy on a rusty old bicycle. He was struggling to ride through the gate while maneuvering around me. On his face was a sweet, intent expression, but when I scrutinized him, I saw that his left arm was only a short stump. It was just long enough to reach the handlebar in order for him to keep his balance, but not quite long enough to be of much use. It was obviously a struggle for him to ride, but in China riding a bike or scooter is very important for personal transportation. The majority of citizens cannot afford to own cars or even pay bus fare.

It made me reflect on what happens to the other disabled children when they leave the orphanage. I've been told they are required to move out at a very early age if their disability is not severe. I have grown so close to so many of these babies that it worries me to think of their futures. I'm always trying to picture them as adults and imagine what they will be doing with their lives.

I see people about town who are disabled and wonder if they grew up in an orphanage. Sometimes these people are collecting trash, sweeping the road, or begging in the street. It's nothing short of a tragedy that not only do these children miss the treasure of having a family to call their own but also as adults they face a lifetime of discrimination.

Returning home a few nights ago, we watched a Chinese little person stashing his bags in a hole under the elevated road. He was only about three feet tall and evidently homeless. Amanda commented on how "cute" he looked—an odd description, considering he was actually a middle-aged man. He knew he had captured our interest, because he turned and stared directly at us. He looked me straight in the eye and gave a heart-melting smile.

Few programs are available here to help the disabled, but that is not nearly as bad as the fact that I see no compassion given to these people. Frequently, I will sit and observe a beggar just to see how many times a Chinese person actually gives to their cup. To this day, I have never seen anyone but foreigners put money in the cups. While I realize many people advocate that it's wrong to support begging, looking into the eyes of these people and seeing the hunger and desperation, I find it difficult to walk away with money jingling in my pocket.

Often we see women out on the highway with babies strapped to their backs, going from car to car at red lights. They're also scattered about the streets of Beijing, sitting with children in their laps and a cup or bowl in front of them. They bow their heads as we walk by, silently pleading for help. Their pride was long ago shattered; they have only the need to feed their children in mind.

I wish God had not granted me the burden of being so sensitive. These children and adults of poverty invade my thoughts ceaselessly. I would like to help all of them, but I can only keep moving on in the mission of helping one child at a time. Thank goodness for all of the humanitarians out there who come to China and other poor countries to implement charitable foundations. There are so many hurting people just waiting for a helping hand.

As for me, my family is safe, warm, and has food on our table tonight. At this moment, my gratitude exceeds description.

* * *

DECEMBER 24, 2005

Today was Christmas Eve and I was disappointed that Ben was required to work all day. While we waited for him, we watched the DVD of *Cheaper by the Dozen,* with Steve Martin. I enjoyed the movie but kept alternating between laughter and moist eyes. It was all about family, which prompted memories of past Christmases with our large extended families, which in turn made me gloomy and homesick.

Ben arrived home and we headed into town for his company's Christmas dinner and a non-advertised or approved church service to be held at a restaurant. Traffic was impossibly choked; it's strange that the Chinese are out celebrating even though they don't know what the festivities really mean. Since China opened up to the rest of the world and Westerners have come here, the Chinese want to emulate us in everything we do. Today was just a regular day for them, but knowing it was a popular foreign holiday brought them out, making the streets and restaurants busier than usual. Spectacular fireworks displays dazzled us, and children with their parents clogged the streets, their sparklers waving streaks of light through the dark sky. Shop owners have their workers dressed as elves or Santa Clauses, waiting outside hopefully for foreigners shopping for last-minute gifts. (They can't seem to get the elf and Santa colors right—some of them were wearing colors such as baby blue and looked like Smurfs.)

We arrived at the restaurant and filled our plates from the special buffet. The menu was bland turkey, potatoes, salad, soup, and Jell-O. The meal was a flop, but we had fun socializing with several expats we met there.

After dinner, we moved up to a tiny room on the third floor, with nothing but ten chairs and a podium occupying the space. The icy room was narrow with only one window, but we were enjoying ourselves and hardly noticed the cold.

The restaurant's Singaporean owner had expected only eleven people to attend the evening service, but word of mouth spread and people kept coming in—soon I counted more than thirty people in the tiny space. There were seven Americans, two English, some Hong Kong Chinese, some Singaporeans, and several local families. The room was so crowded that some people had to sit in the outside hall, but they didn't seem to mind.

We sang Christmas songs and read the baby Jesus story from the Bible. The owner had a special presentation for the locals, explaining what we were celebrating and how they could become God's children too. We sang more songs and ended with "We Wish You a Merry Christmas," along with hugs and handshakes. It was so gratifying to be with people who shared my faith and knew what Christmas truly stands for.

After we left, we headed to Ben's favorite restaurant, where we nibbled on spring rolls—a shoddy replacement for Christmas cookies, but we reminisced about past holidays to keep our spirits joyful.

After an hour or so, we left to start a fruitless search for a taxi. The traffic had become even worse than earlier and every taxi that passed was occupied. We stood on the corner for at least fifteen minutes to no avail. Next, we decided to walk down to the corner of another popular street to see if we'd have better luck there. The sidewalks were thronged with people on foot and on bicycles, while cars inched along the road. Chaos reigned. Most of the people were in festive moods and we received many greetings of "hello" (the only English word many of them know).

At the next street corner, we met some people who had been

at the service earlier. They said they'd been waiting for a taxi for a long time too.

We decided to forge ahead and take the city bus. With help from a local, we learned where to catch the bus toward our house, and five blocks later, we boarded a very dirty bus. The driver surely wouldn't win any safety awards, but we made it to a stop close to home and walked the remaining distance.

Next, we had fun attempting to take an automatic picture with our new digital camera—we simply could not figure it out. We would pose ourselves and Ben would reach out his long arm to click the button. While the pictures were mostly taken from cockeyed angles, each frame caught us happy and giggling at our efforts.

The mood became more somber as we gathered around the phone to call our family and wish them a merry Christmas. China seems farther away from the rest of the world on this night than on any other of the year.

I'm amazed that I'm still writing, but now we're finally ready to climb into bed. Ben has worked three weeks straight, but tomorrow he'll stay home and we'll enjoy some family time while digging through the several boxes of Christmas gifts that were packed with love by Grandma and sent across the ocean to reach us for this special holiday.

* * *

DECEMBER 28, 2005

When I walked through the orphanage door today, I sang out my usual "Where's my girl, Xiao Gou?" Immediately she spotted me, becoming businesslike and pulling up her sleeve. Her arm was purple with a bad bite mark.

"Oh no! What happened?" I cried out.

She pointed to a child her own age, telling me the girl had bitten her. While the culprit looked on, I made quite a fuss, hoping to make her understand that I was highly disturbed by her biting habit. I hugged and kissed Xiao Gou, rubbing her thin arm; then I produced my cookies. I thought of a plan.

I could almost see the other girl's thoughts as she stared at the cookies longingly. I proceeded to put a cookie in each of Xiao Gou's hands. To the little girl I held out one cookie only. With a "most disappointed in you" expression, I made her understand that Xiao Gou had received two cookies, not just one, because she'd been a good girl who doesn't bite.

I swept Xiao Gou into my arms and took her upstairs with me for some playtime; an hour or so later, she chanted, "*Da bian,*" and a diaper change ensued. When I returned Xiao Gou to her room, the little girl saw me and backed away in tears. I quickly reassured her that I wasn't anyone to be afraid of; I was just the Great Cookie-Keeper!

The *ayi* was laughing, but I felt bad—this is the first time I've had to show dismay to a child here. Biting is a serious offense in a country such as this, where hepatitis and other diseases run rampant. After my little cookie lesson, next time she's contemplating biting my girl, I suspect she'll reconsider.

* * *

DECEMBER 29, 2005

I had a surprising gift come my way this week. It begins with the story of Yue Hua, a darling little girl who had captured my heart. Yue Hua had a most serious face and deep, solemn eyes. During my first year at the orphanage, I'd become quite attached to her, and had comforted her after several traumatizing events. I felt very connected to this child, with a different kind of love than I felt for the others. I knew Yue Hua was on the list to be adopted, but wasn't sure it would ever happen.

One day I arrived at the orphanage to discover that Yue Hua was gone.

"*Xianzai ta zai Meiguo, zhu zai xinde jiating*" (Now she is in America living with new family), the *ayi* said offhandedly.

I was devastated that I hadn't had a chance to say goodbye or hug her one last time. While I was happy she'd been given the gift of a family, part of me ached over the loss of her. For a long time, the room was bereft of Yue Hua's subtle enchantment. I wasn't even allowed to correspond with her new parents, and I wondered if Yue Hua had actually been adopted or if something unspeakable had happened to her. I hated to think the worst, but past experiences had left me mistrustful of much of the information given to me.

In our dining room, I had a framed picture of Yue Hua, in which she wore a shabby red coat and a solemn expression. Many times now, I have passed her face and wondered what might have happened to her. Each time, I felt a wave of sadness for her and all that she'd endured in her brief time at the orphanage.

Several months ago, I received an email from a couple in America wanting to know if I had any information about their soon-to-be son. They sent his file picture, hoping I would recognize him. I discovered this couple were going to be the parents of Le Bai, our little albino boy. The mother was a remarkable woman, and I started up an online friendship with her. We exchanged many emails in which I reassured her of Le Bai's health and sent other snippets of information to ease her mind.

In one email, this mother hooked me up with yet another woman who had recently adopted one of our girls, Le Ci, whom we had sponsored for surgery. I sought out a picture of her post-surgery for the scrapbook the mom was compiling—the adoptive parents treasure any pictures we can provide of the child's orphanage days. For this reason, at any given opportunity we can be found snapping as many pictures as allowed.

Once we'd begun corresponding, an email arrived saying, "I have another daughter whom we adopted from your institution some time ago. Do you perhaps know her?"

Imagine my surprise when I learned her name was Yue Hua. I still didn't get my hopes up, because many children are given the same Chinese names.

When I finally saw a current photo of Yue Hua, I realized we were indeed speaking of the same little girl. She looked much happier but still carried that wistful, dreamy look. I cried tears of relief and joy as I sat at my computer alternately reading the message and staring at her beautiful face. Yue Hua is now over four years old and living a contented life with an adoring family in the U.S.

These emails came to me, halfway around the world, through so many people and across several states. I knew without a doubt that it was a gift telling me our efforts are assuredly not for nothing. The orphanage is like a different place now; over time, it has become a much healthier environment with rare cases of outright abuse. With the day-to-day issues that still arise, it's so easy to lose hope and to forget all we have accomplished. It takes a small miracle such as this for me to remember where we began and realize how far we have come.

Since we've discovered we have something in common—a little nymph of a girl—this mother and I have exchanged many emails. She has continued to make me smile with stories of Yue Hua and her developing personality. In return, I have helped her to understand some of Yue Hua's issues by sharing the early childhood experiences I witnessed her daughter suffer.

Yesterday was our last holiday party for the orphanage, specifically for the foster kids and parents. Thanks to donations from an American organization, each child received a stuffed toy and a bag of goodies. Donations also paid for needed items such as diapers, cream, wipes, socks, and toys. Most of all, we were relieved to see some of the children we love and have missed since they went to live with foster families.

Many children, including Bella, Xiao Li, and several of the cleft palate toddlers for whom we had sponsored surgeries, happily accepted their gifts. It was indescribably wonderful to see them safe and content with foster mothers at their sides. These mothers deserve support and encouragement, and we always make sure to praise them and let them know how grateful we are that they've taken these children into their homes. It is thrilling to see the children's true personalities emerge once they are in a loving environment.

It was a special pleasure to see Bella, the toddler who'd had a phobia of the outside world for the longest time. Claire, our young American volunteer who had come for a year, had sponsored her and taken on the responsibility of helping her overcome her fear. Maggie also played a large part in this story as her surrogate grandmother. Claire and Maggie lived in a dorm and taught English at a Chinese nursing school and gradually Bella became the unofficial school mascot.

Claire recently returned to the U.S., but because of her infinite love for this child, Bella was able to go into foster care, where she now lives a happy life. She even has a foster sister from our institution: the toddler we call Buddha Baby. When Bella's foster mom brought her in to the party, she greeted me exuberantly. Ordinarily, the foster children don't care to interact with us when they visit, but when I called Bella's name, she ran into my arms. We played and I received many hugs before they all had to leave.

At the party, I talked to another foster mother who has taken in eight children in the last nine years.

"Where are those children now?" I asked her.

"They're either back at the orphanage or have been adopted." She wanted to talk about one child who had been with her for over a year and who is now in America. I could not understand which child it was by the Chinese name but longed to know.

"Are you sad when you have to let them go?" I asked.

"Yes . . . I cry and cry and cry!"

I was awed by her commitment and passion; she was an exceptional woman. I could see the love shine in her eyes as she talked about these kids. We've had many success stories, and seeing these children yesterday helped to renew my resolve that I'm in the right place, and what we're doing, as a team, is indeed beneficial to these children.

So many times when we help them, they go into foster care and we never see them again, so we don't get to see the fruits of our labors. We've had to overcome so much frustration, deception, and outright abuse, but to see just one of our kids happy in a home is worth every struggle and heartache of the past few years.

* * *

JANUARY 11, 2006

There are so many beggars here! It is tragic to see small children out in this bitter cold, hungry and begging. Amanda wanted McDonald's today, a treat because it's not close to home, and the long lines and general chaos usually keep us away. Ben and I decided she deserved the reward. When we arrived, before we could even get out of the car, the beggars saw our foreign faces and came running. I dug for change and gave it to Amanda as we fought to get out the door. Outside, three children and a woman with a baby on her back all pushed and shoved to get nearer to us. Amanda was bewildered as to whom to give the change, so she turned and handed it back to me.

I divided it and dropped it in their cups, then grabbed Amanda's hand and pushed through, mumbling, *"Mei you"* (Don't have).

While standing in line to order, Amanda mused, "I wonder if those kids are hungry?"

We decided to order them some food. After we'd finished ours, Amanda excitedly raced for the door, five extra burgers in hand. When we stepped out, we were accosted by the same three children begging for more money with their now emptied cups. Amanda handed each child a burger, and watched in surprise as the kids ran off without opening the wrappers. Another beggar woman appeared with pleading eyes, holding a baby in one arm and an empty cup in the other. Amanda presented her with a burger.

Temporarily free of beggars and with one more burger remaining, we took the opportunity to jump in the car. As we were leaving the crowded parking lot, I saw that two of those children—each about six years of age—had run with their burgers to their "sponsors," who were huddled in a nearby doorway. The sponsors, two relatively healthy-looking women, immediately snatched the burgers from the kids. With a crestfallen face, the little boy returned to the parking lot to beg. As the little girl hungrily reached for some of the burger the woman was wolfing down, the woman smacked her, causing the child to fall backward. Defeated, she came back reluctantly to beg some more.

I could feel the fire rising in my chest. In a low voice, I said to Amanda, "Hand me that last burger." I gestured to Ben to stop the car.

As soon as he did so, I leaped out and made a determined beeline for the two women who were still gulping down the burgers. Marching up to them, I scolded, *"Nimen bu hao ren! Nide haizi leng ye e si le!"* (You are very bad people! Those children are cold and hungry!)

I was shaking all the way to my toes—not from fear but from outrage. I wanted to snatch those burgers from them, but I knew if I got close enough, I'd probably do more than grab the food. After my verbal lashing, I stormed through the cars and crowd until I found the two children. Tearing the burger in two, I urged them to hurry and eat it, but they hesitated, looking back toward the building where the women stood smacking their lips.

I shouted at them one more time, *"Nimen bu hao ren!"*

One of the women put her hand over her eyes as though she was humiliated. Onlookers could see what was happening, so the women were rightfully shamed—they "lost face" in front of the crowd. The other woman looked at me with hatred.

"Way to go, Mama!" Amanda said as I climbed into the van. As we pulled away, we saw that the child who was about eleven had wedged herself between two cars and was furtively eating her burger. She'd been smart enough not to show her benefactors the unexpected treat so I gave her a thumbs-up. She grinned from ear to ear and waved at me. Despite her vagrant clothing and dirty face, her entire demeanor changed when she smiled. She was beautiful.

I am not proud of myself for losing my temper in front of my daughter. It just infuriates me to see children begging for money that they are forced to hand over to adults who won't even feed them. It's outrageous—how can they be so cruel?

I'm no angel, that's for certain, but I know one thing: if my child and I were homeless and someone handed me a hamburger, my kid would get every bite. I wouldn't smack her away and then gobble it down in front of her. Those women should be prosecuted and made to go hungry. Evidently, they've been eating well—they each had enough padding for two people, while their cold, thin, and hungry children were forced to beg.

As I kissed Amanda goodnight a few hours ago, my mind wandered back to the three beggar children outside of McDonald's. They were neither an invention of the media nor a figment of television drama. They were real—and they were cold and hungry.

* * *

FEBRUARY 18, 2006

I've just returned to China after a whirlwind three-week stay in the U.S., where I visited a neurologist about my back and leg. Though I dreaded the many scheduled tests, I was excited about traveling alone. I thought it would be a pleasant break from my role as a mother both at home and at the orphanage, but I found I missed everyone so much that I called China every night, and they called me every morning. I discovered that being "free" from responsibilities is not for me. After the tests, it was concluded I had permanent nerve tissue damage in my leg and a bulging disk in my back.

The doctor suggested physical therapy and possibly exploratory surgery. I declined both because I had to return to China immediately. I was prescribed pain medication—which I won't take—and we planned to explore more options on my next trip.

While there, I was invited to speak to two women's groups

about my work at the orphanage. At those engagements, I met several women who were in the waiting period of the adoption process and intrigued to hear my story.

On the last day, I gladly boarded the plane back to China and my family. When I arrived in Beijing, I was greeted with a bouquet of flowers, hugs, and exclamations of "Yay! Mama's home!" They were so exuberant that people probably imagined they hadn't seen me in years. I am a very lucky woman.

* * *

Heather had a surprise awaiting me upon my return. My beautiful, blond, blue-eyed, fifteen-year-old girl now has jet-black hair and is sporting an eyebrow ring. Her fingernails are painted black and she is begging to have her tongue pierced. How did this happen? I ask myself. The answer is that Heather has a new boyfriend, and not one whom I approve of.

Eli is from Turkey and has already wreaked havoc with several other American girls in our expat circle. He has a wild reputation, and when I first discovered he and Heather were an item, I was filled with dread. Not surprisingly, Eli also has dyed black hair and a fair amount of metal puncturing his face—I've given him the nickname "tackle box."

He, too, wears black nail polish, and for sixteen years of age, he has quite a collection of tattoos. Incredibly, he is the son of the international school's director—a very important man in our community.

It came to my attention that, after curfew on the weekends, Eli has been scaling our house to the second-story window of Heather's room. With Ben leaving for work at dawn, staying up to make sure she is in at curfew was about all he could handle before he surrendered to exhaustion. They just waited until he was in bed for the night before the house-climbing sessions began.

Fortunately, Heather always has her friends stay over, so to my knowledge she and Eli haven't been left alone—or perhaps I've been naïve. I pray this stage will pass and Heather will go back to dating nice boys like the one she met who is from Finland. He was what I call boyfriend material. He always made a point to speak to me and impressed me with his commitment to be at his family table for dinner every night. He was very smart and consistently encouraged Heather to study harder. Doggone it, why did he have to be so boring?

Why didn't God give me boys instead of impressionable, vulnerable girls over whom I must stay awake and worry? The least He could do is send Eli back to Turkey as a special favor to me. *I wonder how much it would cost to install metal bars on all the upstairs windows . . .*

35

FEBRUARY 20, 2006

Last night was our annual Chinese New Year company party. In this country, this is the single most important holiday of the year. It is like American Christmas minus the religious part—the whole country is in party mode with two weeks of fireworks, drinking, extravagant meals, and the famous red envelopes of money being passed around everywhere.

Ben and I purposely arrived a little late. Usually, when we walk in, the room goes silent and then everyone starts applauding. I'm not sure how to interpret this—is it because they like my husband or is it because to them I am some sort of foreign Queen Bee? It is quite embarrassing either way—the first time it happened I was so surprised that I tried to back out of the room!

However, since we were late tonight it didn't happen. When we walked into the restaurant, we were immediately guided to the party room, which was not extraordinarily big but still managed to hold approximately six hundred people. Everyone kept their coats on because it is still winter here and very cold. Most public places don't actually use their heating systems, so the room was icy.

The round tables were laid with fine linens, cutlery, and wine glasses. There wasn't any wine, however, only beer or Coke. People were seated according to status, putting us at the first most-honorable table next to the stage. That also meant we were next to the speakers and the wrestling arena, which I'll get to in a minute.

The food was brought out in order of cold dishes, hot dishes, soups, and then rice and fruit. (Rice is not considered part of the meal but rather an end to the meal.) We arrived after the cold dishes, and the table with its convenient turntable for passing the food around was soon full of duck tongue, eel, deep-fried baby chicks, turtle, and many other foreign delicacies.

I didn't even bother picking up my chopsticks. My stomach sent me a silent rolling message to wait for the rice.

A young woman onstage was singing karaoke, and with the speaker box only about two feet away, her shrill voice made the hair stand up on my neck. I bumped Ben's leg under the table and we both struggled not to show any expression; instead we clapped like crazy when she finished the song. I was applauding her exit, while everyone else gave her false hope for her future singing career.

Between each butchered karaoke song, the two announcers called out numbers from the Draw Door Pull Box, as it was confusingly labeled. People in the crowd surged around the stage— and us—to get closer in case their name was called.

For some inexplicable reason, the announcer girl only gave them to the count of four to get there, which was hard for the people far in the back and caused even more chaos as they tried to shove their way though the masses as quickly as possible. Most of the time we didn't have a clue what was going on—we were the only non-Chinese in the room, and with the static and poor quality of the sound system, I could not understand the Mandarin being spoken.

In just a short time, things started getting even crazier. Men were becoming increasingly drunk, louder, and more obnoxious from all their *gambeis* ("bottoms up" toasts), particularly our driver, who also wielded a can of the Chinese version of Silly String and was not afraid to use it.

As the emcee continued calling out names, the employees began yelling and throwing things at the stage. A few empty Coke bottles went over our heads, and Ben was clobbered on the back of the neck by a huge cucumber torpedo. Using tissue, I wiped away what I could while mentally scheduling a trip to the dry cleaners to rescue his new suit.

Onstage, each time a man was called and shoved through to receive his box of whatever it was, another guy would try to wrestle it out of his hands. If he succeeded, he threw it into the crowd, causing even more mayhem. At one point, the two announcers decided to throw scarves as door prizes. Who knew the Chinese loved scarves so much? They went mad; the colorful scarves were landing on food and glasses of beer as the Chinese dove for them and yanked them out of each other's hands. It was utter insanity! The girl threw about twenty of these, and when it was over, I was just relieved to be sitting with no beer, food, or people in my lap.

After the scarves had been thrown, a diminutive young man in a very nice suit politely walked up to the microphone. Ben whispered in my ear that the man was a machine operator and always showed up to work dressed nicely—then changed into his work clothes in the bathroom. He was the only non-manager wearing a suit, so he stood out in the crowd of hundreds. The women were obviously smitten with this young man and his dimple-accented smile.

When he took the mike and began speaking, I almost choked on my Coke. His squeaky voice sounded like Speedy Gonzales's. I couldn't help but picture the silly cartoon mouse zooming around and had to turn away to keep from laughing. Imagine my surprise, then, when he broke out into his song with a deep and strong baritone! He was five minutes into a Chinese opera aria when the crowd went wild, showing their approval by whistling, hooting, applauding, and running up to thrust flowers or gifts into his arms. He was good, and I was so astounded I could not stop smiling from ear to ear. By the end of the song, he held three roses and a gift box and wore a new scarf—all from his new, adoring fans.

Despite Ben's presence, the singer approached me and gave me a rose, which set off more whistling and catcalls. As he handed over the mike and tried to leave the stage, three big bullies grabbed him by his suit and dragged him back to the mike. Everyone wanted him to continue singing, but he wanted to sit down. It's unusual for a Chinese person to give up the microphone willingly and I really think he would have sung another song if it weren't for the drunks yanking on his suit. I could tell by his red ears and scowl he didn't appreciate the roughhousing and wouldn't be doing anymore crooning for the women.

While another draw began, Ben got up to begin his tradition of toasting with all of the people in his department. According to Chinese custom, as their manager, Ben was expected to approach each table and fill each person's glass of beer and *gambei*. He did this in three different intervals, but instead of filling his own glass with beer, he furtively chose the unused bottles of Coke sitting on the tables.

While he was gone on the last round, the bedlam around me escalated and I feared I was going to be caught in the middle of a group of wrestling drunks. The thick fog of smoke had my eyes watering and my throat burning—and my stomach was begging for the rice that never made it out of the kitchen.

Intensifying the chaos, the people at the table next to me had turned the speakers to blare even louder in my ears. Other drunken partiers snapped picture after picture of me with their mobile-phone cameras. No one was brave enough to talk to me, and I sat there feeling alone and vulnerable, as if I were on display, with a plastic smile pasted on. I was so tense that my back was aching and my feet were like blocks of ice. Each time I looked, Ben was moving farther from our table, entirely unaware of my need to be rescued.

Finally, I couldn't take it anymore. I had survived two miserable hours—more than enough. I grabbed my purse and shoved my way past the throngs with my cell phone in hand, pretending I had an important phone call. As I talked to my imaginary friend, I continued moving away from the banquet room until the noise was just a buzz in my ear. I ended up standing at the open front doors, where it was blissfully quiet and private but cold.

A few minutes later, Ben sent me a text message: "Where are you?"

"Outside and I'm *not* coming back."

He found me shivering by the doors.

"I didn't feel safe where I was sitting. Everyone was just too drunk. I can either taxi home alone or just wait out here." I stood with my arms crossed and waited on his answer. I knew he had already toasted everyone he needed to for etiquette's sake and I wanted him to say that we could just leave together.

To my surprise, Ben didn't agree; instead, he became irritated. It wouldn't appear "correct" for him to remain there without me. I was trying to explain why I refused to enter that lion's den again, when, in a rare fit of pique, he turned and stalked out of the building, leaving me standing there looking like an idiot.

Outside, he walked about twenty feet ahead of me until we found a taxi. On the way home, the silence made the short ride last an eternity. I was fuming at his inability to sympathize with my feelings; he was irritated at me for not recognizing the importance of his position and the way he was expected to act.

In those moments of frustration, I didn't want to hear any nonsense about accepting the culture and traditions of China. In my opinion, this was not Chinese culture—it was just people losing their inhibitions by consuming copious quantities of alcohol.

Ben was undoubtedly worried that leaving early would offend

someone. But what about the flying food and bottles and the mass of bodies offending me? What about the thick haze of cigarette smoke floating around my head? What about people chattering and staring and snapping endless photos of me? What about the screeching *Chinese Idol* karaoke wannabes?

When we arrived home, I stomped up to our room in disgust and stripped off my reeking clothes and stood under the scalding hot water until I was sure I had used every ounce of it. I had to get one last sting in there and leave Mr. All-Important with only a cold shower.

It is morning now and Ben and I have made up. We weren't really mad at each other; we were irritated about the situation and how things had gotten out of hand. Thankfully, we didn't stick around for the grand-prize draws of luggage and a new scooter; there was probably bloodshed over those!

36

Isn't it strange how a key can just lose itself? Awakening this morning to a gorgeous, sunny day, I decided that since I had just spent three days in bed with a stubborn flu, I was going to ride my bike to the Ling Li, our local market, to buy vegetables for a salad. I haven't ridden all winter, and it was time to begin my spring exercise regimen. However, since experiencing how rampant the theft of bikes is here, I first needed to find the key to my bicycle lock.

After a frustratingly unsuccessful search, I opted to walk— the day was lovely. As a writer, I am constantly formulating little essays in my head, and ideas come much more easily when I observe things at a slower pace.

But how is one expected to cross six lanes of traffic and two lanes of bicycles before the light turns red? I tried twice at different intersections, walking as fast as I could, but it was simply impossible. I would get perhaps halfway before the light changed, and then I'd have to race for the opposite sidewalk. How did others less nimble than me fare?

It was heartwarming to see many grandparents strolling hand in hand with their grandchildren. In China, it is customary for the grandparents to care for the small children while their parents work, unlike in developed countries, where day care is prevalent.

It's a practical concept if you don't mind your parents living with you under the same roof, which is a sacrifice many young couples here must make.

I passed several locals leaving the market carrying small bags of raw meat, which explained all the red splotches on the sidewalk that I delicately stepped over. They carry the meat home unwrapped and bloody—a dangerous bacterial breeding ground, particularly in this warm weather. The meat at the market hangs in the open, humid air; flies swarm everywhere, invariably settling on the meat no matter what the temperature outside or in. Ordinarily, I avoid the meat side of the markets because of the nauseating smells, choking throngs of people, and thousands of aggravating flies.

I strolled toward the market, trying to ignore the exuberant calls of "Hello, *laowai!*" (foreigner) from a group of construction men.

I yelled back at them in Chinese, *"Wo bushi laowai, wo ju zai zhe li!"* (I'm not a foreigner, I live here!)

This prompted hysterical laughter; they weren't expecting a sarcastic retort in Chinese from a tall, blond American. Not wanting to encourage them further, I continued past without turning my head.

Nearing the market, I decided I'd better eat lunch before going to the open food area; the experience always ruins my appetite. I stopped at KFC, where I practiced ordering in Mandarin while the cashier practiced her limited English. The scene would have made for a great comedic skit, with both of us struggling to prove we could speak the other's language.

I sat down to eat and quickly became the center of attention as people began staring, pointing, and commenting to their companions. I could almost hear their thoughts: What country is she from? Why is she alone? What is she doing here among us?

A few years ago, I would never have been able to withstand the pressure of being alone in a public place full of curious, gawking Chinese. Time has made me immune to this kind of attention. I stare right back and even have the language skills to tell them to quit staring. I'm learning to live through all the frustrations. Even better, I can keep a smile on my face and, if I choose, engage in conversation. I have come a long way from the naïve, idealistic woman who first landed in this country three years ago. Who was that person?

As I finished my meal, I realized I should not have gulped the entire cup of strange-tasting Coke. I headed to the bathroom, knowing I'd be extremely lucky if it contained a toilet.

Luck was not on today's agenda, and in any case, I needed to get over my squatter phobia. I hooked my bag over my shoulder and squatted like a local, not even bothering to look down and see if my aim was on—my shoes needed a good wash anyway. Afterward I scrubbed my hands vigorously and strode out with my head held high—glad to have an empty bladder and a full belly to launch me on to the next mission.

I walked out of the department area and into the open food market. Upon entering, I was immediately harassed by dozens of vendors wanting me to stop at their vegetables. I ignored the overly aggressive hawkers and sought out a polite shop owner, a scarce commodity here, where every *kuai* (Chinese dollar) earned means a decent meal or a bus ride. Eventually, I found one who smiled warmly as I stopped to browse her cucumbers.

When I stepped over to the fruits, a woman pointed at some strange objects and asked if I wanted any. They were round and yellowish and unlike anything I'd ever seen.

"*Wo hai pa. Bu zhi dao*" (I am afraid. I don't know what they are), I said uncertainly, and she handed me one to sample.

She laughed good-humoredly. "Don't be afraid," she said in Mandarin. I decided to live dangerously and bit into it. Delicious! It was sweet like a peach but not fuzzy, small like a Ping-Pong ball but oblong shaped. I bought a dollar's worth—Amanda is sure to love them. I wish I could remember what the woman called them.

Succulent-looking oranges, grapes, and apples beckoned enticingly, but my hands were full and I had to get everything home. I left laden with the strange fruit, tomatoes, and cucumbers. It all cost less than two dollars, a remarkable deal by American standards. Heading to the street, I contemplated walking home for all of five seconds before waving down a taxi. I was weary from the stress of dealing with another so-called ordinary day in China.

This week I begin another Mandarin language class with a new teacher. It's a group class, so I'm anticipating that it will be lots of fun, and several of my best friends have also joined. Now my calendar each week is loaded up for the next two months. I know myself well enough to appreciate a full schedule; I'm not made for sitting around idly.

* * *

APRIL 11, 2006

Last Friday I received a call from the local television station. They were interested in doing a story on Xiao Gou and wanted to come to our house to take photos. I declined. I've been on local television several times, but for security reasons I do not want everyone knowing where we live. You never know who might be out there harboring a grudge against foreigners or Christians and might just recognize our compound.

Next, the TV people asked if I'd consent to an interview at the orphanage. I agreed, but only if the purpose was to attempt to find Xiao Gou a foster family.

When we arrived at the orphanage today, we were put to work dressing the babies after baths and tidying the room. It was disgusting to watch them procure all new sets of baby clothes, slap on powder, produce an array of toys, and shove the babies in the bouncer seats—a real song-and-dance show, and completely false. We joked grimly that we should have visitors here every day so the babies could be better cared for more frequently. I'll admit, it's a pleasure to hold a freshly bathed baby instead of one who has worn the same soiled clothes for several days.

The disruption clearly stressed the staff, but the only one to vent it on the babies was Tilly. Evidently overworked today, she rushed back and forth, dropping babies roughly in their beds, hitting their heads on the metal rungs, and dumping powder haphazardly, which resulted in several infants choking for breath. She left each crib with a wailing baby, and we tried to console them as we dressed them.

By the time the bottles came out, the babies were famished—it was an hour past their usual breakfast time. We busied ourselves with feeding, and afterward I scooped up Xiao Gou to return her to her room. Just as we were leaving, we met the camera crew in the hall; they wanted the interview right away. Xiao Gou instantly became shy and hard to handle, just like any normal kid among strangers. We did the interview, during which I struggled to provide informative responses and prevent Xiao Gou from becoming too rambunctious. I made sure to emphasize what a pleasant and animated child she is ordinarily, how she loves to get "girly" and dress up, how she delights in singing children's songs, and how easy she is to care for. I wanted people to understand that she is just a normal little girl.

One of the questions near the end of the interview revealed a common mind-set one faces in China.

"What is your motive for trying to help Xiao Gou?" the reporter asked.

Motive? What an odd word for what we do. The local media always think we volunteers have secret, underhanded motives for everything.

I was prepared. Through a translator, I answered, "I believe that every child should belong to a loving family. There are many generous Chinese people in Shengxi who can open their hearts and their homes to these children. God intended for children to have parents and it's not their fault that unfortunate circumstances brought them here. I just want them to have a chance to experience the love of a mother and father."

The reporter likely walked away still trying to figure out my ulterior motive. In any case, the show is a three-part series called *Now I Am Five* being presented on consecutive nights. I hope someone will see Xiao Gou and want to foster her, and that it will introduce many people to the idea of fostering the babies.

* * *

MAY 22, 2006

We have decided that at the end of our home leave, Heather will not return to China for the next school year. After a stormy few weeks and some heartache over Eli's continual betrayals, Heather got smart and dumped him. She also feels she cannot handle the pressure of the intense international school curriculum and she misses her friends from home. She's had fun here and formed friendships that I feel will remain strong for years to come. I am just happy she had the chance to experience another part of the world and to see how another culture lives.

Sometimes I wish things were different and my family did not have to be broken apart. In this respect, life is not easy; it's difficult to keep our relationships intact with such distance between us. I tried to talk Heather into staying, but she reminded me she'd fulfilled her promise to try it for one year, and now she's ready to return to what she calls "normal" living. She has also reached the age to apply for a driver's license, which has a good deal to do with her decision.

Heather has a streak of stubborn independence that often makes it difficult for her to find her place in certain situations. She refuses to take my advice and doesn't want to hear of my own experiences, which so often mirror hers. An unexplainable, constant restless battle rages in her, and she is always ready to explode over life's smallest pressures. I hurt for her but know that one day she'll find peace, though she's certainly taking the hard road to get there.

I recall how, when she was a small child, she'd let me hold her in my arms and comfort her. She wanted me to sing her favorite song over and over: Rod Stewart's "Have I Told You Lately That I Love You." These days I can only stand back and helplessly watch as she careers recklessly through her teen years.

37

Things at the orphanage are as usual—the temperature is soaring and mosquitoes have begun their annual feasting on our babies. Recently Ben paid a visit and suggested new screening for the windows; the current screens appear to be decades old. Now, why didn't I think of that? We also bought two bug zappers to test. If they work, we'll buy them for all the children's rooms. Many of the babies have bites on their heads, faces, and arms. I know the bites will only get worse, so this year we're going to fight back!

Before feeding time, Elizabeth asked me to look at a little boy, about two years old, on the other side of the room. He was standing against a crib with his chubby bare feet on the floor and his hands wrapped around the bars. His dark brown face was pressed to the crib and he appeared to be asleep.

I went to him, crouched down, and spoke softly. I didn't want to startle him. With the touch of light massaging on his legs bringing him alert, he slowly turned to face me and I immediately realized he was blind. His eyes were gray and covered by a milky substance that impeded his sight entirely. He was completely still, standing obediently where the *ayi* had put him.

Using my limited local dialect skills, I was able to piece together a few details about his life. He had come to the orphanage only one month ago, and the *ayis* had nicknamed him Fei Fei. When he heard a gentle voice in his ear, a shy smile broke across his face. He was likely confused about where he was and why he was there. I assumed he'd been isolated in the observation room for the first month, as this was my first time seeing him.

I was inexplicably drawn to this quiet boy. His dark skin and coarse hair, combined with his inability to understand Mandarin or the Shengxi dialect, made it obvious he was from a faraway province or farming community. He appeared frightened, which was confirmed when the *ayi* told me he had cried incessantly for the first three days. I can't imagine the trauma he must have undergone being separated from his family and brought to live amid such chaos. What had the orphanage staff told him? Had they explained that this was his new home? Was he aware that his parents had left him? The unknown answers in these situations always arouse my curiosity.

I picked him up and took him to the eating area. He became very agitated at being moved, but I continued speaking to him softly while rubbing his face and head. Soon he seemed to understand that I wouldn't harm him and he began to relax. He was quite plump and ate his rice porridge with gusto; clearly, someone had taken great care of him until his abandonment.

After we emptied the bowl, I picked up a stuffed rabbit and placed it in his hands. With the furry fabric rubbing against his face, he perked up and started babbling to me. The *ayis* were amazed; I suppose because he hadn't talked much so far. I only understood one word, *jie jie* (big sister). Elizabeth and I assumed he had an older sister and must be missing her.

Elizabeth brought him a ball, put it in his hand, and told him *qiu* (ball). Holding the ball and rabbit, his face lit up. What a change from the silent, motionless boy we'd first encountered.

We didn't want to leave him behind. So young and in total darkness, he has been thrown into a strange place with people who don't speak his dialect and are calling him by an unfamiliar name. How terrifying it must be to him! Yet just a little attention and affection proved he was capable of adjusting.

We had to leave Fei Fei to begin bath time. The room was stifling with the heat and smell of sweat and soiled diapers, causing my stomach to cramp and my head to pound. Some babies have open head sores from lying on dirty bamboo mats while perspiring profusely. The sores looked painful, so we placed cloth diapers under their heads, which the workers removed almost immediately, apparently not wanting us to waste clean diapers.

The *ayis* were strangely subdued and quiet today. Xiao Jenny kept sitting down to put her head between her knees; she said she was sick with dizziness and diarrhea. It's going to be a tough summer for all of them.

On the way home, my mind raced as Elizabeth and I discussed how we could possibly help Fei Fei. He is a beautiful boy and I'm thankful that, if he couldn't stay with his family, he somehow made it to our orphanage where my team can do what we can to ensure that a little sunshine penetrates his dark world. We plan to contact the local blind and deaf school—perhaps we can pull some strings to get Fei Fei into their program. Someone must teach him how to live as a blind person so he isn't forced to stand in one spot while listening to the world move by around him.

After a little digging, we uncovered more information about how Fei Fei came to us. He was found wandering near a famous bridge in town by a police officer. I can't imagine someone abandoning such a charming child, but perhaps his mother thought someone else could give him the help and care that she couldn't.

* * *

We are losing many volunteers this summer. Elizabeth and Lucy, the women who usually accompany me on Tuesdays, are leaving China permanently. Many tearful goodbyes have been exchanged lately. As for myself, I would like to go back to the States because of my family, but it's going to be very hard to leave these kids. I hope when the time comes, I am emotionally prepared.

We are now working on an affiliation between our volunteer group and the expatriate association in order to give our group more credibility and future stability. After several meetings to accomplish this, the board votes tomorrow on whether to collaborate with us. If they do, it should help us recruit more volunteers to take on some of the leadership roles I am currently filling. That will mean more organizational support for me, which would be a definite respite from the overwhelming load of communication, scheduling, and financial issues I have juggled for so long.

38

Lucy's adoption of Jia Jia has been finalized, making this week extra special. At last, all the documents have been completed, the passport and visa have been issued, and tomorrow they leave for the States to pursue a new life for Jia Jia. The entire process has been a miracle, one that Director Yao was instrumental in making happen. Normally, in China, you cannot pick which child you want to adopt. Lucy came to the orphanage planning only to volunteer, but she quickly fell in love with Jia Jia and wanted to make her part of their family. At first, she was told it wasn't possible. However, with plenty of prayers and teamwork the adoption was finalized in record time.

Jia Jia is severely handicapped; she needs access to doctors who specialize in spina bifida and can evaluate her case and future prognosis. Additionally, Jia Jia was abused in the orphanage; we saw it many times with our own eyes. In her first two years, this child has endured more discrimination than the average disabled person does in their entire life. Director Yao was relentless in pushing the paperwork through and used all of her connections and resources to make this adoption happen. I can't help but wish she would do the same with Xiao Gou.

We have seen a multitude of improvements in the orphanage's

administration, but with every two steps forward, there is one step back. For instance, I received an email from Sheila yesterday, in which she relayed that Xu Yang, who is struggling with a defective heart, had just taken a turn for the worse. She was feeding him when suddenly his eyes rolled back and his lips turned blue. An *ayi* subsequently told her they knew he was very sick and had given him medicine.

The following day, Sheila found Xu Yang in the sick room. The *ayi* in charge said he had almost died during the night. They had rushed him to the hospital, where he was stabilized. According to the *ayi*, the hospital wanted to perform surgery on him, but instead he was brought back to the orphanage to await approval from the top directors. I was sickened—this baby is hanging on by a thread! He should be in ICU or being prepared for surgery, not sitting in a dark room with an incompetent, exhausted *ayi* tending him. The orphanage administration knows our group will pick up any medical costs, so it's not an issue of funding. One of the most frustrating aspects of our work here is awaiting the many approvals from the endless tiers of directors.

While many improvements have happened over the past three years, we still must continually emphasize that the top priority is saving lives. It's a two-way street filled with red tape; with our donations we give them the things they want, and in exchange they allow us to intervene with sick children. In the past year, donations have bought indoor playground equipment, three new air conditioners, a television, new mosquito netting in all rooms, clothes and shoes, monthly bundles of diapers, and many more necessities.

Two steps forward and one step back, but it's all right, I'm wearing my dancing shoes.

* * *

Recently we had very good news about Xiao Gou. We inquired about her adoption status once again, and this time the answer was more encouraging. Director Fu said that since they have already run the mandatory newspaper notice about her abandonment and no one came forward to claim her, they can now proceed with getting her approved for adoption. Xiao Gou's dossier will be sent to the China Center of Adoption Affairs (CCAA) in July. This is wonderful news! I have prayed for this, and for the right family to see her pixie face and fall in love with her.

Xiao Gou has finally had her colostomy surgery, eliminating interminable hours sitting on a chamber pot. After I sent numerous emails to many contacts, one of my messages made it to the in-box of a doctor in the U.S. who knew of a foundation group coming to China. The group does admirable charity work, visiting China twice a year to perform surgeries on children from various provinces at no cost to the orphanages.

This compassionate doctor took the time to forward Xiao Gou's story and picture to the group and, astonishingly, she was approved. We arranged for her to go to Nanjing and, after many cancellations and obstacles, she finally made the trip and had the surgery. The team performed her operation free of charge and a benefactor paid for transportation, supplies, and *ayi* care while she was hospitalized.

Post-surgery, she contracted a painful infection around the incision and had to remain in the hospital for three weeks. On a cold and drizzling day, I arranged to visit her. When I arrived, my driver asked the security guard for directions and then acted as my guide, navigating us through the maze of floors and corridors in the hospital. After squeezing into several overcrowded elevators and trudging down innumerable bleak halls, we realized we were in the wrong building. At one point, an elevator had so many people pushing to squeeze in behind me that the alarm sounded. I felt a moment of panic, grabbed my driver's arm, and squeezed out through the crush of people. I would rather take four flights of stairs than chance crashing because of too much weight in the ancient lift.

As we left that building and entered the next, I thought about how lucky I am to be a native of a country that strives to offer clean and efficient medical facilities. The shabby, run-down hospital was utterly depressing; I couldn't imagine it being my only option for medical care. The walls and hallways were dark and dirty, and while many people wandered about, a scarcity of doctors or nurses made me wonder where they were hiding. The few I saw appeared to be exhausted and in poor spirits. Interestingly, the nurses wore nursing caps and dresses similar to the ones shown in old movies.

We finally found the designated building and, after asking for endless directions, arrived at Xiao Gou's room. She was happy to see me and produced a shy but adorable grin. Because everyone in the room was so curious to know who I was, they all crowded around and overwhelmed Xiao Gou. She then refused to talk to anyone, and the more they persisted pelting her with questions, the more she withdrew into herself.

The cramped room held six beds and six patients; all except Xiao Gou had several family members camped out around them. She was the only child and, judging by the way they acted protectively toward her, I believe she was their chosen mascot. One frail, grandfatherly man came over and tried to give her some chicken. It was obvious from their interaction he felt very protective of her.

Ultimately, the surgery was successful and she was returned to the orphanage for recovery. We arranged for a retired expatriate from Australia to demonstrate colostomy bag care to the *ayis* in charge of caring for Xiao Gou; however, it seemed they did not absorb the instructions very well. In the isolation room, she lay in a huge bed without television, books, or toys to pass the time. Her colostomy bag hung from a string over her bed to air out, leaving nothing to cover the opening in her abdomen. The staff didn't realize the bag was a disposable item until we urged them to throw it away. The *ayis* were relieved to see we had brought a new supply with us.

While the visiting Australian nurse explained the procedure to the young *ayis*, they grimaced each time they touched the colostomy bag. Listening to their histrionics, Xiao Gou hung her head in humiliation. After Elizabeth and I cheered her with some cartoon stickers and potato chips, we left to finish our shift in the baby room, still wondering what was to become of poor Xiao Gou.

* * *

When I returned to the orphanage this week, Xiao Gou had returned to her normal routine and sat quietly in the classroom. Her condition appeared much improved and she was clearly relieved to be away from the monotony of the isolation room. The next step is to continue reminding the staff to submit her dossier to the CCAA—what a long, twisted journey this little nymph has had. I sometimes wonder if pushing for her colostomy surgery was the right thing. A bag attached to one's body is not an easy thing to live with, but the alternative is for her to sit on the pot for hours each day to alleviate the *ayis'* work. This would be humiliating for anyone, but particularly for this spirited child who has captured the hearts of so many foreigners.

The dedicated foundation doctors who arranged and performed the colostomy surgery also want to help find Xiao Gou a family. I've never seen their faces, but I know this group is sincere, compassionate, and caring. Although they are busy, they still take their precious time to write, inquiring after Xiao Gou and guiding us along in her post-operation care.

* * *

OCTOBER 1, 2006

I've been in a grumpy mood all day, prowling around and accomplishing nothing. Heather turned sixteen today and I am disheartened that I can't be with her. During our summer visit home, I shopped for presents and left them with her grandmother. Since we couldn't give her a party, we included a gift card with which she could buy a new stereo. She's grown into a young woman in an incomprehensible flash. She is doing well in school and appears to have matured from her year overseas. Everyone had her attention on this important day except me, the one who spent twenty-two painful hours bringing her into the world all those years ago. I wish I could have given her a sweet sixteen party, or at least taken her out to make her day extra special. I am so sad that I cannot be there—I hope she knows how much I love her and wish to be with her.

* * *

OCTOBER 10, 2006

We've recently had updates on some of the children who were adopted. Le Men, our first little patient and now almost four years old, is thriving and happy in the U.S. One of a handful of siblings, he has a brother close to his own age who was also adopted from China.

After the first few weeks of getting Le Men settled were over and it was time for the other children to return to school, his new mom reported that he was upset when all the children boarded the bus and left him behind. As he wept, she explained to him that he would soon be joining them.

I can still recall holding him in my arms when he was only nine months old and urging him to fight for his life. After his surgery, he spent a few years in foster care; whenever he'd return to the orphanage for a health check he looked frightened, clinging to his foster mom tightly. He had been such a solemn, quiet child here in China, but from his appearance in photos of him with his new family, a more extroverted personality has emerged.

The orphanage social worker, Ji An, recently asked me about Le Men, telling me that his Chinese foster mom is still sad about him leaving her. She has declined to foster any more children because her heart is still aching over Le Men. I've written to Le Men's mother and asked her to provide a letter about him and a picture, so perhaps we can ease the sorrow for his devoted foster mom. It's good to know he was so loved while here in China.

Not all foster parents are ideal. From the information I can piece together, screening policies for fostering are very loose and many times the children are placed with questionable families.

Our little Le Bai, the boy with albinism, is now six years old and living in the New Jersey area. He bonded immediately with his new parents. He was calling them Mama and Baba as soon as he left the orphanage with them. In my eyes, it was definitely a suitable match. Recently, his mom wrote me an update that affected me deeply. She said:

> I have attached two pictures from the orphanage. Can you tell me if the cook/foster mother is the one wearing the blue shirt?
>
> Le Bai saw her and said she was *Zhongguo* (China) Mama. He said a lot of other things that make me want to go beat her up. This is the first time he talked about what happened in China.

I'm glad I already knew she wasn't a nice person and that many staff members are rough on the kids. Not that I wanted it to be true, but at least I wasn't blindsided when all this came pouring out. Le Bai is a typical little man in that he talks a lot but never gives much detail on anything, but last night he kept going on and on. It didn't all make sense to me—at first I wasn't sure if he was talking about his biological parents, his foster mother, or someone who worked at the institution.

He said he lived with *Zhongguo* Mama and *Zhongguo* Baba (he added the *Zhongguo*/China label to them, not me). He said he had an older sister (*jie jie*) and no brother.

He said, "*Zhongguo* Mama was no nice. *Zhongguo* Mama *da* (hit) Le Bai . . . *da* face and *da* tushy. *Zhongguo* Baba *da* Le Bai, too. *Jie Jie* not *da* Le Bai."

Then he stood with his face against the wall and said, "*Zhongguo* Mama *da* Le Bai and then Le Bai do this" [stands against the wall].

"If Le Bai no good, Le Bai no eat. Le Bai good, Le Bai eat."

He also acted out her cutting his fingers with scissors. He said he slept on the floor and did not have a bed. He said *Zhongguo* Baba was a truck driver. I only had one or two pictures with men in it from the institution. One is the director and the other I don't know. I showed them to Le Bai.

Le Bai said, "No, not *Zhongguo* Baba, because *Zhongguo* Baba not go there."

He doesn't have a word for the institution, but when we were looking at the pictures, he said that was not his home. I pretty much let him do the talking, just asked a few questions to try to get a feel for if what he was saying was true. I knew *he* thought it was true, but I was wondering if he possibly didn't know what really happened.

Already knowing that she didn't, I asked if Xiao Gou lived with *Zhongguo* Mama.

He said, "No, Xiao Gou live upstairs."

I asked if *Zhongguo* Mama wore pink.

"No, she wear blue." (So cute—he says baaa-loooo.) I was testing to see if possibly an *ayi* was the one abusing him, but the *ayis* wear pink and the cooks wear blue. Everything he was telling me fit with my knowledge of the institution.

I asked him if you ever "*da* Le Bai," knowing you never would, but again doing fact-checking.

He emphatically said, *"No,"* and added, "Ti Ti nice, *Zhongguo* Mama no nice."

I tell you, it was so hard. I wanted to cry but I was trying to keep a neutral tone of voice—I didn't want him shaping his answers to what he thought I was looking for. I think the worst part of it was he was saying it in such a matter-of-fact way, as if being treated that way were common.

He said I was a nice mommy and he wanted to stay here, not go back to China. This morning over Cheerios, he asked if he was going to school or back to China. That's the first time he has asked anything like that. All this has probably been on his mind, but I guess he didn't have the language to tell us before, or didn't have enough confidence in us. I guess it's good he was willing to tell us, but it's still so rotten he had anything like that to tell.

* * *

This is the hard thing about promoting foster care. Many of us had suspected the cook of treating the children roughly, but we had no proof of abuse. The way the children acted around her indicated they were frightened of her. I don't know what is best; questionable foster care or the certain desolation of the orphanage.

If I had known Le Bai was being abused by his foster family, I'd have been the first to demand he be pulled out. At least now, his adoptive parents are working hard to smother him with the love he lacked for the first five years of his life. How awful he must have felt sleeping on a cold floor or doing without food because he had supposedly misbehaved.

Sitting outside Starbucks this morning, I tried to explain to Ben about the letter and suspected abuse. Halfway through the story, with tears stinging my eyes, I simply couldn't go on. Ben didn't understand why it affected me so; this sort of abuse was mild compared with some things I've seen. Knowing Le Bai's heart and his affectionate personality, it was almost as though I'd learned one of my own children had been abused.

On a better note, I received an email from Lucy about Jia Jia. She is doing well and is thrilled that she never has to return to the orphanage. It is inspiring to receive pictures of these children in their new homes with their adoptive families. I study every detail: the expressions on their faces, the clothes they're wearing, and their surroundings. These are treasured gifts for me—they're the only way I know the hurdles we've overcome have been worth the struggles. To know these children are now loved and will never again have to experience the harsh, unfeeling atmosphere of an institution makes it worthwhile for us to continue fighting battles for other children.

These are only a few children we have cared for over the years who have gone on to find contentment with foreign families. I am grateful to all their new parents for going out of their comfort zones to adopt and love these children. Their reasons for adopting are not important; some adopt because they can't have children and others because they don't want to bring more children into the world when so many already need homes. Many reasons prompt international adoption and it makes no difference as long as the children are well taken care of and loved.

When surfing Web forums on the controversial practice of adopting foreign children, I read the asinine comments of people who post things like, "You should adopt from your own country," or "Why not spend the money to help children in your own backyard?"

I never respond to these irrational people. Don't they see? The birth country isn't the point at all. If they could see what I see, or hold one of these children in their arms for a minute, they'd realize that it doesn't matter what nationality these kids are or what country they come from—they just need a home.

39

OCTOBER 15, 2006

Often we're asked how long we plan to stay in China and how we are faring in this foreign land. It's been quite a journey, and we've all undergone great changes because of this experience. I have discovered positive aspects of a much more forceful personality than I knew I possessed. This trait emerged because what began as a desire to work with these needy children evolved into a passion.

Along with my new streak of stubbornness, I have also developed patience and tenacity. I will not take no for an answer when working on behalf of a helpless child. Years ago, I'd only go so far before backing down in the face of adversity. My experiences here have taught me not to give up.

I'll admit the traffic, crowds, unfamiliar food, and constant putrid odors will never cease to frustrate me. Another sore point is the hordes of beggars everywhere we go. Avoiding eye contact is a technique I've never mastered; I'm always the one digging for small change. Even so, I have learned to deal with the poverty and am thankful for the good things living here as an expat brings.

The living conditions for expatriates have greatly improved since our arrival a few years ago, making life not only pleasant but actually coveted by some. Several small stores carry various imported items of comfort food, though the price is sometimes double or triple what we'd pay in America.

With more Western restaurants to choose from, our weekends out are more enjoyable. Our social life is much more hectic than it was in the States; the expatriates spend a lot of time—sometimes too much time—with each other as a coping mechanism. But getting together and comparing views on the local culture is always interesting. Since there isn't a lot to do here for the kids, we also spend more time as a family just hanging out, taking walks, or cycling around the community.

I do more to focus on myself now. When I was a working mother in the U.S., my days were filled with work, carpooling, homework, cooking, and cleaning; all with the thought of blessed bedtime pushing me on to the daily finish line. It was an existence of exhaustion, with no time to sit back and contemplate whether my life was all I wanted it to be.

Here in China I've had the opportunity to follow my dreams: work with children, learn a new language, and embark on a writing career. I make time to enjoy an hour of music, a glass of wine, or a quiet walk alone to sift through my thoughts. It has been a time for me to reflect on all the ways my experiences here have enriched my life.

To broaden my knowledge, I have spent countless hours examining every available piece of information about Chinese abandonment of children—a difficult process because China has blocked most websites related to the subject. Only with creativity and tips from others have I been successful in obtaining data to delve into this issue.

Through my research, I've learned that traditional Chinese society blames the mother of a child who is physically disabled or born with deformities. It is still widely believed that birth defects are the direct result of the mother's activities during pregnancy. If the mother is able to obtain an ultrasound exam—they are illegal but not impossible to get here—and a problem is discovered, abortions or infanticide often occur. This is to avoid shame, public humiliation, and ostracism of the mother. Additionally, many children are abandoned after they are a few months or even years old because their problems or disabilities are not known until they have grown a measure.

In traditional Chinese culture, the wife is absorbed into the husband's family and is no longer a part of her own. The government strongly emphasizes having only one child, and male babies are coveted because they will carry on the family name. Keeping a girl child causes uncertainty and fear in parents who wonder who will care for them in their senior years. Frequently, for the sake of trying again for a boy, baby girls are abandoned.

* * *

NOVEMBER 1, 2006

Nine-year-old Dai An and her adoptive mother, Macy, will leave tomorrow for the U.S., and we threw a farewell party for them tonight. We've waited for this moment for a long time. Two years ago, Macy was still a volunteer here in Shengxi, when she was forced to return to the States for a personal medical emergency. Before she left, she promised the heartbroken Dai An she would come back for her.

Though Macy was told the adoption of a child with cerebral palsy would be impossible, she never gave up trying. Meanwhile, Dai An was having emotional problems because of the cruel warnings from her physical therapy teacher that if she didn't learn to walk, she'd never see Macy again. After many frustrating attempts at maneuvering around the orphanage halls, Dai An learned to get around with her walker. Fortunately, each day after her workout, she was allowed to go to a loving foster home.

At the farewell party tonight, what stood out most was the foster mother's anguish as she clutched Dai An's hand while softly telling her goodbye. With a stoic expression, the foster father stood protectively behind them. For him to attend the foreign party was proof of how much he cares for Dai An.

The foster mother worked with a translator to tell Macy what kind of foods Dai An was fond of and that she didn't like milk. During the discussion the foster mother would walk away to dry her tears every few minutes. Dai An was very quiet and overwhelmed with all that was going on—she likely did not understand the scope of what was about to happen.

Diverting some of Dai An's attention away from the heavy emotional atmosphere was the money tree to which people had been clipping donations of renminbi and dollars. All the donations were to be used to launch Dai An into a successful new life. I saw the foster father eyeing it and wondered what he thought of such generosity from foreign people to a Chinese child. He was probably questioning where we all had been for the past year when he was struggling to support his foster daughter. I'm not sure why, but the longer he stared at the tree, the more embarrassed I felt. It was useless to explain that Macy was a single parent and all that implied financially; it would have alarmed him even more.

Sitting close enough to Dai An to drape my arm around her, I whispered that she was going to be very happy in America with her forever mom. With my hand on the foster mother's knee, I asked the translator to tell her she had done a wonderful job taking care of Dai An and preparing her for the next phase in her life. Struggling to find comforting words, I realized nothing I could say would make this any easier for her. I put on my coat and bid them all a teary goodbye.

Outside, as I trudged along the busy street to find a taxi, I alternated between joy for Macy and her new daughter and sad-

ness for the foster parents who would return to a home void of Dai
An's infectious smile.

* * *

Our volunteer group has grown at a phenomenal rate. Every
morning time slot and all but two in the afternoon are filled with
volunteers from all over the world.

It wasn't so long ago that Regina and I dreamed of the day that
we could entice more women to be part of our team. When God
began sending them, they just kept coming! Since we are only
permitted four women per shift, we now have a waiting list of
interested volunteers. With ongoing donations, we keep the baby
room stocked with diapers and other supplies needed to make
running a nursery easier.

This orphanage has changed considerably over the years. It
has gone from being a dark and depressing institution to an often
cheerful children's home. The crisp white cribs are a big improvement over the old, rusty baby cradles that had been used for so
many years. The new sky-blue curtains hanging in the nursery
add pizzazz to the dirty concrete walls. The donated plastic chairs
and tables are safe and comfortable for the mentally challenged
children's room, where the residents have to stay for every hour
of every day.

The painted hallways make a great difference over their previous bleak incarnation. Thanks to many donations, the babies are
now more comfortable and dry in disposable diapers. The stimulation and attention they receive has changed personalities from
silent and vacant to joyful and rambunctious.

During our volunteer time, we strive to make the workload
lighter for the *ayis*; in turn, this makes life much easier for the
babies. The *ayis* are happier and have more time to give each child

individual attention. It is remarkable how people can change by the examples of others. Perhaps they wanted to be this way long ago, but were so overloaded with their duties that it wasn't possible.

It is now rare to see any outright abuse and more common to see workers who genuinely care for the children. This week there was a little tension after one of the toddlers was found in the pit of colored balls at nap time. The volunteers were blamed for leaving him unattended, but they denied doing such an irresponsible thing. The *ayis* were hostile for the next few days, but that soon passed. In the meantime, we discovered that the boy in question has learned to push a stool to the pit and dive in. We assume this is what he did when we found him there, but no one witnessed it. It wasn't until all the children were put down for naps that he was even discovered missing, with just an arm and leg poking from the colorful balls indicating his whereabouts. He wasn't hurt but had become sleepy and was content to be put down for his nap.

Another positive change—we are now allowed to feed all the babies in both rooms. Some children still appear to be wasting away from malnutrition, but we are not prevented from attempting to feed them. Many of these children have problems that keep them from taking in nutrition, no matter the efforts of any caregiver.

Four years ago, there wasn't enough food to go around and the babies shared bottles. Now every baby gets a bottle and every toddler a bowl of rice. Perhaps this is because we have supported the medical needs and many other wished-for items for the past couple of years, so more money is available to spend on food.

Our volunteer from New Zealand, Alex, teaches basic English to the small group of children who don't attend school. With help from his wife and other volunteers, he also treats the group to occasional field trips to the park or the video-game room located in our neighborhood center. When I hand out my snacks, it's amusing to hear the children say, "Thank you very much," or if I ask them, "How are you?" they return with "I'm fine, and you?" They know all the letters of the alphabet, as well as the names of colors. Alex has taught them to say, "I love chocolate." He makes learning a fun experience for the children, and they thoroughly enjoy the class.

Another volunteer, a nurse from America, is putting together material to give workshops for the *ayis*. These will consist of several sessions during which they'll learn basic hygiene and disease control measures like hand-washing and utensil care. We have found another foreign nurse who's fluent in Chinese and English and who will assist the American nurse when the material is ready to present.

Our surgery fund is building every week and we continue to fight the system to get the babies into the hospital for urgent care. This week I held a tiny infant girl named Xin Xin in my arms. Her forehead beaded with perspiration, she struggled to breathe while gazing into my eyes. She is suffering from a congenital heart defect and we are encouraging the orphanage to find a doctor who can perform the delicate necessary surgery. In the past few weeks, Xin Xin has had to be stabilized in three different hospitals, while the orphanage directors take their time deciding how to proceed. The funding is already secured, but if what the director says is true, each hospital has declined to move forward with her case. I find this utterly baffling.

Baby boy Xu Yang died of a heart problem last week. I held him six days before his death while he was in the ICU of the children's hospital. The doctor told Ben and me that Xu Yang was improving and might possibly be ready for surgery the next week. When he unexpectedly died, we became more aggressive in pushing for Xin Xin's operation to happen. We have spent a huge amount of time since then on the phone each day making inquiries.

Continuing donations have financed numerous operations and procedures. We regularly receive financial support from the local Happy Fund as well as from various individuals overseas who hear of our work. We are currently working on finding funding to buy the orphanage a much-needed van. It will cost thousands of dollars, but if we can satisfy the administration by fulfilling some of their wishes for better equipment, clothing, and transportation, they will reward us by allowing us more flexibility with the children.

Another ongoing project is our work with an overseas group to buy a six-year-old boy named Xu Cao an expensive hearing aid. I've emailed the group his picture and details of his handicap. I hope to hear soon if they will approve the donation. So many children have needs like these, and new ones develop every month.

I have been told that the institution does not turn away any orphaned children, which helps keep the already high number of street children down. Evidently, the Chinese government is making a concerted attempt to change its reputation regarding its child welfare systems. It has implemented many new programs and projects to assist orphaned children. However, it will probably take years before these projects are successfully implemented in the smaller orphanages in cities like this one that do not receive international attention.

With enough effort, China is capable of succeeding in turning its welfare systems around. I have seen the intriguing Terracotta Warriors in Xi'an and climbed the famous Great Wall; these people can do nearly impossible things when they set their minds to it. We need to strive to support them with advice and leadership.

They've made many strides but issues remain, as they do with similar institutions throughout the third world. Comparing where we were with where we are now, the improvements are too many to number. Looking back over the almost four years we've spent in China, I know this experience has changed me profoundly.

I am thankful to have had the chance to come here and take on this challenge; I feel I have matured into the woman God intended me to be. I'm no longer the weak and helpless creature who arrived and immediately wilted from culture shock; I'm now strong and stand tall for what I believe in, no matter how difficult it may be.

I've met amazing women who have joined my volunteer group and helped to lead it to success. What began as a personal mission has become a group effort of many people of multiple nationalities who have joined to help change the lives of these children.

Faces of babies who have left us are stashed permanently in the corners of my memory. Sad eyes that my own have shed tears over are embedded in my soul forever. Every child who has passed on took with them a piece of the old me to make room for the new me to grow. Facing these images is only possible with the faith that God has taken each child in His arms and comforted them as they left this earth. For years I thought of the orphanage babies as the Forgotten Children of China, but I know now that this is not so. We have been brought here to ensure these children will know love and that they have meaning in this world. When they are grown and out on their own, I hope some of what they learned from us will stay in their hearts and encourage them to make a difference in the lives of the future children of China.

* * *

NOVEMBER 21, 2006

Xin Xin died last week. Those five words are easy to write but look shocking to me on paper. I was not surprised by her death, only angry and depressed at the ineptitude and carelessness that resulted in the end of this child's life. Only two weeks before, she had been admitted to the local hospital and the surgeon finally attempted to repair her heart damage. After her chest was opened, she went into cardiac arrest and the doctors had to abort the surgery. She was sewn up and then stabilized after four days in the intensive care unit.

One of our volunteers who had worked in pediatrics in the U.S. was outraged that this child was opened up and subjected to invasive procedures before the doctors had a plan or had completed enough testing. After many meetings with the attending physician, we insisted Xin Xin should not return to the orphanage, but instead be transferred to the better hospital in Beijing. The doctor agreed with this, and a few days later, we came to the local hospital to pick her up and transport her to Beijing.

Director Fu, Ji An, and the *ayi* holding Xin Xin climbed into my van for the long ride to the children's hospital. Xin Xin struggled to breathe but she never cried. She was such an adorable girl, frequently giving me the "bye-bye" wave and looking at me with her dark eyes. Her name means "little heart," and it was a constant reminder of the burden she had to bear.

Not surprisingly, the *ayi* had overdressed Xin Xin in too many layers, which caused a film of sweat to break over her entire head. It's common in China for the babies to be dressed in multiple layers, something I still fail to comprehend. We couldn't really blame the *ayi*; she was only a poor woman from the countryside the orphanage had hired to care for Xin Xin. She was doing what she had learned to do from early childhood. She was having a difficult time herself, immediately becoming nauseated from the unfamiliar ride in a vehicle. Most people of her class use bicycles for transportation; for long distances they take a city bus.

Halfway there, after continuously wiping perspiration from Xin Xin's head, I insisted that the *ayi* remove a sweater and one blanket to reduce the little girl's efforts at breathing.

In Beijing, after a round of the usual red tape and chaos, we met with the chief director of cardiology. He examined Xin Xin's X-rays, confirmed she had a very complicated heart problem, and determined he would need to meet with his team to decide how to proceed. Alarmingly, he did not have a bed available in his ward; instead, Xin Xin would have to go on a waiting list.

I told him how Xin Xin had been rushed to the hospital in Shengxi several times in respiratory distress. We did not want her returned to the orphanage, fearing she would not survive there. After some convincing, the doctor asked us to wait while he would see what he could do, and much to our relief, he came back with the news he could admit her. We settled her with the *ayi* and left with the plan that in a few days we would have another meeting to discuss her surgery.

I felt confident Xin Xin was in competent hands and would finally receive adequate medical care. On our way out, we repeatedly expressed gratitude to the doctor for pulling the strings to get her in.

Three days later, the orphanage director called me with the upsetting news that the Beijing hospital was going to discharge Xin Xin because of a rash on her body. Until it cleared up, she could not be considered for the delicate heart surgery. This made no sense, so I frantically called around to get a proper English translation of the ailment. Why couldn't she stay in the hospital where they could treat the rash? Why did they want to discharge her knowing how dangerous it was for her to be without constant medical supervision?

I received no answers to these questions but instead had a feeling of déjà vu. So often we finally reach the point where we think we have accomplished something positive for a child, just to have it fall apart for inexplicable reasons. They knew we were paying for the expenses, so finances should not have played a part in the decision to discharge Xin Xin.

That evening, calls flew back and forth between the director, my translator, and me. I insisted Xin Xin would not be safe at the orphanage with her current problems. The director finally agreed that Ji An would take Xin Xin and the *ayi* home with her. This wasn't ideal either, but was better than placing her back in the understaffed orphanage nursery. Then, after two days at Ji An's apartment, the *ayi* moved Xin Xin to her home. We were not happy with this arrangement at all, considering the delicate state of Xin Xin's heart.

For several days, we received reports of the improvement of her skin rash. We continued to inquire about her so the staff would understand that we were not backing down about returning her to Beijing for the surgery.

Tragically, after four days in the home of the *ayi*, Xin Xin fell into acute distress once again and was taken to the local hospital, where she was pronounced dead.

When my translator called to tell me the news, it was as if all my breath had been sucked out of me. The wave of numbing sadness was quickly replaced by a pent-up fury that I'd kept contained for some time.

To my translator I spoke the words no one likes to hear: "I *told* you so."

She stayed quiet on the line.

"I *told* you they would keep sending her around until it was too late to help her—and then she'd die." All at once, I was drained of all energy and emotion.

In my heart, I had known this would happen. Perhaps it was Xin Xin's destiny to die, but I truly believe she was not given a fair chance. With all the orphanage's accomplishments over the past few years, the staff still has not reached the place where they value every human life placed in their care. The children who will receive a future are hand-picked based on their beauty, gender, or lack of physical or mental handicaps. This child should have had the same chance at life as our own children are so freely given. It is a horrible injustice that she was neglected because she was an orphan and a girl with a heart problem.

Director Fu tried to offer consolation by telling us we were allowed to supply the clothes Xin Xin would be cremated in, but this did not placate me at all. I wanted to hold her small body close to mine and make her feel as though she mattered. I wanted to let her know that someone would grieve for her, that her life was important to me and to the other volunteers.

Thoughts of her last minutes have played over and over in my mind until they've made me ill. How long had the *ayi* waited before she could get the distressed Xin Xin to the hospital? Perhaps the *ayi* hadn't had the taxi fare? Had she consoled Xin Xin as her frail heart was giving up? Had the *ayi* shed a single tear? Had Xin Xin felt alone as she left this world? The vision of her petite body lying on a cold slab in the hospital has haunted me for the past few nights. Why could they not have left her in the hospital to recover from the skin problem? They'd known how delicate she was!

Sifting through memories, reflecting on the children who have lost their lives in the past few years, I know without a doubt that many of the deaths could have been prevented.

Last week, I told Amanda I was going back to the hospital to visit Xin Xin. She hugged me tightly and whispered, "Okay, Mama, but please don't come home sad again." With her words, suddenly I knew I had deceived myself all along by imagining I'd been successful in hiding my feelings from her. My anguish was so clearly reflected in my own child's eyes.

What memories am I giving my daughter of our time in China? Will she remember the fun, the new experiences we had, and the things she learned, or will she dwell only on the times her mother was frustrated and grief-stricken? I hope the positive experiences will outweigh the negative in her mind, and I pray that my courage and not my sorrow will be remembered.

* * *

Yesterday I received another blow to add to my despondent mood. It came by way of a brief email telling me the adoption process for Xiao Gou has been dropped. Her parents will not relinquish their rights because of the ongoing lawsuit against the driver who struck and maimed their daughter. This means the orphanage does not have legal guardianship of her; therefore, she cannot be considered for adoption.

This was bewildering because months ago the orphanage said they had petitioned the government for guardianship and it was approved. I saw the required newspaper advertisement of a plea to the parents to come forward if they were opposed to Xiao Gou's being considered for international adoption. Now the orphanage people are saying they never applied for guardianship and did not run the mandatory newspaper advertisement.

Because of her situation, Xiao Gou's parents had abandoned her. Yet they will not relinquish guardianship because they want to win a lawsuit, ostensibly on their daughter's behalf.

It wasn't easy getting approval for the operation to cure the life-threatening infection that raged in Xiao Gou's body, nor did the orphanage's directors easily comply with the colostomy surgery requests. Pushing for the orphanage to appeal for guardianship so that we could get Xiao Gou's adoption dossier to Beijing was supposed to be our final gift to her. After all this, I'm informed we are back at the beginning with no hopes of ever having her live anywhere but the institution; that she'll never have a family to witness what a remarkable little spirit she is. How can the government be so heartless?

After making a few frantic phone calls and sending emails, I was told nothing further could be done for Xiao Gou. With the finality of those words, my life changed course.

It has been a difficult decision, but it's wrong for me to continue leading this group with the cynical attitude that has overtaken me of late. Witnessing children suffering needlessly and silently tolerating the bureaucratic obstacles for every small goal we want to accomplish has taken its toll. Walking away will be difficult, but my family deserves to see more of the joyful me they knew before I was altered by this endeavor. Memories of cleft palates, twisted limbs, and innocent eyes will follow me the rest of my life. The children I've nurtured, the tragedies I've seen, and the emotions I've felt over the past four years will never be forgotten; they have shaped me into the more compassionate, patient, and mature woman I am today, albeit more jaded and realistic.

I resigned my position.

Epilogue

JULY 2009

I have been back in the States long enough now to experience two summers and a winter. My life has changed drastically since I left China. With trepidation, I have rejoined the frantic pace of American life that I had gladly left behind so many years ago.

I noticed a peculiar pattern upon my return. Friends and family frequently ask about my time in China, but I don't believe they really want to hear the truth. In the beginning, I would tell them about things I witnessed in the orphanage, about the babies and what they meant to me. Soon I realized the bored expressions and glazed-over eyes meant they expected the response to be, "Everything is fine." They didn't want details of anything unpleasant that might make them *uncomfortable*.

I decided it was better for me to leave my memories of China behind—I felt like no one really wanted to know. I did my best to move on with my life. Unfortunately, the more I fought to push away the thoughts of the children, the more I was plagued by flashbacks, dreams, and haunting dark eyes. I missed the children and China so desperately—no matter what I doing, part of me was always thinking about the orphans or the life I had left behind. In the winter, I worried they were too cold or didn't have enough socks. In the summer, I worried about their heat rashes and thought about the mosquitoes that were most likely plaguing them. In the streets or stores it only took a small child with dark hair to bring the memories flooding back. My family repeatedly told me I had changed—that I was more serious and they missed the old me. It is accurate to say that I was grieving for China. It took some deep searching, but I soon realized I was wrong to avoid the truth. Just because someone refuses to hear about things that need changing, it doesn't make them cease to exist. The children's stories deserve to be told, and despite the sadness I experience with each memory, I want to spend my life finding ways to speak for the children—to speak for those who cannot speak for themselves.

It took me a year at home to come to that moment of realization and to stop trying to force myself to forget. Since then, I have plowed forward and never looked back. Keeping my promise, I published *Silent Tears*. By building relationships with readers of my book, I continue to advocate for the children of China. And I found out another interesting tidbit about myself—that despite my daily exhaustion of juggling two worlds, my passion is ignited when I am advocating for those who have no voice. Each time I gain a sponsor to rescue a child from the orphanage and place them in foster care, I feel a burst of energy and a fleeting moment of satisfaction. This is what I am meant to do, I know that for certain. And on this side of the ocean it is very liberating that I can write what I want and not have it blocked, censored, or banned— so I use that freedom to bring together people who want to help, and connect them with children who need the outreached hand. I spend every spare moment and use every avenue available to raise awareness about the travesty of institutional care for children.

I am not suggesting all Chinese orphanages are abusive or lacking in professionalism. My story is based on what I observed myself. Others who have experience in this field have told me that efficient and nurturing orphanages *do* exist, and I know some

Chinese welfare professionals genuinely care for the children, even at the institution where I volunteered.

Through the many exchanges, I found a few of the directors of the institution to be largely compassionate people. They obviously have difficulties trying to please both sides. On one hand, they work to give the children a better life; on the other, they are severely hampered by stringent restrictions, low budgets, and endless outdated and ridiculous laws. They're often unaware of much of the neglect, as they do not spend much time in the children's quarters, and when they do, the workers are on their best behavior.

I admit I find offense in the false show the administration puts on for the media and for visiting adoptive parents. Before outsiders are allowed in for a tour, the children are bathed and dressed in fresh clothing. Rooms are thoroughly cleaned and flowers set out around the courtyard, making the usually gray surroundings appear more cheerful. Toys are brought in and the older children placed in the most up-to-date and well-equipped classroom, where they are treated to a rare few hours of music and games—all an ostentatious production to make the orphanage appear as though the children live in a world of structured learning, developmental encouragement, and nurturing attention.

Despite the constructed facade of normalcy, the administration deserves some credit for progress made in the quality of life for some of the children. They made renovations to brighten the surroundings, and our recommendation to switch to disposable diapers was accepted—no more pieces of cloth secured by strips of sheets means fewer wet bottoms and painful rashes.

Most important was the gift of trust—which was given each time they allowed my team of volunteers to work closely alongside their staff. Upon our arrival we could see the children's eyes brighten and feel their anticipation of a break in their usual monotonous existence, even if only for a few hours. And because we were allowed to intervene and provide needed medical care in critical situations, many lives were improved and sometimes even saved.

Even though I am no longer a part of the team, the volunteers have continued on with new leadership and are still making positive changes for the children and staff. The last time I received an update, the directors were allowing even more time with the children.

My hope is that my story will inspire people to reach out to children in institutional care and also be used as an educational tool to create awareness among future adoptive parents on possible post-institutional issues. Following is an email from an adoptive mother concerning her daughter's condition on Gotcha Day:

> Hi. We were in China for two weeks around the end of October. We were in Guangzhou the entire time, except for three days in Beijing. Many adoptive families were touring around, so thankfully we didn't experience the curious stares we had heard so much about. Our daughter did not smile for a couple days after we received her. She looked at us as if to say, "Who on earth are you?" In fact, she would not eat for five days. Most of our group found our daughters were not described very accurately in the referral information we received. They told us our daughter easily cruised around using furniture. Not quite so: the poor baby had very little muscle in her legs and could not even crawl, much less stand or walk. She finally warmed up to us and is doing very well now, jumping and running at high speed all day!

For parents who have long awaited the day their child is placed in their arms, they can think of nothing but a joyful and satisfying experience. Often the parents are shocked to find that their children's developmental skills are far behind those of other children in the same age group. When I first started in the orphanage, most of the babies were not accustomed to doing anything except lying in a bed all day, which resulted in serious muscle atrophy.

Some adoptive parents are bewildered by the children's grief at parting with the orphanage *ayis* or their foster parents. If the child is older, he or she may hide toys or hoard food, because that is what they'd do in the orphanage if given the chance. In extreme cases, some adoptees act out in anger, are violent, or appear totally detached. Many times they suffer from night terrors because of their tumultuous early months or years.

These kinds of behaviors need to be approached with patience and a positive, comforting attitude; this will reassure the child that he or she will be taken care of every moment of every day. Many children will have emotional issues to work through that may require counseling.

Yet sometimes these issues do not arise. Since the release of *Silent Tears,* I've received hundreds of heartwarming stories of children who were fine once united with their forever families.

If your adopted child is obviously traumatized or hurting, do not lose hope. A child who appears fragile, withdrawn, or listless during the first few days or months after Gotcha Day, can, with lots of unconditional love, bloom into an outgoing, stable child. Patience, affection, and understanding during those first few months (and sometimes years) can work miracles.

I have seen the marvel that love can provide. I saw it in Xiao Gou when I took on the responsibility of advocating for her. After my departure from China, it was finally arranged for Xiao Gou to travel to America to be fitted for a prosthetic leg. While there, the owner of the company that was creating the leg met Xiao Gou and instantly made a connection with her. After spending time with Xiao Gou, he and his family decided they wanted to adopt her and entered into the treacherous waters of her case.

Way past the medical-visa return date, Xiao Gou was forced to return to China. At first the directors gave the family the same false hope they had repeatedly given me. After a year of stringing them along, the directors finally declared that adoption for Xiao Gou was not possible.

Our next step in the endeavor to get Xiao Gou placed with a family was to involve a Chinese businessman, who promised to do what he could to help us work through the complicated legal constraints holding Xiao Gou prisoner. After several months of correspondence and phone calls between him, his legal consultant, and the orphanage directors, he was also unsuccessful in helping us change her status.

Not long after that, Lily, my Mandarin tutor and good friend, emailed me an article about Xiao Gou that was published in China. It said she had started school, where she endured teasing about her colostomy bag and leg. Her classmates even repeatedly tried to follow her into the bathroom to see how it all worked!

Despite years of obstacles, I was still not ready to give up on Xiao Gou. I didn't understand why she could not be adopted if her parents did not want her. So I engaged Lily to do some investigative work on my behalf. She and I made a plan; with her aspiring journalistic skills she was the perfect one to pull it off.

Lily and her coworker, who pretended to be her husband, made a trip to the orphanage to inquire about adopting a child. At first they were treated very well—served green tea and fruit while the director assessed their intentions. They were taken to stroll through the halls and look into the windows of the various children's rooms. Lily, furtively searching for Xiao Gou, finally asked, "Can we meet the child who was depicted on the news—the one named Xiao Gou who has only one leg?"

The director's warm welcome suddenly turned icy cold. She informed Lily that Xiao Gou was not able to be adopted. The tour was quickly ended and Lily departed with no more information than she went in with. The next week, I emailed Xiao Gou's original finding notice to Lily. Starting at the hospital where Xiao Gou was taken after her accident, Lily began another investigation to find the parents.

At the police station, she was lucky to discover that, because of the media attention, Xiao Gou was well remembered by the officers. Lily was pleased when they recommended her to the police station in another town, where the original accident reports were filed. I hoped this new information would finally lead to Xiao Gou's parents and the possibility of reuniting them with their child.

Pushed on by promises from me to make it worth her while, Lily continued to play spy girl. The next week she hopped a train to the city where Xiao Gou's parents were thought to reside. At the police station there, she was told the parents did indeed live nearby and knew their daughter's circumstances. Lily pleaded for their names, but was told to leave and not return. When she explained Xiao Gou could be adopted if her parents would relinquish their rights, she was told the parents would never do that—a mind-boggling answer that probably has to do with the parents' expectation of compensation for the damage done to their daughter.

At that point, we all admitted defeat—until I received an email from a couple who had read my story. They were interested in Xiao Gou and wanted to inquire about possibly adopting her. I explained to them all that had happened, and they said they just might be able to get help from a very prominent political figure.

With the thought we might have a chance due to the importance of their colleague, I asked someone to call the orphanage to inquire about Xiao Gou's status. They were told that Xiao Gou was no longer in the care of the institute. After a few more weeks, I reached out via email to the director of the orphanage. She replied, "Xiao Gou's aunt came for her months ago and we have not seen her again." I wrote back, asking for the name of the town but received no response.

I would have loved to believe that this latest tale was true and that Xiao Gou is indeed living happily ever after with someone who loves her and can appreciate how special she is. However, the part of me that was introduced to the many definitions of corruption and neglect relentlessly whispered that they may have concocted the story to stop all further inquiries about Xiao Gou and the possibility of her adoption. After many sleepless nights, I again contacted Lily and asked her to resume her investigation.

After making several calls to the orphanage, Lily was not able to obtain any more information than we already had. She turned to the Internet and, after a few days of research, found an online article from a hospital newsletter that mentioned a girl matching the description of Xiao Gou. In the article, it was written that the child had come to the new city with her aunt, who had rescued her from years spent in the orphanage in Shengxi. After only three months with her aunt, the child had been in an accident and was brought to the hospital where she spent weeks in the intensive care department. Lily felt sure, from the details given about the girl, that the resemblance to Xiao Gou was too close to be coincidental, even though the hospital was located far from Shengxi.

Lily immediately called the hospital, but the child mentioned in the article had been discharged months before. Lily asked for the ICU department and, after speaking to several staff members, was finally transferred to a doctor who remembered the girl. He informed Lily that the girl (who had been renamed by her aunt) had been abandoned at the hospital and upon her recovery was released to the local orphanage.

Lily called the orphanage and, based on information given by the director, felt strongly that she had found Xiao Gou. She was told Xiao Gou was doing well but had outgrown her prosthetic leg. The director mentioned that Xiao Gou was very clever and a great student. She also informed Lucy that Xiao Gou's grandparents live nearby and make frequent visits to check on their granddaughter. I had emphasized to Lily not to mention the involvement of foreigners, so Lily told her that Xiao Gou was something of a celebrity in her hometown and asked if she could visit her. She was told the request would have to go through an approval process.

Given the circumstances of Xiao Gou's situation and second abandonment, I began making calls to those who had been involved in her life. With the emails and calls circulating, I was contacted by the founder of an organization that had sponsored one of her surgeries. With the information I provided her, she has now started the process of requesting Xiao Gou once again come to the States on a medical visa in order to be examined and fitted for a new leg. As for the possibility of adopting her, our first desire would be to make it possible for her family to care for her, but if that isn't an option there are currently three families (including ours) who would love to welcome her home. While the chances of Xiao Gou finally being free of institutional life seem slim, we will not give up on her.

* * *

Please visit me at
WWW.KAYBRATT.COM
for ways you can help raise awareness for
children in institutional care.

Letters to Kay

Dear Kay,

I am happy to have had the opportunity to meet you at the conference and felt a connection when you spoke about your passion for China's orphans. Over the past four years, my husband, Clay, and I have experienced two adoptions from China. We adopted Sophie May in December 2005 at the age of ten months, and our son, Garrett, in May 2007, at the age of eight years. Both adoptions were completely ordained and orchestrated by the hand of God, but at the same time, both adoptions left us with many questions surrounding behavioral issues in both of these children's lives.

The day I received *Silent Tears* in the mail, I couldn't put it down. So much of what Clay and I were experiencing was being backed up right on the very pages of your book. One moment of clarity came as I read the passage about how the babies there are fed their bottles. As we were sitting in the meeting room, holding our baby girl for the first time, one of the orphanage workers poured very hot water in her bottle to mix with her formula. As she handed the bottle to me, I was afraid to give it to our new daughter because it was so hot to the touch. As Sophie May cried loudly for the bottle, the worker forced it from my hand to her mouth. To my amazement, she gulped the mixture down in less than two minutes. She didn't seem fazed by the hot water, and my family stood there wondering if it was okay for her to take it that quickly. How heart-wrenching to think that our baby girl was afraid her bottle might be taken away if she didn't drink it quickly enough.

A few years later, as we stand on the other side of the ocean, holding this gift from God wrapped in the form of a little, precious brown-eyed girl, I can't help but think of the thousands of others who are still living that sad reality on a daily basis.

Thank you for capturing the culture, rituals, and daily life of many orphans and of the workers in your specific orphanage. And while I sensed the frustration in your words at times, I have to commend you for loving the people you came in contact with, with the love of Christ. You didn't go in as a boisterous American, bent on changing their ways. Instead you went in to serve the people and the orphans of China. What an extraordinary difference you made in the lives of so many!

Whether people are planning to adopt or not, *Silent Tears* will be an inspiration. At the end of the day, most of us can sit down in our comfortable homes with our families and enjoy the life we lead. Oh, if only our eyes could be opened to the suffering of so many helpless children across the world. There is much we can do! As I saw these children through your eyes, Kay, I visualized you holding a baby and whispering words of encouragement and love into their ears.

Renee Crosse is a wife, mother, author, and speaker with HolyHomes Ministries (holyhomes.org). Her husband is Christian recording artist, author, and speaker Clay Crosse. They have been married since 1990 and reside in Tennessee with their four children.

Dear Kay,

Hello to you once again. Now it's my turn to cry! I have gone through all of your emails and looked at all the pictures, and, yes, Yue Hua is indeed my Ruthie. Her name is now Ruth Elizabeth, and she was named by my husband after the biblical Ruth.

We considered the name appropriate since Ruth Elizabeth was adopted into a group that stated, "Your people will be my people, and your God will be my God." This has always been our prayer for Ruthie, and I have loved her from the first time I saw her picture.

Ruthie is still a quiet and shy little girl, and I have always felt like she had a history that extended beyond her years. I'm not even sure what I mean by that, other than to say there is a lot, including much sadness, which we will never be able to share with her.

She is an incredible little girl, and I can't tell you enough how much she means to us. She was the answer to many prayers and came to us at a time of great sadness in our lives. To say we needed each other is an understatement! We were ready to help a child in need, and she was ready to be taken in by a family. She adores our third son, who is now sixteen and our only "original" child still living at home.

Your note about sharing the toys is very interesting because we are seeing much of the same behavior with the addition of our second adopted daughter, Abby. Ruthie is having a hard time with the sharing of time, toys, love, etc., and now I am beginning to get more of a picture as to why. You would be welcome to visit her at any time. I cannot thank you enough for the love you showed her while she was an orphaned child.

Not all of the questions related to Ruthie speaking Chinese can be answered. From the time we got her, she never spoke another word of Chinese. In fact, she had a way of looking into space when others spoke to her, as if to say she didn't understand anything.

Initially, she was so very angry. She was angry with the workers who were leaving her with us, and she was angry with me for just being there. She was the least angry with my husband. Something about him intrigued her, and for the first three or four days, he was the only one she wanted to hold her. Even saying that, she was still very angry and tended to suddenly pinch him or pull on his beard. For such a little thing, she went out of her way to be downright hateful and let us know that she had very little use for us.

We returned to the orphanage to see the facility the day after we got her, and they asked that Ruthie wait in the secretarial offices with the personnel. We met the little girl whom you named as her best/worst friend, and we watched the "doctor" tease Ruthie in a way that just about broke our hearts. We had brought some toys and children's clothing donated by our church, and she wanted a small stuffed animal very badly. They were incredibly cruel in the way they gave it to her, then jerked it away and dangled it over the railing. They kept telling her that she had to go home with us or she would not get the toy. By the time we left, she was crying and terrified of us. We wondered even then what may have been done to Yue Hua.

We were united on a Monday, I believe, and we stayed in Nanjing through Friday. On the Saturday morning that we flew to Guangzhou, something changed in this child's heart. She suddenly let me hold her hand and show her things. We walked back

and forth in the small airport, looking out the windows and pointing at things. She was very quiet, but kept watching me and holding my hand. I was afraid that it would not last, but it did.

Everything was very slow going, and my husband and I did
not push for much. Little by little, Ruthie acted as though she
really wanted to be with us. I should mention that other than the
initial crying not to be left with us, she did not cry again. The
early pictures we have of her show so much sadness in her eyes
that they just about break my heart. We adopted her in July, and
frankly, the majority of her pictures look very sad through much
of November or so.

She met her new brother at the airport and was fascinated by
him from the very beginning. He is small for his age, and I think
that helped. We wondered how he would do with her, but we
should never have worried. He became her friend and protector
and has remained such to this day. He spent hours teaching her
words and getting her to speak with various accents.

She especially sounded funny saying, "What's up, mate?" with
an Aussie accent. She will do anything for him!

One time, about eight or nine months after she had been with
us, we went to an adoption gathering. A couple from Taiwan were
fascinated by Ruthie. Once again, she pretended she could not
understand Chinese and took no apparent interest in them. Finally,
they said something that made her look up with shock and horror,
and she ran behind my husband Bob's legs and grabbed hold of
him. The couple said that they had told her that she was very pretty
and asked if she would like to go home with them. This indicated
to us that she understood quite well but refused to acknowledge.

We had a similar experience when we were in a furniture
store and noticed a young Chinese couple. They began to talk to
us, and through the conversation, we learned they were originally
from China. The young woman's mother walked up and began to
talk with the girls. Abby chatted back excitedly, but Ruthie took

on that vacant look and actually turned her head. (She normally is very nosy and quite interested in listening to what is being said.)

Ruthie quit eating Chinese food right after we returned home. She will pick at it if she has to, but she has decided that it is not her favorite. Actually, she likes anything with pasta, and thinks Mexican food is to die for!

Back to her language skills: I talked to Ruthie and sang to her from the very beginning, and she just seemed to know what I was saying. Her English is still a bit of a struggle, and some sounds, such as hard Ks, are very difficult for her. Even still, most people understand her if they try. She loves music, and she requests that the radio be turned to a Christian FM station that she likes, when she takes naps, etc. When Sam (son No. 2) came home to visit from Fort Bragg, she became very interested in his piano playing. He is in the band at Fort Bragg and plays both trumpet and piano—he allowed her to sit at the piano bench, where she was engrossed in the songs he played.

Soon after Ruthie came home, we set up an appointment with the local children's hospital for her spina bifida. We took her in August, and she began acting very mean while we were in the waiting room, not at all like the sweet little girl we were beginning to see. We were very surprised. Ruthie was back to pinching, slapping, etc.

After the appointment, she just stood there glaring at us. We said, "Come on, Ruthie, let's go." She instantly grabbed our hands, smiled, and transformed again. I honestly believe that the sterile environment of the hospital reminded her of the orphanage, and she thought we were going to leave her there. She just clung to our hands and smiled as we walked around downtown, window-shopping.

The neurosurgeon wanted to perform her surgery as soon as possible, as he has seen huge growth spurts in adopted children once they are in a loving home environment. If I remember correctly, the surgery was done in mid-September. She was a real little trouper and did very well. She was beginning to be just a little bit hunchbacked, but that disappeared right after the procedure. She is now catheterized about four times a day, which she can almost do herself. She will always have bowel and bladder problems, but she is doing very well and is quite functional. Her doctor states it appears at this stage that she will be able to bear children as an adult, should she choose to.

You asked what her favorite thing to do is. Ruthie is really a little homebody. She loves having her *stuff* to mess with. She has always loved the junk mail that comes in, and she plays secretary. Since I do transcription during the day, she sits at a little desk next to mine and plays with an old nonworking keyboard.

She loves going to Sunday school. It is the highlight of her week, and every Sunday evening she starts counting down the days until the next Sunday. She is a type-A personality and likes things neat and tidy. She can be a bit neurotic about having all things, including the rest of the family, in their place at all times.

You asked if she was affectionate. Yes, very much so. After she got over her initial anger, she couldn't get enough cuddling. She loves to sit on our laps. Every night she has one of us read her a story, and she sits as close as possible.

I told you about my other two sons who died, one from birth defects and the other in an accident. She often looks at their pictures and talks about them. We try to avoid making it a sad thing, but rather something wonderful for both of them. Sometimes I am unable to hold back tears in front of her, but I tell her that even though I miss them very much, they are happy living with Jesus.

We have told her Danny was in an accident and got hurt very badly, but Jesus made him all better and now he lives with Him. Ben was severely handicapped and died from his birth defects, and we have told her that he, too, went to live with Jesus, and now he is all better. She accepts this very readily. She will tell you Jesus loves her, and he wanted her to have a mom and a dad—so he told us to come to China to get her. This pleases her greatly, and she talks about it often.

Regarding being away from the orphanage, after her initial tears, she never cried again. When our travel pictures were developed about one month later, she looked pensively at the ones of the orphanage staff and her little friend. She was quiet and subdued for several hours afterward, and we have made a point not to show her those again until she is a little older.

I think I will close for tonight. I am so happy to know that she had you and your friends. I have pondered on this all day and how faithful God has been to have answered these prayers and to allow me to know part of the "behind the scenes" of His workings.

Goodnight for now,
Ruthie's Mommy

Dear Kay,

Ruthie was adopted in July 2004, and since there was a twelve-year age difference between her and our youngest son, we knew early on we would be adopting at least one more time. Both Bob and I wanted Ruthie to grow up having at least one other sibling to lean on. Ruthie has spina bifida, and my thought was perhaps we could watch the waiting child lists for a little girl with some type of eye problem. Since I do medical transcription for an ophthalmology group, I knew that good eye care would be easy to come by. The agency we had previously used received a new listing, and there were nine or ten beautiful children, including a little girl with an eye disability.

The agency sent us her file, but we returned it without making a decision. Another month passed, and we began looking at several different agency lists. There were lots of wonderful kids, but there seemed to be no specific child who called out to us. After looking once again at available listings, I saw a little girl we had not noticed before. I'm not sure how we missed her, but we did. Our son, Nathan, was immediately convinced that this little girl was our "Abby," and my husband tended to agree. However, her medical condition was spina bifida, and I was not quite as sure. The thought of caring for two little girls with SB was scary. I cried because I feared she might not be placed, and I cried because I felt selfish and not sure if I wanted to give up more of my freedom. For

two weeks, I agonized and cried every time I considered the rami-
fications, and I prayed that God would give me a clear direction.

One day Nathan walked into my room and said, "Mom, if you
don't feel like you can handle another kid with spina bifida, I guess
I understand, and I'll accept it if you choose the little girl with the
eye problem, but do you remember how you felt about Ruthie?
How you felt that God was leading you to adopt her? Well, that's
how I feel about this little girl, and I'll always care about her."
Okay—I dissolved into tears, but this time it was because I had my
answer. God had given me His "sign." How often does a fifteen-
year-old boy allow you to see into his heart? We called the agency
and made a commitment to Le Ci—our Abigail Hope.

Bob and Nathan brought this frightened little two-and-a-half-
year old girl home on the Saturday before Mother's Day 2006.
The first two months she cried a lot. She had apparently lived in a
foster home, and was missing someone very deeply. As she came to
trust and then love us, she became a little ray of sunshine.

Abby talks loudly and laughs often. She dances and sings and
dearly loves her family. She can work a 100-piece jigsaw puzzle,
but struggles with memory issues. She is also incontinent, which
was my greatest fear, but that doesn't matter—she is perfect. Abby
is the buried treasure that we almost passed right over.

In closing, let me mention that Abby was brought to the
orphanage at the age of one day old. As Abby's mom, I want to
thank you and the other volunteers who gave so selflessly to advocate for her to have the surgery she needed. I will never know
most of you, but you were a blessing in Abby's life and in ours!

Warm regards,
Linda

Dear Kay,

My first adoption from China was in August 1996. In the world of Chinese adoption, that would be considered "the old days." My daughter, Hua Ming Sha, came from an obscure little city called Gejiu, in the southern province of Yunnan. Most people have never even heard of Gejiu, which has the distinction of being the largest tin-mining city in China. It is also the home of the first AIDS clinic in China.

We were not taken to visit the Gejiu Social Welfare Institute on our trip. Our babies were brought to Kunming, the capital of Yunnan. At that time, Gejiu was a seven-hour trip from Kunming, on bumpy dirt roads. Our guides did not feel we'd be up to a trip like that (they were probably right!). So I have to judge the orphanage by the condition of the eight-month-old baby that was placed in my arms on the afternoon of August 13, 1996.

Little Hua Ming Sha became Olivia Lee Mingsha in the fourth-floor office of the Civil Affairs Bureau in Kunming. When she was placed in my arms, she looked at me quizzically for a moment, then smiled from ear to ear and snuggled her head down on my shoulder. It was the most magical moment of my life . . . I was finally a mom! It was also obvious to me that this little girl had been given both attention and affection. She was very alert and interactive, and attached to me almost immediately. Twelve years later, she is still as affectionate as she was on that first day, and she still has the same smile.

On the other side of the coin, however, there was physical evidence that the care she had received was somewhat substandard. At eight months of age, she weighed just eleven pounds and had legs as skinny as knitting needles. Her head had been shaved at some point. She was very developmentally delayed—unable to roll over, sit up on her own, grasp an object in her hand, or babble. She also wheezed from some kind of upper respiratory ailment.

It took almost two years to overcome the early issues of insufficient nutrition and lack of development. She could roll over (almost) by the time we left China. She crawled at thirteen months, walked at sixteen months, and at age two had only about ten spoken words. But at two and a half, everything clicked into place for her in a BIG way! She could spell her first name, could name nine colors, was speaking in long sentences with a very rich vocabulary, and was even potty trained!

Today, one would never know that Olivia had begun her life in poverty and nutritional deprivation. She is a top student in her eighth-grade class, a black belt in karate, and a sweet, loving bundle of kindness. In retrospect, I would have to say that while her care in the orphanage was not quite what one would desire, it could have been a lot worse. I think the orphanage staff did the best they could under the circumstances. The other five baby girls who were adopted at the same time as Olivia were all in similar condition when they came home, and are now all doing beautifully with no learning issues or developmental problems. I guess we were among the truly lucky families!

Marie

Dear Kay,

I read your book with tears in my eyes and a hand on my heart. Having been to China to adopt two beautiful little girls in the past three years, I am reminded of the stark realities of life and the conditions in an institution in my daughter's birth country. Thank you for offering yet another view into the lives of those left behind. I have never been a member of the "sunshine and ladybugs" contingent that hopes that their children are from "a good orphanage." I was one that made the decision to adopt after seeing *The Dying Rooms* documentary. My expectations were, let's say, low to start.

Your book allowed me to step inside the daily life of the children and staff in an orphanage without all the hype, and your account of the time spent among the children was extremely insightful. I ordered a signed version of your book and felt compelled to share it with another adoptive mother, one yet to begin her journey. I will no doubt read through your experiences in the years to come, and hope that in time the good work you and your volunteers do will trickle down to the staff and caretakers in all of China's institutions. I believe firmly that one person can make an impact that can be felt around the world. In your case I think this is evident.

Our story . . .

In March 2008 my husband and I and our three-year-old

daughter (also from China) sat in a stuffy conference room in an "upscale" hotel in Nanchang. Jiangxi anxiously awaited the arrival of baby sister ZiZi. Ten other families milled around the crowded room waiting for their children to arrive. We were the only ones to be receiving a child from this particular social welfare institute as we were adopting a waiting child and had been "piggybacked" on to a non-special-needs travel group. Nervous excitement hung like heavy velvet drapes, stifling anything more than idle chitchat and nervous laughter.

After a few minutes, a woman hurried into the room, called out our baby's name, made eye contact, and thrust a screaming ball of dirt and tears into our arms. We were elated, yet also extremely aware of the loss that Z would be feeling in her new environment.

We tried to comfort her, but she was terrified. Having been told for the previous four months that our daughter was living at the institute, we were shocked to find out minutes later, with babe in arms, that she had been in foster care for the past ten of the eleven short months of her life and taken that very day from the arms of her foster mother to be placed into ours.

The following five days are a blur of paperwork, takeout food, unwashed hair (mostly mine), all amidst the undeniable soundtrack of wailing. Our daughter cried—no, wailed—for almost five full days. Her lament of choice was repeated over and over until I would hear it in my sleep: "Ahma, Ahma, Ahma." She was calling for her foster mother. Grieving is an understatement. She wouldn't eat or drink until the last day, an hour before the deadline to hospitalize her. Coupled with the heart-wrenching wails, our daughter relentlessly scratched at her body. She drew blood, and then scratched until her skin was no longer visible beneath the blood. The streaked lines spelled out her grief and the loss of the only mother she had ever known.

It was a tough time for all of us; we knew we needed to bring our daughter home for the treatment she had been denied in the country of her birth. We were still unsure of her actual medical prognosis due to a translation issue that neither China nor our agency representatives were willing to clarify. God had whispered softly into my heart long before we ever saw her face, and we knew no matter the outcome, this child needed to come home with us.

It has been eight months and our daughter has bloomed! Her condition, which was feared to be extreme by top international adoption physicians, turned out to be a cosmetic issue that was corrected with a twenty-minute surgery once home. Her prognosis is excellent! Even the Early Interventions team is surprised at her progress, which blew their estimations out of the water!

She is now 100 percent on target and up to six months ahead in many areas. People tell us we are lucky it wasn't something worse, they tell us she is lucky, but we know she is blessed beyond measure, as are we. So many other adoptive parents would have walked away from her condition due to the translation issues and the advice from the professionals—I am so glad we persevered.

I am filled with sorrow for her birth parents, not knowing that their daughter's birth defect wouldn't stop her from living a wonderful life.

Sincere regards,
Hayley

Dear Kay,

By the time each of my sons were born, I felt like I already knew them. I knew how active they were, how busy they were, and how much they liked to sleep (or not), and I was completely head over heels in love with them. These children, who had been inside of me, had been real to me from the moment I first felt them move within me. And when we saw our first daughter's face in her referral picture on August 25, 2006, and then met Katie for the first time on November 7 in the Bureau of Civil Affairs of Guangzhou, Guangdong province, my first thought was incredibly similar: There you are . . . I *know* you!

However, as I reflect on the day we met Ella, who was also adopted from China, I can only describe my initial reaction: for the briefest of seconds I felt like I was meeting a stranger. Ella was a special-needs referral, and we found her on an agency's Waiting Child list. We worked hard to make Ella our daughter and endured an emotionally exhausting nine months from our initial review of her file until we were able to travel to meet her and bring her home.

For nine long months I'd been staring at pictures of our little girl bundled up in layers upon layers of clothing, with only her chubby face peeking out at me. During our wait, we received three sets of updated pictures, and in every one of them she looked like a plump little dumpling with a sweet round face.

So, twenty months after bringing our first daughter into our family, on June 23, 2008, at the Jin Feng Hotel in Nanchang, Jiangxi province, I had a completely surprising revelation: that the nanny was handing me a child I loved with all my heart but didn't feel like I *knew*.

As I held out my arms, the nanny placed in them a scared, sweaty little girl wearing a tiny frilly shirt and split shorts over her diaper. Only her face was somewhat familiar to me, but even then, she looked different enough that there was a split second when my mind questioned if *this child* was really she—our long-awaited daughter. This thought was no more than a heartbeat long before my mind overrode the irrationality of it.

Ella was as light as a feather at nineteen and a half months old, but seemed impossibly long and lean to me, completely without the adorable rolls of fat one is accustomed to seeing on healthy babies. Once she settled into my arms, however, I knew in my soul that she was my daughter—she was the child I had prayed daily for since I'd first seen her precious face.

With her somber eyes looking at me and her fingers clutching her name tag as if it were a lifeline, I looked into the eyes of my daughter and began the process of getting to know her.

I feel a bit guilty, four months later, putting those first, fleeting thoughts of mine in writing, for all to see. I don't want my precious child to ever think, for even one second, that she wasn't meant to be my child, to think that for even one brief period of time I didn't love her. But I want to be honest at the same time, as my feelings, as brief as they were, were real at the time. Just because I didn't feel like I *knew* her the first second she was placed in my arms, it only took a heartbeat for me to realize that she was my daughter and she was right where she was supposed to be.

Kelly
Mom to three teenage sons and two toddler daughters

Dear Kay,

I am compelled to write to you after reading your book, *Silent Tears*. I want to thank you for shedding light on so many behaviors that my four adopted Chinese children have exhibited at times after their adoptions, and that I had suspected the reasons for. Now I know that my instinct was correct. My husband and I are the parents of four biological children and four from China. Our oldest Chinese daughter, from Fujian province, was adopted as a non-special-needs baby through the traditional method. Our second daughter is from Guangxi Zhuang Autonomous Region and is considered special needs because of a very minor port-wine stain birthmark on her jaw. Our third and fourth children were adopted simultaneously, through a very rare instance of the CCAA granting us not only a family size waiver but also the permission to adopt two unrelated children at the same time. Both children were adopted in March 2007, from Anhui province, at the age of thirty-three months.

Our son is missing a foot and a big toe on his remaining foot, but nothing slows him down, and he has his own Lightning McQueen prosthetic leg/foot.

Our youngest daughter has cerebral palsy. Until we adopted her, she had spent all of her life lying in a bed with little interaction or physical therapy. A team of American pediatricians saw her in China and advised that she would be severely handicapped her entire life, and was unadoptable. She could not hold her head up, roll over, sit up, or stand at almost three years of age. We were not swayed in our pursuit of adopting her, and she is now our beautiful, happy daughter. In just a little over a year, she has learned to sit up, crawl, feed herself, partially dress herself, walk in a walker, ride a horse, is potty trained, sings beautifully, speaks perfect English, and knows all of our dogs' names—something not even my husband has a grasp of! She will be starting piano lessons within the next year, as she is very musically inclined.

All this to say, I can now envision the life that they had before we came, how those with disabilities were treated, and how our youngest daughter very likely would not have lived to be an adult. Their orphanage had no heat, no cooling, no running water, not enough food for the babies, and a single cooktop burner to prepare the food for thirty-plus children and caretakers.

The children were all afflicted with dysentery in late summer 2006. This caused much concern, and several, including our daughter, were hospitalized in the ICU. Through charitable organizations, and the people who gave so generously, this poor SWI was able to receive a new well for fresh water, a refrigerator, stove, baby formula, food for the older children, heating/air-conditioning, and new cribs. Some college students from Hefei came and painted murals on the walls to cover the dismal mold. All such a blessing, and it came at a critical time in the lives of so many children.

I have all of their abandonment information tucked away to share with them when the time comes, all such different places, the stoop of the SWI, a busy train station, a bridge, the mouth of a coal mine . . . but all with the same ending: a warm, nurturing home full of love and encouragement so that they can and will be all that God created them to be, with a family to love and help them down that path.

Take care, and may God bless you,
Kim

Hi Mrs. Bratt,

This is Hunter. My Chinese name is Le Men. Four of us have Chinese names. But not my oldest sisters.

I am about to have my birthday. I will be six. I want a new bicycle like Parker got. Parker is my brother. He is older, but I am bigger.

I asked my dad who my mom and dad were in China. Dad didn't know. I was very sick in China. Dad said they loved me a lot but couldn't fix me. They took me to a place to get well. Mom said you took care of me in China. I was very sick. My heart didn't work right. You got them to fix my heart. Thanks!

When I came to Colorado I had a new family with six sisters and one brother. My mom and dad took me to the heart doctor and they smeared stuff on my chest and I got to see my heart. The doctor said it worked great—like it was brand-new. They fixed it great in China!

I like to run and jump and play all day long. Parker and I pretend we are karate guys. We kick and jump. We are very good and very fast. I want to be a firefighter.

Mom gave us haircuts last week. The clippers tickle on my neck. And Dad used the big vacuum cleaner tube to suck the hair off of us. It tickled so much!

Mom says I make a face when she tells me no. She tells me to stop "the face." Dad says I look like a very old army guy that isn't happy. I wish they wouldn't say no. It is just my face.

I love my family very much—even my sisters.

I am very smart. Dad says so. I know lots of big words. I start full-day kindergarten next week. I will go to school all day. We are all going back to school. School is fun, except when they make us sit around.

The ice cream man comes in his truck to our house! He stops in the driveway. Dad chased him one day and now he comes to our house. We get to pick our ice cream and then we wave bye-bye. I love ice cream. I love cake, but not the icing stuff.

I eat anything (except icing). Parker too. We eat lots. Macaroni and cheese is great. Vietnamese egg rolls are great too. And pizza. Sometimes we get a soda. Parker drinks it too fast and feels sick.

Dad says, "That's enough, say goodbye." When are you coming to visit? We have fish tanks. We had bears in the driveway the other night. And fawns. They run fast. Kind of jumping.

Okay, Dad! That's all I can say.

Let me know when you are coming. Don't come while I am at school. Come on Wednesday when the ice cream truck comes. You will love it!

From Hunter

Dear Kay,

It's August and Le Bai's ninth birthday. A few weeks earlier we celebrated the third anniversary of his becoming part of our family. It's hard to believe three whole years have passed already. He's grown tremendously and his language has exploded. He loves school and has blown his teachers away with his drive to learn. He speaks English as if he were born here, even has a bit of a local accent! He's a natural charmer and has a sharp (if dry) sense of humor. Everywhere we go we run into someone that knows him.

Le Bai has embraced all things American—pizza, Halloween, birthday parties, cartoons about talking sponges, and mischievous monkeys. Once terrified of our elderly golden retriever, he now romps around at the dog park with our two young greyhounds. We are getting a handle on his vision issues and starting to fine-tune the accommodations he needs for that.

He doesn't talk about his time in China much these days. He does have some good memories and we try to keep those alive. The bad memories are still there too; he doesn't want to talk about those much, but they do creep out sometimes. He says he doesn't remember, but we know he does.

He's finally starting to understand there will be enough. Enough food, clothes, attention, and love. While he understands it most days, there are still lingering doubts that we haven't been able to chase away yet—mostly about the love.

He's still not entirely sure this is forever. He *wants* it to be so very much. He does love us and I love him to the bottom of my soul. He's still afraid that we might be wrong though—that something might happen and we won't be able to keep our promises and maybe this time next year he might find himself someplace else. Even after all this time, when he's pushing the limits I sometimes see him bracing for the hit he's sure is going to come. Even though we never have struck him and assure him we never will, he's still convinced that it's just a matter of time.

Only a few weeks ago, at the end of a rather trying day, he crept into my lap. He didn't say anything, but I could tell there was something on his mind. I held him and waited. It finally came.

"Mommy, can I ask you a question?"

"You can always ask me anything," I said as I stroked his back.

"When I'm bad, do you want to get another boy to replace me?"

I suppose all children sometimes wonder if their parents really love them enough and if their place really is permanent. Usually it's typical childhood fears that can easily be soothed away with a hug and kiss. But Le Bai has genuine reasons to worry. Hundreds of hugs and kisses have only made the smallest dent in his fear. He has every reason to be skeptical when I tell him there is nothing he could do that would make us send him away—he's been sent away before. Not because he was bad, of course, but nine is too young to fully grasp that. He doesn't know what permanence is, and I imagine it will be several more years before we have even begun to prove ourselves to him, or for him to be able to let down his guard permanently. I wish I could take that on for him, to be able to do something to let him relax and not have these worries that no child should have. All I can do is continue to give one more hug, one more kiss, and one more promise.

Adopting an older child comes with challenges, but it comes with so many rewards as well. I have learned a lot about myself, learned how to be patient when I didn't think I had any patience left. Learned how to think on my feet and answer questions I never dreamed of being asked.

I've learned how to truly appreciate what life brings, even when it's not what was expected. I know people mean well when they exclaim, "Oh, he's so lucky to have found you!" but really, we are the lucky ones.

Le Bai's Mommy

Survival Mandarin
for
New Parents

BING GAN (been gahn) – a cookie or biscuit

CHI FAN (chr fawn) – Used to indicate you want to eat. With "le" as a suffix, it indicates you have already eaten.

MI FAN (me fahn) – rice

ZHA SHU PIAN (ja shoe pee-an) – potato chips

NIU NAI (nee-oh nie) – milk

BU YAO (boo yow) – Don't want. Your child may say, "Bu yao!" if he doesn't want a certain food or object, or doesn't want to do something you have told him to. Also used to tell a child not to do something. If he is throwing an object, you can say sternly, "Bu yao!"

WEI SHENG JIAN (way sheng gee-an) – bathroom

XIAO BIAN/DA BIAN (shall bee-an/da bee-an) – Refers to having to urinate or defecate; mostly children use these two terms. "Xiao" translates as "small," meaning urinate. "Da" translates as "big," meaning defecate. Find a bathroom immediately!

ZAI NALI (tsai na-lee) – Where? If you need to find a bathroom, you'll ask, "Wei sheng jian zai nali?"

ERZI (are-tzuh) – son

NUER (new-are) – daughter

WO (whoa) – I

WO DE (whoa duh) – mine

NI (nee) – You

NI DE (nee duh) – yours

WO AI NI (whoa I nee) – I love you

NI HAO (nee how) – Hello

TA (ta) – He, she, or it. "Ta sure" means "he/she is." "Ta shi wo de nuer" means "she is my daughter."

BAO BAO (bow bow) – Baby. I often say to a baby as I hold them, "Ni wo de bao bao." Meaning, "You are my baby." This is to help them feel loved.

BU KU (boo koo) – Don't cry

BU HAO (boo how) – bad

BU SHU FU (boo shoe foo) – Doesn't feel well. "Ta bu shu fu" means "he/she doesn't feel well."

DUI BU QI (doy boo chee) – Excuse me; pardon; sorry

DENG YI HUIR (dung ee hwar) – Later; wait a while

DENG YI XIA (dung ee shaw) – Just a minute; wait a bit

Acknowledgments

This story could not have been written without my journey to the Chinese orphanage. With the involvement of my fellow volunteers, we were able to make a difference in the lives of many children; a million thanks to that group of amazing women for standing by me, especially to our rosy Regina, who kept me focused during my most emotional moments. Thank you to John and Elaine Dargan, Jim Bell, and the rest of the Happy Fund crew who financially supported many of our endeavors. More generous supporters include Danny and Connie Peelman, Randy and Carolyn Marcum, Tyrone and Kim Ball, as well as many others from around the world who offered up prayers and encouragement. Thanks to my agent, Kevan Lyon, for guiding me through the publishing process and to the team at AmazonEncore, for believing in my story and giving me the opportunity to reach a wider audience. I am indebted to the adoption community for kindly allowing me to feel a part of their online family and I must acknowledge the *ayis* at the orphanage who did their best to care for the children, despite their circumstances of being overworked and underappreciated.

To Xiao Gou, I thought I was the survivor until I met you and realized my life was a fairy tale compared to what you have endured; your resilience amazes me.

To my warrior daughter Heather, it is you that unknowingly taught me to accept my failings and look to the future. And, finally, a resounding thanks to my husband, Ben, and daughter Amanda, for their help. I pulled through the hardest experiences of my life and was encouraged to put it all in writing. It wasn't needed but my biggest reward came from the words of my youngest daughter, "Mama, I want to be just like you when I grow up because you always want to help people." I only hope I can continue to live up to that compliment.

About the Author

Kay Bratt grew up in the Midwest as the child of a broken home and, later, a survivor of abuse. Facing these obstacles in her own life instilled in Kay a passionate drive to fight for those that had been dealt an unfair hand. Upon arriving in China on an expatriate assignment with her husband in 2003, she was immediately drawn to the cause of China's forgotten orphans. Moved beyond tears by the stories of these children, she promised to give them the voice they did not have. In 2008, she self-published her memoir, *Silent Tears: A Journey of Hope in a Chinese Orphanage*, to do just that. With the help of her readers, Kay continues to raise awareness and advocate for at-risk children. In China, she was honored with the 2006 Pride of the City award for her humanitarian work. She is the founder of the Mifan Mommy Club, an online organization that provides rice for children in China's orphanages, and is also an active volunteer for Court Appointed Special Advocates (CASA) for abused and neglected children. Kay currently resides in Georgia with her husband and her daughter.